Delete Me:

An Argument Against Facebook

Ronald Read

Delete Me: An Argument Against Facebook

This book is dedicated to all the people in my life who asked me to get on Facebook.

Contents

Introduction

As of this writing, Facebook has approximately 1.1 billion monthly active users worldwide. This makes it not only the biggest social network on the internet, but the biggest ever. No social network, not MySpace, not RenRen, or even Google+ is or was larger than Facebook. And for all we know, no other social network will ever be larger than Facebook. Their membership along with their daily usage numbers have been going steadily upward since their founding in 2004.[1] It would seem at this moment that Facebook could be the social network of the 21st Century.

Facebook's success however is not the same as their concern for their users. The network routinely collects massive amounts of data on individuals to run their advertisement targeting business. This targeting works by using information to send advertisements to users based on their demographic and interests. In 2012 Facebook made over $4,279 billion dollars in revenue from advertising. When other fees that Facebook collects are added in, Facebook made $5.32 for every person on their network.[2]

On the surface, this deal might sound great. After all Facebook is providing their users free services in exchange for making them see a few ads on their Newsfeed. But despite how innocuous this deal might sound, there is a lot more to the situation than just free service for information. And the reason why is because there is a lot more that can be done with information than just sell advertisements.

Consider for instance that a Lexis Nexis study found that over 80% of police departments in America use Facebook to conduct law enforcement investigations. These investigations include both real world and online crimes that may have no direct relationship to Facebook whatsoever.[3] Facebook gets so many requests from the government in fact that they put a special guide on their website for how law enforcement agencies can obtain Facebook user data.[4]

This example is just one of many that demonstrate the unintended consequences of using Facebook on a regular basis. A person logs-in to Facebook expecting to a get a social experience. And they may very well get that experience by talking to friends and updating their profile. But at the same time, they are a product for advertisers and as an informant for police officers. This should make it clear that Facebook is not just a social networking site.

What is presented in the following chapters is an argument against Facebook. It details the numerous problems that stem from Facebook's excessive collection of information and why that system of collection will never change. Facebook wants to know everything about everyone in the world. Until users leave Facebook in massive numbers, Facebook will continue to progress towards achieving this goal.

The solution of leaving the network is a simple one to implement. First go to the Facebook log in screen. Then look in the bottom right hand corner and click the small lettering that says HELP. Click on the Manage Account option. It will include an option that says "how to delete my account. After clicking on that screen, it will then say to click on a link that will ask for log in information. There will also be a form that Facebook has departing users fill out. Facebook will then receive a request for a permanent deletion. The request will take 14 days to complete. Do not return to Facebook in the 14-day period, or else they will reinstate the account.

But many users have discovered that this process of deletion is not as easy it sounds. The real dilemma is in the decision to delete ones Facebook profile, not in the action itself. The measurement of reasons for why one should leave and why one should stay can be difficult. People may even suspect that there is something wrong with Facebook but they have no significant reason to leave so they don't. The objective of this book is to give every Facebook user a reason to leave. And if that is what you have come looking for here, rest assured that it is here where you will find it.

Part I

1. Benefits

So why do people use Facebook? What makes this one social network so great compared to all the others? After all Facebook is not radically different from a network like Google+ or Twitter. But for some reason Facebook has more members than they do. And the average Facebook user uses the network longer than the others do. There is something special about Facebook that we need to discover, if we haven't already.

It is important that we understand why people love Facebook so much so we can understand why Facebook is something that should be abandoned. When people point out the flaws in Facebook, the counterargument always uses the positive aspects of Facebook to downplay the negatives. These positive aspects are real for the most part and are not hard to obtain for the average user. But when we are done looking at all that Facebook offers, we will see that the bad far outweighs the good. This imbalance is not clear on the surface so we must take the time to examine both sides of the equation.

An Excellent Product

There are numerous ways for people to communicate over the internet, but Facebook is a cut above the rest. We know this because people are always using Facebook. Users will typically stay logged into the site for a half an hour at a time and they will log into the site multiple times throughout the day.[1] Not every Facebook user is this loyal, but enough are so that there is always someone to talk to when you log into Facebook.

And what allows those people to visit the network so often is that it is compatible with a wide array of devices. Facebook is available not just on desktops, but also on a variety of smart phones, tablets, and gaming platforms. This compatibility of Facebook with other platforms makes the network easy to access regardless of what machine the user has. As a result, people use Facebook whether they are at home, at school, at work, or anywhere else that has a good internet connection.

The ways that people can communicate with each other on Facebook are not one dimensional either   There are plenty of different avenues to exchange information on the network other than just simple messaging. While logged into Facebook, a user can comment on someone's wall, make a post to the Newsfeed, chat in a private session, like another user's content, and make use of numerous other features that Facebook gives to its users.[2] This range of ways to communicate expands the type of conversations that can occur on Facebook while keeping the site from getting stale over time. It also shows Facebook's commitment to innovation despite being on top of the market.

And if there happens to be a feature that Facebook doesn't already have, there are always applications that users can download. Applications are essentially programs that provide the user with a unique feature that they may or may not already have access to on the platform they are using.[3] Facebook's Platform allows users to download millions of applications from developers from all over the world. These applications give users more out of the Facebook experience than what Facebook Inc. can give them. At the same time, the platform also allows application developers to test out their projects on one the most popular social networks on the internet. Everyone, in a sense, gets something out of the deal.

Along with giving users access to an excellent product, Facebook also gives access to it 24/7. Facebook is always available barring any serious mishaps or updates. This constant availability requires a dedication to engineering that other social networks in the past have struggled to accomplish.[4] By going the extra mile however, Facebook gives their users an experience that they can tap into whenever they want. And that means they are going to use it more often than the other sites that go down every time the wind shifts.

Facebook's uncomplicated design partly allows for this constant access. For instance, Facebook does not encourage users to have backgrounds on all their pages the way other social networks like MySpace did. There are also no glitter tags and flashing icons that fill up profile screens. And if things such as notifications begin to fill that space, the user has the option of turning off those annoying Farmville reward posts.[5] This plain design keeps Facebook manageable while still giving users what they want out of a social network.

Despite the costs that Facebook experiences from running the site constantly, Facebook is free for those who wish to use it. Free registration has become the norm for modern social networking and Facebook has stuck by the trend. People who wish to join Facebook right now can register for an account free of charge if they wish. The only exception to this free policy is when the user is trying to advertise their brand or product on the network. Otherwise a person can interact with people on Facebook as long as they want, where ever they want, when they want, and to a limited extent how they want.

Social Interaction

Facebook is an excellent network not just because of how easy it is to use, but because of the benefits that it makes possible. One of the best of these benefits is social interaction. Facebook gives individuals the opportunity to talk with friends and family who they might normally be unable to see. With Facebook people can continue the story of their relationship even if they are not geographically close to each other. It is this enhancement of social interaction that makes other benefits possible.

With increased interaction between peers, Facebook users are given increased accessed to knowledge about their real world social networks. Because people are constantly posting information about themselves on Facebook, users are given access to their friend's inner thoughts and desires. Ideas and actions that would normally stay hidden from the world are brought to light through Facebook. The result of this sharing of ideas is a more descriptive look at who the user is compared to what a typical email or phone call might reveal.

The social information that is exchanged between peers can also allow for users to browse profiles that they might find interesting. While on the network, the user can examine the photo albums and Timelines of users that are basically strangers. The information Facebook provides can allow the user to determine whether the person is "friend material" before making the decision to friend them. Facebook will also occasionally give users recommendations for who they should become friends with based on the information contained in the profile.[6] The recommendation system is not perfect, but it is an effective way to identify people who the user may have forgotten to add to their friends list.

The activity of adding and engaging friends on Facebook leads to the construction of an online social community. This community offers people the chance to come together and communicate with each other in a convenient way in social distant world. Users may not see each other often real life, but because they are on Facebook they are still together in a digital sense.

And if the user can learn how to exercise some self-restraint in what information they share in that community, the user can use Facebook to build their reputation. Facebook gives individuals a chance to introduce themselves to people on their own terms. They can present themselves in the best light to show people the person they want to be. This can sometimes lead to incredibly narcissistic posts, but it can also give people a sense self-confidence that they don't get in regular social interaction.

Linked to this role as a reputation builder, Facebook can also serve as a diagnostic tool for a person's social situation. If a user makes a lot of posts that no one ever comments on or likes, it may be a sign that they are doing something wrong in their effort to fit in. Or if a user gets likes when they say or do things on Facebook, it could mean they are doing things right. It isn't exactly a full proof science, but Facebook can at times provide an image of ourselves that we have been unwilling or unable to see through normal social interaction

Having access to a digital community also makes it easy for users to arrange meetings with their contacts in a convenient way. In a matter of minutes a user can send out invitations for an event using Facebook instead taking days to send out the invites through the mail. What makes this feature workable is that users are given customization over the invitations as well. They can name the event, they can say what time it begins, they can post pictures about it, and they can even include a comment stream where people can talk about how big the event will be.

This gives users a better idea of what they are getting themselves into before attending that crazy bar mitzvah or boring dinner party.

Changes to Society

These enhancements that are given to the user's social life are only one example of Facebook's impact on the world. Facebook can also be a major force for social change with online communication. We can see the effects of Facebook in the promotion of cultural exchange between societies to the sparking of revolutions in authoritarian countries. Because of these changes in the world, Facebook has been given an image boost as a source of technological rebellion against the existing order.

One of the major ways Facebook does this is simply be having a diverse set of people all together in the same place. Facebook has a billion members on their network that are scattered throughout 127 countries around the globe. [7] This diversity allows people who might never meet each other to chat about something they saw on Facebook or in the real world. And with Facebook's translation feature, people who speak different languages can communicate with each other in real time. Facebook is not just providing users a way to interact with their local community, it is providing them with a cultural exchange like the world has never seen before.

This ability for individuals to communicate in a global forum has also changed the way stories are told in the media. Facebook has forced news networks and public relations departments to pay attention to publics they would normally ignore. Now individuals have a voice in a global conversation previously exclusive to the elite members of society. Reputable new sources such as CNN are even relying on social networking sites for information about what is happening around the world.[8] Facebook helps to change the perspective in the media from people who only hear about the news to people who experience the events that are being reported on.

This type of reporting, known as citizen journalism, works on Facebook by allowing the user to post links that a mass audience can see in real time. If a person puts a link to a story on the Newsfeed, a sizable portion of their friends list may see it.[9] The same goes for pictures and other forms of content that users share with each other. If enough people comment, share, or like that news post, it might get the attention of the mainstream media. By opening the channels of communication, Facebook offers users a chance to get the world's attention.

The sharing of content is important not just for news stories but also for helping users navigate the web.[10] Users can discover websites hidden in the depths of the internet by following content that their friends have posted. Navigation through Facebook can even be better than a search engine because it has a real person behind the recommendation. Facebook is not just using algorithms to find out what people want, it is using people with real world knowledge about what the user is interested in.

Something that also really adds to the atmosphere on Facebook is its mostly user generated content. The links and pictures that are shared on the Newsfeed are brought to Facebook by the user. Even Facebook's translation feature is created from individuals on the network who have knowledge of native dialects that a computer does yet not understand.[11] By "crowdsourcing" most content and services, Facebook stays out of the way of users who are essentially making their own network, not just using someone else's.

This crowdsourcing of tasks allows Facebook to concentrate on handling the more difficult tasks that keep the site functioning well. Tasks such as developing new features while recruiting world class talent are just a few of the more important things Facebook does in their spare time. It is not easy running the world's largest social networking site, but Facebook gets it done because they don't try to do everything themselves.

An effect of the atmosphere that Facebook has created is that there has been somewhat of an awakening on the internet. For the first time, the internet is alive with people who are connecting to each other and talking about content together. Millions of websites now have Facebook social plugins that offer users the ability to examine and discuss content in a new way.[12] Before with instant messaging and photo sharing people could talk on the internet, but they couldn't experience it all at once in a group setting. Now they can, and because of that the internet is better in many ways.

Business

Facebook's success with users also brings benefits to advertisers who use Facebook. Businesses on Facebook can direct advertisements to their target audience based on information that users have shared.[13] This targeted advertising allows businesses to reach audiences that want to be contacted instead of forcing them to sit through a worthless page takeover ad. It doesn't eliminate annoying advertising altogether, but it does make the experience more useful or at the very least tolerable for those involved.

And not all advertising on Facebook revolves around direct advertising. Facebook also allows businesses to build a relationship with the people they are marketing to. Great public relations work can be done on Facebook when companies try to engage the audiences that are on the network.[14] Facebook PR may not be as good or as a favorable as news story or as an excellent product review, but it does allow for a more intimate relationship between the producer and the consumer. How good that relationship turns out to be depends on how good the organization is at using Facebook.

Engaging social media for public relations work also allows businesses to receive feedback from their audiences about how well their campaign is doing.[15] If users hate a brand, they can go to Facebook to complain about it. If they love the brand, they can go on Facebook to say how great it is. By receiving reports on what users say, companies can make better marketing decisions about their products. Having more knowledge about their audience gives the business a better idea of how they can please their customers by listening to what they must say instead of just focusing on sales figures.

Another benefit from Facebook that many companies are beginning to take advantage of is applicant screening. Facebook offers employers the opportunity to see behind the resume that their applicants turn in. This examination using Facebook gives businesses a better chance of getting the employee they want for the position instead of taking a gamble on someone they really don't know. In a way Facebook helps recruiters save time for both their company and the person they are looking to hire.[16]

Applicants can also find businesses to work for in a shorter amount of time by looking at companies who use Facebook. A quick look at a company profile can give the applicant an idea of who the company is and even the morale of its employees. And if they are already hired at the job they want, then Facebook allows employees to communicate with their coworkers outside the workplace in an easy to use communication platform. This gives employees and managers an efficient and fast way of exchanging information in a face paced world.

Aside from businesses and corporations, a smart celebrity or community organization will also understand the ability to use Facebook for self-promotion. Comedians and musicians use Facebook to promote their tour dates. Activist groups can use Facebook to tell people when their protests will be. Authors can tell people when their new books are coming out. The same applies for actors in television shows and movies. Facebook is a new way for people to tell their fans what they want them to know. This all assumes of course that the celebrity knows how to use Facebook without incriminating themselves in any irresponsible behavior at the same time.

The advertising environment that Facebook has created has resulted in thousands of organizations and celebrities joining Facebook to help promote their brand.[17]   Without Facebook, brand managers would have to go back to the traditional methods of advertising that people have grown sick of hearing.   And without the service they provide to businesses, Facebook could not provide an excellent, free service to its users. It could be said that advertisers and Facebook are made for each other.

Downsides

As with all great products, Facebook also has negative aspects that users must learn to deal with. These downsides are not totally exclusive to Facebook, but they can be larger in magnitude with Facebook because of its size and nature. Facebook generally does not shy away from these setbacks but instead looks at them as challenges that need to be faced to provide an excellent product for the user. Other problems however are presented as a problem that the user needs to handle on their own to best find a solution. These difficulties can occasionally be harmless, but not always.

A usual complaint made of frequent Facebook usage is that it encourages narcissism in those that use it. Users who make posts about every event in their day can seem self-absorbed to their friends and family. This may or may not be true of the user, but surely they would not want to have the label of a narcissist regardless of its validity.

Another complaint made of Facebook is that causes users to spend too much time online.   Studies have even shown that Facebook cuts into work when users have online access at their job.[18] Using Facebook too often can also result in wasted spare time that could be spent doing more useful things. While most people would suggest that Facebook is a great way to communicate, they might also admit that there are other things to do with one's time.

A problem that may not be thought of until it is too late is that Facebook forces users to be in contact with annoying people. By lowering the barrier for social interaction, Facebook lets people into the user's life that they would normally try to keep out. This can apply for the creepy guy in the office as well as the mother in law who likes to keep tabs on everything. Sure, it is nice to say hello to these people at work, but it can become a problem when they try to talk to you every day on Facebook.

The greatest drawback of using Facebook by far however is that its usage requires the sacrifice of personal information. For Facebook to provide their great, free service they must collect large amounts of data from all their users and refine that data to target advertisements to specific users. This system of marketing known as ad targeting makes Facebook billions of dollars every year. They are not about to give it to give up even if they could, which they can't.

While this collection makes Facebook a lot of money, it can also the user personal harm. And because of the severity of danger Facebook puts their users in; information collection by Facebook will be the focus of this book. There are of course other problems that Facebook causes that do require a serious discussion such as society's increasing reliance on digital communication and the social, physical, and environmental drawbacks. There are also concerns about the monetization of personal information and whether users should be paid for the content they generate. These problems are important but they pale in comparison to what Facebook can do to their users based on the information that users provide. To put it simply, some crimes cannot go unpunished.

2. Extraction

Everyone who uses the network by now should know that they are giving information to Facebook whenever they use it. Facebook is not a phone line that just passively relays data to and from the sender. It collects every piece of information that is passed on the network. There are no exceptions to this collection of information. Facebook must receive a certain amount of information on every user and it will store that information until the user tells them specifically to delete it.

There are several reasons why Facebook makes this demand of everyone. The first is that Facebook must have data about the user for security. By asking for certain personal information about the user, Facebook can recognize them when they return to the site. This tracking of users lets Facebook know who most of the people on the network are to make the network somewhat safer. The identification system obviously can be bypassed by registering a fake account, but enough people are honest about who they are to make the process worth implementing.

Another motivation for this collection is that it allows Facebook to provide the user with benefits based on who they are. An example could be making a friend's list recommendation generated by information from the user's location and connections to other users. By knowing who the user is, Facebook can give them additional benefits that would be impossible to do if the user was anonymous. This information-for-convenience model drives a lot of the sharing that takes place on the site.

And the third and major reason for collection once again is for target advertising. By collecting the information that users share on the site, Facebook can direct advertisements more accurately to people who the advertiser wants to reach. Usage of target advertising makes Facebook more profitable than the average website that just displays the same advertisement to everyone. And because Facebook makes billions of dollars from this form of advertising, they are able provide their service for free to billions of people around the world.

A result of this collection for advertising system is that a lot of information is being collected on the 1.11 billion individuals who use the site. In 2012 Facebook reported that its users were sharing approximately 4.75 billion content items every day. That number just includes information like pictures and posts to the Newsfeed and doesn't even touch all the other information that Facebook gets with registration and applications.

[23] When all was said in done it was estimated in 2012 that Facebook had collected over 100 petabytes of data.[24] A petabyte for those that don't know is 1 with fifteen zeros on the end, so Facebook has collected roughly 100,000,000,000,000,000,000 bytes of data on its users.

Understand that the information Facebook collects goes beyond just bytes and instead falls into several categories that strive to capture the total identity of the user. Each category represents the vastness of what Facebook can touch in our society. There is very little that Facebook cannot see about a person who uses their site faithfully. The network was made to collect information on those that use it, there are relatively few exceptions to that rule.

Registration Information

The first set of information that Facebook requires their users to "share" is registration information. The point of collecting this data is to certify that the user is who they claim to be. By filling in a few of the fields that Facebook provides (name, birthday, password, email, method of access); the user creates an online entity that the network will recognize when they log in. An example of this could be: John O'Neal, 6/17/1987, Cobra33, joneal@yahoo.com, logging in from "Work". After this registration is complete, everything that John O'Neal does on Facebook will be attached to that identity.

While this information is important to establishing an online persona, individual pieces of registration information are more critical than others. A name for instance is something that can be important or it can be ambiguous. Knowing John O'Neal's name for instance only tells us so much in a world with numerous John O'Neal's. Each one of them has a completely different identity. They have different friends, different locations, and different lives. So it is important that Facebook know the difference between each John O'Neal by asking for more information.

The next place to verify someone's identity is their birthday. This field is important because there are only so many John O'Neal's who are born on June 17, 1987. Having the user's birthday helps Facebook to determine if the user can be a member. For the time being Facebook still has a 13 and older age policy, but that may change in the future.

Another reason for the birthday requirement is so Facebook can direct ads toward the user based off their age. This prevents Facebook from wasting their time and the user's time with ads about Viagra when they are only 16. Of course, the user could lie about the age and birthday by providing a false one, but most probably won't. A reason for telling the truth is that friends will be notified of the user's birthday when it comes around. When you lie, people will remind you with birthday wishes on the wrong day. When you tell the truth, someone wishes you an appropriate happy birthday.

To provide even more uniqueness to the Facebook identity of John O'Neal, Facebook also asks the user to create a password. The password will serve the purpose of protecting the user's information from unauthorized users while providing a unique identifier about him or her. As many users probably know, Facebook passwords are easy to crack for the average hacker. But they do serve to make the user feel safe, which is what is most important for information collection.

Asking for a password from the user may also allow Facebook to guess other passwords that they use for other websites. After all there are so many websites that ask for passwords these days it can be difficult for the user to come up with an original one for each website. While every internet user should know not to do this, many do and as a result they are more susceptible to online impersonation. As we will see in later chapters, founder Mark Zuckerberg is no stranger to this form of hacking. He used it to break into a Facebook users email account that also happened to be a reporter at Harvard...but that is another matter.[25]

In case users forget their password, Facebook also asks for an email address so they can send the user a reset application. This application will provide the user with a way to get back in after supplying a security question answer.[26] The user's email address is also one of the requirements for registration because it creates a link between the user and a second registration that is obtained when the user got their email address. The email requirement is kind of like an anchor to weigh down the identity of the user. A user can of course provide a fake email address, but that takes a slight degree of added effort that most users won't give for the sake of security.

Unless the user adjusts their account settings, they will receive an email notification every time they receive a Facebook notification.[27] This feature is incredibly annoying, and it also serves as a backup for Facebook in case the user deletes their account and the information on it. Even after their time at Facebook is over, their email provider will still have the emails Facebook sent the user about their notifications. This is a particularly clever tool for storing information on people who provide fake or spam email accounts. Because the person who gave the bogus email probably never checks their inbox, the information will probably go unnoticed and not get deleted. So giving a fake email is a bad idea if the user is not proactive enough to turn off the email notification setting.

But regardless of the individual importance of each piece of the identity like a name or email, with registration Facebook has created an entity that is now attached to the actions the user takes on Facebook and elsewhere. Everything that the user does while logged into Facebook or while visiting a website with a Facebook social plugin will be attached to that identity.[28] This is very important because the creation of an online identification system has never been done before. And as we progress through this investigation it will become clear why this should not ever be attempted.

Machine Information

To access the network a user must have a machine that is connected to the internet. When the user accesses their account, the machine will give information about itself to

Facebook. This will include: IP Address, machine type, and location.[29]   After this collection is completed our example will look something like this: John O'Neal, 6/17/1987, password: Cobra33, joneal@yahoo.com, logging in from "Work", IP Address: 136.15.142.3, using an iPhone, in Scottsdale Arizona. That is a lot of information to have on a person, so let's explore some of the new pieces of data in detail.

An IP Address, more specifically Internet Protocol address, is a unique numerical code used to label devices that use a computer network functioning on Internet protocol. Unless a person takes special precaution, a website can see the IP address of the device the person is using to access that website. Without more information to identify the user, the only thing the IP address would identify is the machine.   And unless the IP address was combined with legally protected internet service provider data, there is usually no link to the individual through the address number.

Now almost every website takes down IP addresses, but they normally have no idea who those IP addresses belong to. Facebook is unique in that not only do they get a device's IP address, but they also have a plethora of information to attach to that address. Facebook has a name, a profile picture, the friends of the user, and lots of other unique identifiers to certify that the address not only belongs to the user, but that it is the user.

To help with identifying the device, Facebook immediately asks the user once they initially log in the name of the location where they are logging in from.[30] Without answering this question, the user cannot gain access to their account. Examples of logins that could be given to Facebook are "home" and "mobile", and perhaps even "work", or "library." Once they give this device a name, Facebook it turns that random IP address number of 154.34.2311 into "Library Computer."

The location question feature comes in handy when someone decides to break into a user's Facebook account from an unrecognized device. When this happens, Facebook will tell the user where that person logged in from, such as the city and state.[31] The negative implication of the user sharing their method of access is that it reveals how the user typically accesses the internet.   From that piece of information more information could be discerned. If the user gets online with a desktop it could mean that they only get on when they have time at home. If they use a mobile to log in it could mean the user is online every chance they get. Information frequently leads to more information.

Other than for security purposes, Facebook can of course use the locations of members to give them advertisements. With their location Facebook can send the user information about restaurants in their area or stores that sell products nearby. While this use of a user's location is a nice benefit, it is not outweighed by the fact that the user's physical location is being collected and stored without their permission. It is simply taken, and there is nothing they can do about it.[32]

Another feature of Facebook that the user has no voice in is cookies. Every Facebook user must accept cookies on to their browser when they log in to Facebook. Cookies are pieces of HTML code that tell the website being visited what other websites the browser has visited. Once the cookie is on the browser it reports information about what the user does on the internet back to Facebook.[33] It is basically an internet tracking device.

Facebook requires cookies for many reasons, some of which will be familiar. By having cookies placed on their browser, Facebook can tell whether the user is who they say they are. Cookies also allow Facebook to service users with advertisements based off the websites they have visited. Additionally, the cookies will tell Facebook specific information about the user's geographic location to provide relevant advertisements. And Facebook also makes the claim that by keeping their cookies on a user's browser allows for them to route traffic faster based on knowledge of their preferences.[34]

If the user wants to eliminate these cookies they should delete them from their browser. The problem is that when a user visits a site like Facebook every day, their cookies will get replaced every day. This means they must manually delete the cookies every time they log in and log out to keep Facebook and other sites from tracking them. This is a problem for not just Facebook users but for internet users in general who wish to maintain a degree of browsing privacy. To combat cookies Do Not Track options are available on most browsers. Safari, Internet Explorer, Mozilla, and Google Chrome all give users the option of blocking cookies.[35] Some sites can however defeat these do not track options making it a cat mouse game between the user and the cookies.

Aside from cookies, the other forms of collection by Facebook during the registration process and afterward is not a totally uncommon occurrence. Outside of naming the machine that their members are using and taking down their location, Facebook is like most websites that require users to register their identity. What makes Facebook different is that they transcend what the other websites do every chance they get. Keep in mind that Facebook wants everything. If you wish to see this desire in full swing the best place look is in profile information.

Profiles

A Facebook profile is a basic description of the user. Users create this profile so that their friends will recognize them based on the information that they have provided. This information is also shared by the user in the hope that it will increase social interaction with people who look at their data. Information such as interests or activities may stimulate conversation between the person who shares it and the person who sees it. Facebook may even provide recommendations to the user based on the information included in the profile.

The costs are that there is a wide range of information given to Facebook when users build their profile. In the beginning a person will typically upload a profile picture of themselves to show people who they are. The profile picture is a photo of the user that serves as the icon over their name. When a friend or relative looks up the user by their name, seeing the profile picture helps them identify that this is the user they are looking for. In the beginning Facebook used to make profile pictures mandatory but now profile pictures are optional because most users do not need to be told to share their image, they do it voluntarily.

The profile picture the user shares will typically be a recent photo. If the user has changed their appearance in a moderate way it is hoped that they will take a new picture for their profile so that people will recognize the new look. This is especially important if they have had a change in weight or hairstyle that radically altered the user's appearance. Not keeping the photo recent and accurate can lead to gossip of inauthenticity which may poorly serve the user's reputation.

This does not mean that people must provide a picture of themselves. Plenty of people upload pictures of landscapes and animals and all sorts of things in place of their own image. These people who use a picture of something else will probably be recognized by their friends anyway because they have other information about themselves on their profile. But if the user wants to receive the benefit of having more distant associates recognize them immediately it is best if they upload their actual image.

Along with the profile picture, users spend a lot of time uploading photos to their albums that can be seen on their profile.[36] Albums help provide a look at the user in a variety of situations instead of just their best pose. On average Facebook receives 350 million of photos day from users who are uploading their pictures to these albums.[37] What makes this feature revealing is that unless a user makes these albums private they will be visible to whoever is on the network.

In addition to visual representations, users are given the option of writing a short biography of themselves that will be shown on their profile. A bio will typically say what the user looks like or what they do for a living. For people who use Facebook for their career this box will probably be more detailed than a user who is just on the network for social interaction. And for some people they will just leave it blank. But for those that do not they give up just one more piece of the puzzle as to who they are.

Facebook also encourages users to add their high school or college into their profile because it will help Facebook recommend friends.[38] By giving this information, the user tells Facebook not only where they went to high school, but the quality of education they received. It says whether they went to a private or public or a magnet or a charter school. The high school information also allows Facebook to draw connections between former classmates which the user may or may not want made known. It is a piece of information that can seem worthless in everyday conversation but on Facebook it can be very revealing.

If the user continued with their schooling, then more data will pile up about them. They will make new contacts at the college or university they attend, and those contacts will probably be on Facebook. The person may have to join class groups that share information on Facebook. The number of times the individual logs into the group can also say what type of student that user is. If the student comments about their classes or professors, this can also say how they behave in school. The photos and posts they are tagged in will say what kinds of groups they were in and what type of parties they went to, if any. Much like MySpace, Facebook is a window into the high school/college experience.

To provide even more academic detail Facebook also has a box for saying what the person is studying.[39] While this information may serve as a source of the pride for the individual in pursuit of their degree, it can also have consequences as well. The area of study can give a reasonable assumption about the interests of the user as well as concerns they may have about the outside world. For instance, a political science major is more likely to care about political matters than a medical technology major would. What a person studies can say a lot about who they are.

Depending on what degree the individual graduated with, a reasonable prediction can be made of employment and level of salary. A philosophy graduate is probably in trouble with their student loans, while an information technology graduate is probably employed with a good salary. If the student goes on from there to get their master's degree or another degree of some kind, they will increase their chances of success greatly from their bachelor degree peers. And of course, the degree will say what kind of job the individual will have or at least try to get. A journalism graduate will probably try to write for a paper, while a medical technology graduate will try to get a job in a laboratory.

A much easier way of determining a user's place of employment and salary is for the user to post it on Facebook. Along with having a field for school, Facebook has a field right below it for work.[40] It is encouraged that the users share where they work so they can add their co-workers. While this action has benefits for social networking among business contacts, it can also help Facebook draw inferences about the salary and status of the user who shares their workplace and position. This is not to mention the unintended consequence of sharing Newsfeed information with people who may have a personal interest in seeing the user fired for what could be considered unprofessional behavior.

An equally important piece of information that can be used to describe the user is their religion. Facebook includes a space on the profile for users to proclaim which religion they are, and users can also like pages dealing with their religion of choice. The amount of insight that can be gained on a user varies depending on religion, but they all say something. I will stop there.

Close but not quite as extreme as religions are political affiliations. Facebook allows political parties, candidates, and even ideologies to have pages on the social network. If the user likes or subscribes to these pages it can denote what their political stance is on many issues. Including these political affiliations on one's profile gives users access to information from those pages about issues that they care about. Being a fan of certain political entities may also help the user meet like-minded people on the network who hold similar beliefs.

When the user isn't on Facebook they can still tell Facebook about what they do in their spare time. Activities are included on Facebook for users to tell their friends not just what they like, but what they do. To elaborate, they might like soccer but they play hockey. Activities say a lot about a person such as whether they are athletic, popular, healthy, intelligent, extroverted, or any number of things that go along with the completion of activities.

A part of the activities that people do are the things they are interested in. A person might put under their activities that they like reading, and in their interests, they might say what books they like. People tell Facebook their interests for three possible reasons: To help their reputation, to facilitate discussion, and to receive updates on that information in the form of advertisements. This information typically includes but is not limited to music, movies, and books which can reveal the personal beliefs and attitudes that the user holds.

The second part of the profile information and arguably the largest piece is a user's Timeline. The Timeline feature of the Facebook profile is not really an addition so much as a change in the way information is presented. Before Timeline, a person's Facebook history was stored in a gigantic list that went all the way down the profile page. With the creation of Timeline, that same information is presented in a format that jumps out at the user. But along with creating a galvanized process, the Timeline encourages the sharing of more information about a user's history. This is because the Timeline will look plain without additional information.[41] The spaces that litter a new account's Timeline almost ask to be filled in.

The information that Timeline collects falls into two categories: personal history and logged activity. The user's personal history includes events that happened in real life that the wish to share with Facebook in a thorough chronological format. Sharing of this information could be done so that the user lets their friends know where they came from and who they are.[42] Putting on Timeline the day your child was born is a way to tell people you are a parent and how old that child is for example.

An interesting aspect of personal history Timeline is the reports application. The reports application asks the user to share information about something they enjoy doing.[43] This makes their Timeline richer from an observer stand point. An example of a report might be a runner who reports how many miles they ran that week. By using reports the runner can track how their weekly mileage has increased or decreased over the years.

The activity log of what someone does on Facebook is also an intriguing part of Timeline. Storing and showing a person's online activity is beneficial to the user because it allows them to look back at past actions for personal reflection. At the same time however, the log stores every action that the user has not chosen to manually delete or hide. The record means that if there is an embarrassing action that the user is unaware of at the current moment, that piece of information can be looked up by someone else.[44] Hopefully, the user checks their log frequently or else the embarrassment can last for a long time.

When we combine this Timeline feature with profile data the user has chosen to describe themselves with, we gain an understanding of who the user thinks they are and how they wish to be seen. This information provides a complete look at how the person's self-image has changed overtime in an easy to read format. While this information is all very telling, how the user views themselves is only part of the story. It is also essential to know how they interact with others.

Communications

To begin communicating with other users on Facebook, the user must first add them to their friends list. A friends list will tell visitors of the user's profile how many friends the user has and who those friends are. An addition is made to this list when the user sends the targeted person a friend request. The person who receives that request has four options: they can do nothing, they can say no to it, they can ignore it, or they can accept it.[45] By doing nothing they continue the non-existent relationship they had with the person on Facebook before they got the request. By doing nothing with the request the receiver shows that they do not want to be bothered with the person whatsoever. It is the cold shoulder of the Facebook world.

The next option is for the receiver to ignore it. Ignoring a friend's request is an actual button a user can press on the friend request.[46] This action will make it seem to the sender that they have accepted. The sender will be able to see posts made on the Newsfeed but they will not be able to interact. This ability will last for a limited time until the sender forgets about sending the friend request. Ignoring the request is the passive aggressive way of doing things on Facebook.

The third option is to say no. This option is obviously a very direct way for the receiver to say to the sender that they want nothing to do with them. Not only will the sender not be able to see the receiver's information, but they will be sent a notification that the receiver said no. The "no" firmly establishes a wall between the two parties. It says, "I do not want you as my friend, go away." Some people go away; other people keep sending friend requests.

The last and most used option is to accept the friend request. By accepting the request, the receiver allows the sender to see all their information and vice versa unless the receiver adjusts their security settings. The two parties can then talk to each other in every way Facebook allows. A Facebook friendship is born.

For every addition and acceptance of friends, a profile link will be added to the user's friends list. By having these links, the user tells Facebook that these are the people they want to communicate with. These people are considered acceptable enough by the user to be given access to their information. Everyone who is not on this list is either a person who has been denied a friend request or who has not sent or received one yet. Of course, the users who click on friends lists see only the acceptances; Facebook however gets to see the acceptances and the denials.

Users can organize their friends into special sections once they have been added to the lists. An example could be a "family" section that displays each family member and their relationship to the user.[47] For everyone else, there are plenty of other groups that their friends can be put into. The groups can vary from close friends to spouses to team members to same political party to whatever they can think of. In the end, the designations help Facebook understand not just that two users are connected, but how they are connected in the real world.

Once the link has been made between the two users, there is a variety of ways that they can communicate. Interacting simultaneously with every person on the friends list is best done by making a post to the Newsfeed. The Newsfeed is an ever-changing list that documents the posts made by users throughout the day.[48] It is probably one of the biggest attractions for the website and major reason why Facebook collects information.

Along with being added to the Newsfeed, posts are also visible on a person's Timeline after they click "submit". This way every action that takes place on the Newsfeed is subdivided into the individuals that take those actions. It serves to organize a mass of information that could seem almost incomprehensible if the observable could only look at posts that are grouped with everyone else's data.

This is important because posts reveal a lot of information about who the user is. A post can capture what the person is thinking at that very moment and a series of posts can also capture the feelings a person had over an extended period. When looked at over a long enough time frame, posts can map out the ups and downs of a person's life. An emotional breakup for instance would have several posts about loss of love and mistrust. A rekindling of that love would show the user singing their praises for their significant other.

Posts to the Newsfeed also show how intelligent the user is. The way the post is written along with the content of that post can speak volumes about the way a person thinks. A person who posts using incomplete sentences and slang may not be very smart. A person who posts information about politics and current events may be intelligent depending on their sources of information. Writing the posts off as trivial ramblings disregards how important our thoughts are in saying who we are.

From the posts that users make, communication is generated between the user and those that read their posts. There are three actions that users can take on posts that they see. They can ignore the post and go about reading the Newsfeed. They can like the post which says that they agree with the information. Or they can comment on the post to add more information to the discussion.[49] For people that do not have time to interact with every post, the can elect to just read the Newsfeed and log out when they are done.

The like button is an option that allows users to agree with a post that they see on the Newsfeed or Timeline. This button is convenient because it allows the user to just click instead of having to type a reason as to why they agree or like the post. This also transforms communication by creating a rating system for thoughts. Posts that get more likes are seen as worth reading and are put to the top of the Newsfeed. Posts that no one likes will disappear from the Newsfeed in a quicker amount of time. The rating system encourages more posting and more quality posting by turning the act of communication into some sort of game that users can play. Likes could be considered points for using Facebook.

Likes come heavily into play when we start discussing Pages that are run by organizations on Facebook. These pages help businesses and groups raise awareness about whatever they are trying to do. By having a page, a business for instance gives users the ability to like the business. From the action of liking that businesses page, the user will now receive information about the business. And thus, a social channel between the user and the business entity is formed.[50]

In addition to likes, commenting on posts is also very popular with users. Comments are like posts in that they capture a brief statement from a person about what they are thinking. The difference is that comments are always directed toward something. A comment is a user's opinion about something they see on the network.   This could include posts, pictures, and videos...whatever a user can see. However, the comments are always attached to something.[51]

Comments reveal the same characteristics that posts do as far as intelligence and attitude, but they also help explain the piece of content the user is seeing. A comment about a photo may reveal where the photo was taken. A comment about a post may reveal the relationship the user has to the commenter. Comments help explain what the user does on Facebook to the casual observer. But more importantly, it gives the site more vitality. People don't just post videos; they talk about them over prolonged periods of time occasionally with large groups of people. In many ways, Facebook gives the content a life of its own.

When it comes to making posts, users can also tag their friends in the posts they make. Tagging occurs when the user designates who the user is in the content that they post. "I am at the store with James Farelly and Thomas Edwards" is an example of tagging someone in a post. In the post, the names will be written in blue. That is done so the people who read the post see the names first. Along with tagging in text posts, the other big feature with tagging is in pictures. When a user tags someone in a picture they draw a box around the person's face and label the box. This serves the same function with the post. It says who the person is with and it includes a link to their page.[52]

But if the user wants to communicate more privately with their Facebook friend, they can always use private messaging.[53] The messaging feature gives users a faster way to talk to each other while not worrying about what other people are seeing or fearing that someone will butt in on the conversation. This allows Facebook to collect more personal thoughts on the user than the public communication features would allow. The collection is aided by users being given the impression that only the people in the conversation can see the posts. But as we will see later there are numerous exceptions to the security of private Facebook messages.

A more advanced form of messaging beyond that of text communication is video calling. Video calling allows the user to talk with a friend or several friends through a video display.[54] Apart from allowing the user to see their loved ones while talking to them, video calling also provides another certification that the person said what they said over the message. Not only did they audibly say something to the person, but they recorded it on video.

The last way for individuals to communicate over Facebook is through poking. A poke is the simplest feature of all on Facebook. The user presses the poke button on another person's page and then the person is notified that they have been poked.[55] It is more of a novelty if anything. But it does something about the relationship between the poker and the receiver of the poke. It says that maybe the relationship is one where pokes are acceptable.

Because of its numerous communication features, Facebook brings in information that would have been left to dissipate into the darkness of the offline world. Normally the break up fight would have to happen over the phone or in person. But now with Facebook it can be recorded for the world to see as it unfolds over the Newsfeed. In a way users are soliciting their friends for the information that Facebook wants. There are benefits to the solicitation, but the result is that Facebook gets to monitor the user's interactions with the people they know. To put it simply, this is voluntary surveillance.

Social Plugins

Whether a person is a member of Facebook or not they have probably seen a social plugin before. A social plugin is a piece of HTML code that is written into a web page to serve as a link back to a host website.[56] The social plugins that Facebook gives to web pages allows the user to post information or activity they do on the website back to their Facebook page. Facebook currently has 13 social plugins that include: the Like Button, the Comment Box, the Send Button, the Login Button, the Activity feed, Share Dialog , Embedded Posts, Recommended Posts, the Recommendations List, the Like Box, the Face Pile, Instant Personalization, and Registration.[57]   The plugins are Facebook's way of expanding their website beyond their own webpage and into the rest of the internet. Facebook wants everything they can get, and this is just one of the ways they are doing it.

To get the benefit of the social plug-ins the user must be logged in to their account. By logging in, users combine their Facebook account with the activity they engage in off the site. Any time there are one of these social plugins on a website outside of Facebook, it means that website sends Facebook information. Even without being logged in, the social plugin reports the IP address, what type of machine they logged in from, what browser they used, and the activity the user engaged in while on the website.

These social plugins are all designed to record different pieces of information, but they all share a similar feature in that they give Facebook a presence on almost every website. By having these plugins, a site gives Facebook intelligence about what happens on that site. The IP addresses that visit and what those machines attached to those addresses do is recorded by every social plug in and sent back to Facebook servers. The plugins act like little spies that stand on every corner of the internet watching every move we make.

When a website decides to include one of the social plugins on their page, they allow themselves to become a part of Facebook's Open Graph. The Open Graph is essentially a system the tracks all the connections that exist inside of Facebook's network. These connections include everything from websites, applications, users, pages, and anything else that enters a relationship with Facebook. This Graph is constructed with the purpose of helping developers and advertisers reach users based on the information they give to the Graph.[58] While it may not seem important now, in later chapters we will see just how powerful a tool the graph can be.

Applications

It is important to remember however that Facebook cannot give the user everything they want. Facebook can only do so much, and for everything else there are applications. Applications are ways for users to get more out of the Facebook experience by sharing certain pieces of information with third parties that operate on Facebook. These people, often referred to as developers, create additions to Facebook that give user's access to certain benefits in exchange for the user making information available to the application. This information in turn will be used by the developer to promote the app to other people the user may know.[59] If the developer is successful in designing and targeting their applications, a lot of people will download it and make it profitable for advertising and digital purchases.[60] If this sounds a lot like Facebook, it should because Facebook is also an application itself.

In addition to being a major internet application, Facebook is known in the internet development world as a platform. A platform is a place that developers use to build their applications on.[61] There are various platforms throughout the world such as gaming platforms like Xbox Live. There are mobile platforms such as Android which is owned by Google. Facebook is a platform for internet as well as mobile and gaming applications that can integrate with the other platforms that were previously mentioned. What these platforms have in common is that they sit underneath a sea of activity that they can tap into whenever they want.

Facebook is a good example of this when we look at just how successful some of their applications are. An individual application such as Texas Hold'em can capture over ten million users. Farmville is another application that has over ten million subscribers. With a potential market of a billion people, Facebook is the place to develop. This is not only because it allows for the application to reach a lot of people, but Facebook's size allows for a variety of people who want to use a variety of applications. Not everyone wants to play Farmville, so there is room for other developers who do other things.[62]

The result of this massive market place for development is the creation of numerous applications that collect user data. Facebook has not just game applications but applications for news organizations such as CNN or FOX. These apps take the users news interests and give them stories about news they like. There are travel applications such as Foursquare that will take the users location and tell them where their nearby friends are. There are even sports applications such as ESPN that will take the users sports interests in exchange for information about the user's favorite sports teams.[63]

The other applications made available to users for download range from the silly to the essential. There are music applications that recommend songs to users based on their music interests. Facebook also has lifestyle applications that record how often someone works out so they can track their fitness progress. For the avid reader, there are applications that record every book the person reads and from that list recommends more books to the user.[64] The list is endless for what these applications can do.

Remember that applications in a way are like patches on software. They fill in the gaps of what the core version of Facebook leaves out. Facebook as a program can only change so many ways to extract the maximum amount of information from users. They know they have a good core product, and they cannot create a master type program that would be better than what they have already. Facebook needs add-ons to fill in everything else. That is where applications come in. They expand the range of where Facebook can go beyond that of the internet. The Platform makes Facebook an active part of the user's real-world experience.

Intrusive

The result of this mapping of connections and this endless expansion for information is a total look at the user's world. Facebook has become an information gathering machine that extracts data from everything it touches. To even suggest that this level of information collection is not intrusive is naive. Facebook is making a strong effort to know everything they can about everything they come in contact with. The possibilities of what information Facebook can collect on a single person or organization dwarf what most websites can even dream of obtaining. It doesn't just eliminate anonymity; Facebook is trying to get rid of privacy all together.

Some people may be bothered by seeing this behavior. The idea that Facebook is an ever-expanding net that picks up information is certainly is a terrifying one. But for many, this behavior is not a concern at all. While there are people who care and who have chosen to leave, they are far outnumbered by those who have chosen to stay.   These people do not stay because they are totally ignorant of what Facebook does. They do not live in some bubble that blocks out all discussion of Facebook's effects. No, they stay at Facebook for a different reason. They stay because they are addicted to Facebook.

3. Addiction

What makes the data collection process so lucrative for Facebook is that they have created a very addictive website. Users of the network are in a cycle of Facebook usage that can be difficult for them to break out of. This cycle stimulates the collection of more information on the user than if they were only casual visitors. Most people are not casual visitors however. They log on when they wake up, when they are at work, before they go to sleep, and whenever else they get a chance. The last thing they care about is how much information they sacrifice when they are on Facebook.

The label of addict does not apply to every user, but it is pushed on every user. Facebook takes many steps to encourage an obsession with their website for the sake of gathering as much information as possible on their users. These addictive qualities are built on top of an already excellent social networking experience. This makes Facebook strategy seem blurred between making an addictive website and making a reliable website. The truth is that they do both and they do them very well.

To foster the addiction, Facebook has embraced a tactic in web page development known as gamification. Gamification involves turning a website from just a simple source of information or communication into a more game-like atmosphere that encourages frequent usage.[65] Features that encourage this type of transformation include things such as: page view counts, rating systems, and comment streams that allow for people to be judged on how they use the website. Sometimes users will get a favorable grade such as many likes, and other times they will not. The result of this reward system is that the user will share more information with the network because they have an expectation of getting a favorable rating for what they do.

This way of increasing usage is like the design of classic arcade video games. First the arcade game's screen was made very large so the player not only saw the game well, but so that other people could see what was happening on the screen. The score that the player achieved for the game was also written very large on the screen once the player finished. This caused the player to have a concern for how successful they were thus causing them to have a concern for how much effort they put into the game. And depending on how successful the player was, they may have received a high score or perhaps even tickets that were redeemable for a prize at the front desk.

If the player failed to achieve their desired score, then they would put more quarters into the machine to start the game over again. Some arcade games were even made purposely difficult as to play on this need for achievement by the player. Because the player could not achieve the high score the first or second time, they kept putting quarters into the machine hoping to master the game. In the end, they would either have given up or they would have conquered the game, but the owner of the machine would have captured the player's money which was the goal from the beginning.

When looking at Facebook we should think of it as a game because it was designed to be a game. Social interaction is the intention for the user, and collecting information is the intention of the owner. And the way for the owner of the game to get more information is to encourage the player to use the game more frequently. Whether the user achieves quality social interaction is immaterial as long they are encouraged to keep playing the game and share plenty of information.

Get Them to Join

Before the Facebook machine can begin mining information out of the user, the user must first join the site. To encourage registration Facebook makes the site incredibly easy for everyone to join. Facebook is available in hundreds of countries around the world in a variety of languages. It is also available on many platforms such PCs, mobiles, and tablets while at the same time being free to all users. So a lot of people will join simply because it is easy to do. This goes along with the wide range of benefits that were discussed in previous chapters that make playing the game very enticing to begin with.

But for people who still haven't registered for the site, Facebook has several other ways of encouraging their membership. Peer pressure is a strong encouragement to join Facebook. People are encouraged by their friends to join the site so that they can communicate with them online. Because Facebook has developed such a monopoly over digital social interaction, Facebook may be the only way two people can stay in touch on a frequent basis. Facebook's games also play a role in encouraging users to recruit non-members in exchange for game rewards. And aside from encouraging recruitment, Facebook has so many members to pressure non-members with that it can be hard for the targeted user to say no.

In addition to receiving pressure from friends, the non-user is also tempted by the millions of sites on the internet that have Facebook's social plug-ins. As of December 2012, over 10 million websites were integrated with Facebook's platform to allow for some sort of plugin to be placed on their site.[66] Along with the internet there are also reminders of Facebook that are placed on advertisements in the real world. These ads typically encourage the viewer to visit their Facebook page to receive more information about the brand or product. This bombardment amounts to a lot of free advertising for Facebook that forces the non-user to pay attention to something they would typically ignore. Much like the large screens in the arcade or perhaps the big slot machines you might see in a casino, Facebook is constantly baiting users to come in and play.

While voluntary membership to Facebook is the usual route that a user takes, there are also many forces that push individuals into involuntary Facebook membership. Employers may ask their employees to have Facebook accounts to encourage more office communication and better representation of the company. Teachers and professors also may ask their students to become members of Facebook for discussion and distribution of class materials. Some websites on the internet now require that the user be a Facebook member instead of registering for an average membership. This requirement for Facebook or any social network profile is a result of Facebook becoming intertwined with the society that it exists in.

These numerous factors come together to pressure individuals to join Facebook whether they want to or not. The effectiveness of all the pressures and temptations that Facebook puts on the public is evidenced by Facebook having over 1.06 billion users as of December 2012 which was a 25% increase from the year before.[67] Facebook's recruiting works very well even after the site has been around for nine years. Because of that ability Facebook has a little over a billion chances to collect information from each individual account.

It is safe to say that Facebook's marketing techniques have allowed them to capture a sizable portion of the online social networking market. CEO Mark Zuckerberg has stated that Facebook wishes to have every person in the world on Facebook within the next five to ten years. The way they intend to do this is through cheap mobile devices that would allow even individuals in poor, developing countries to be a member of Facebook.[68] They certainly have a long way to go in reaching that goal, but right now they have more registered users than any website has ever had in the world.

Keep Them Logged In and Keep Them Coming Back

Once a user is registered, it is important for Facebook to keep them on the site for as long as possible. By keeping their traffic numbers high, Facebook stays attractive to advertisers who may be concerned about usage rates. This high level of engagement is important so that users see the advertisements they are being shown. Keeping users logged in also serves to promote the sharing of massive amounts of information that helps to direct these advertisements. Facebook's retention of users for long durations of time also serves as advertising for Facebook to other individuals who see the user logging in on their phone or laptop. There are plenty of reasons for Facebook to keep people on the network, but to do so they must take the necessary steps to keep them there.

One move that Facebook does to keep users logged in is giving them the impression that they have logged off. A user that is logged in will continue to give information to Facebook until they specifically log out of their account, not just open a new browser window or exiting out of the existing on.[69] This slightly deceptive trick allows Facebook to collect information such as browsing habits that the user might normally choose not to share directly with the network. A user could potentially be online all day long without recognizing that they are still logged in. And the entire time Facebook would be collecting information on the user which they assumed was being kept private.

Whether they are aware of it or not, when the user engages in logged-in browsing they can interact with social plugins on other websites. These plugins as we discussed earlier let the user have more personal interaction with the site and its visitors. What happens here is that the user is on Facebook without really being on Facebook in a way.[70] If the user turns on Instant Personalization, the website will get even more information about the user. This allows for the website to make recommendations based on the information the user makes available.[71] It is this type expansion that could lead to Facebook not existing in a singular website format in the future. Instead it could be a part of every website on the internet.

But after the user logs out, which they all must do eventually, Facebook has on its side the natural desire to return. When a user interacts with someone on Facebook it creates a reason to check back into the website. Once a post is made on the Newsfeed for instance, the user must check back in within a reasonable amount of time to respond to whoever may comment on that post in a timely manner. When the user's friend responds to the post, Facebook will alert the user with a red flag over the notification button to get their attention. This system of send, wait, receive, respond, wait, is one of the most addictive traits of Facebook.

The loop that is created is like a tennis match between two people on a court. A player hits the ball over the net. That player must stay alert and wait until the ball returns them. When the ball does return, they hit it back and the process starts over again. Users are playing a game, and they must constantly be alert for when the ball will come back to them.

What also helps Facebook is the increasing number of users who log into Facebook with their smartphone. Currently that number stands at 680 million.[72] This is important because it means those users can access Facebook quickly and discreetly which will encourage frequent usage. All Facebook must do is get them to download the application first, the phone in many ways will do the rest.

Along with outside technology, this addictive cycle of communication is aided by Facebook's creation of an artificial social environment that entices users to return. What makes the environment alluring is that it prevents the proliferation of arguments and exclusion over Facebook's social channels to allow for a more user friendly, fantasy like atmosphere. A more realistic social environment could scare away users who fear rejection as well as advertisers who may fear people who would bash their brands. To protect the fantasy, Facebook takes care to keep things more peaceful than realistic on the network regardless of any negative social effects this might cause.

A way that Facebook propagates this fake social experience is through the encouragement of excessive friending. Facebook frequently pushes users to add large numbers of people by suggesting individuals that the user might already know. They also push for excessive friends by showing the user the comments made by strangers on their Newsfeed.[73] These factors are in addition to the large friend list numbers that promotes self-consciousness about how many friends the user has on their profile.[74] By having this substantial number of friends the user is led to believe that they are more popular and well liked than they really are. The truth as many will guess is less attractive.

A problem that arises when users have too many friends is that they must listen to people that annoy them. To remedy the situation Facebook offers users the option of blocking individuals so that they do not have to see the designated person's posts.[75] The user will still show up on their friends list, but in name only. This feature of Facebook is what holds everything together. Without the ability to block people, users would have to resort to such pesky actions as deletion and perhaps even confrontation through interaction. Conflict and pain is something that Facebook does not want to happen on the network, so they let users block as much as they want.

Preventing people from being annoying however is only a secondary goal of what Facebook wants to see on the network. The idea behind using Facebook is for the user to create a better impression of themselves than how they are perceived in real life. Done properly users can achieve a sense of confidence and self-esteem that may have been unattainable in the real world.[76] The problem with this ability to put one's best foot forward is that it gives people a false impression of the user. As some may have discovered already, the person the user knows on Facebook could be far different from the person they know in real life.

Facebook also protects the boundaries of this artificial world by creating content policies that shield users from the ugliness of reality. These policies place prohibitions on material such as violence, offensive language, or sexual content. Users are even encouraged to report any content that they deem reprehensible.[77] This control does have legitimate uses such as the reporting of child pornography or acts of harassment that happen on the network. But at the same time the policy serves to limit reasonable freedom of expression. This creates an artificial environment where certain ideas such as sex, violence, or self-harm appear not to exist.

Out of this demanding, fake social scene that Facebook has created, users spend egregious amounts of time on the site. The average amount of time spent in a typical visit to the network is approximately 33 minutes a day and over 15 hours a week.[78] This is a substantial in comparison to other websites whose average visit time is only a few minutes a day. From an observer's prospective it is safe to say that Facebook's engagement numbers are doing just fine.

Get Them to Share Lots of Information

While Facebook does an impressive job at recruiting users and getting them to stay logged in, the whole point of this process is to get information out of them. As iterated earlier, information is what fuels target advertising and that is what makes Facebook the bulk of its revenue. But along with getting the raw product of information for advertising, the information also serves to entice users to stay on the site.

Much like the way advertisers feel, users also enjoy looking at the information that Facebook has on individuals. One could almost call the information that Facebook has "irresistible" in comparison to what the other websites must offer. So, there is a strong incentive not just from an advertising point of view but also from an addiction perspective to have plenty of user data on hand.

Facebook has several ways to get information out of the user. They could just take it by creating deceptive features that collect information without the user knowing it. An example used earlier could be keeping users logged in without them knowing it. Facebook also gets information through their cookies that they force users to accept upon log in.[79] Regardless of the method used, when a user is logged in to Facebook they are giving Facebook information whether they like it or not.

The design of Facebook's layout can also be a major force for information collection. Facebook is filled with blank spaces that the user is encouraged to put their information into when they see them. The post box on the Newsfeed, the comment box under photos, and the blank spaces on the Timeline are all examples of holes that need to be filled with information. They just stare at the user waiting to receive an input. After the user does give the hole some information, the hole empties itself again waiting for more. It is never enough.

As a result communication is no longer just communication, but instead a reputation competition that causes some users to share lots of information with the hopes of getting recognition. Managing one's reputation can be a tireless task that is never really finished. Being preoccupied with who is commenting on a status that was made earlier in the day is something a person should not have to be worried about. Every time someone is on Facebook they must worry about their account and what they do while they are logged in. This requires a steady stream of information to be shared by the user.

Outside of whatever neurosis the features might cause, the user's friends also encourage them to share information all the time. A study completed by *Pew Internet Research* shows that friendship numbers drive Facebook user activity.[80] This happens because friends are constantly commenting on walls and sending messages to interact with the user. Since the user wants to maintain favorable relations with those people, they are probably going to respond. Out of that exchange information has then been successfully solicited out of the user.

The friends of the Facebook user also have a significant role to play in encouraging the user to feel safe in sharing information. Being somewhere with friends can create the impression of safety in times when a person should feel in danger. This type of thinking helps soften the user's sense of awareness at a time when it should be heightened on the internet. Being in an area surrounded by friends could be why people feel okay with sharing information on Facebook while hesitant to share it with other less friendly websites.

This environment that mimics a real social life while collecting massive amounts of information helps to create what is known in the tech world as a digital doppelganger. Essentially the doppelganger looks like the person would on paper, but they are not that person in real life. A Facebook profile is a good demonstration of this because it allows a person to highlight their best qualities, leave out their worst ones, and still look authentic to themselves and their peers. This works because even if the user is entirely truthful with all the information that they put down, they are still just impersonating an identity that they have created. The doppelganger is less than what they are, which is why it can be more attractive to be the doppelganger than the person.

Communicating through the doppelganger gives the user the ability to have "vicarious lives" as Oxford Professor Robert Scruton would say.[81] Those lives might feel very real, but it is still someone else that is doing the talking. The illusion is made to feel real because the person has included so much information about themselves on the profile to make it real. A better identity can be just as good as a better life.

When we add up all the information that is pulled from the user, we see that Facebook is incredibly successful in their collection of data. Every month Facebook users share over 70 billion pieces of information on the network.[82] In content alone people share almost a billion pieces of information at day with Facebook's Open Graph.[83] For the fourth quarter of 2012, there were 350 million photos being uploaded every day to Facebook.[84] While this may seem like a lot of data, we can assume that Facebook will try to collect even more as time goes on.

Don't let them Leave

Because users are constantly communicating on Facebook, there is a tendency for users to grow tired of the site. This "Facebook Fatigue" as it is known is something that Facebook must prevent if they wish to maintain their place as the world's largest social network.[85] After accumulating all their users and taking their information, Facebook can't just let it all slip away. They need those users to be members of the site for as long as possible. And sometimes being a great website just isn't enough to make that commitment happen.

The first thing that many users do when they want to end their Facebook life is to deactivate their account. Deactivation is different from deletion in that it only prevents other users from seeing their account and it forces the user to enter in specific information to gain access again. Otherwise Facebook still remembers all the user's information and can recall it all with only a few keystrokes by the user. Actual deletion on the other hand means the end of the user's account. Everything known about the user is gone, and there is no turning back.[86]

There are two important roles that deactivation serves for Facebook. The first role is that it lets users take a break from Facebook before they get burned out from using it. Deactivation is almost like a vacation that users can take when they need to slip away for a while. And when the user wants to come back, Facebook will be ready and waiting for them. No information will be lost, and no friends will have to be re-added. The user's account will be the same as when they deactivated it.

The deactivation button also serves as a delay before the user exits Facebook entirely. Whenever a user falsely chooses the deactivation button under the assumption that they are deleting their account, Facebook has successfully delayed the user's exit. This mistake gives the user time to cool down and think about what they will be leaving behind. Once they realize that the deactivation button is just a decoy, they may even develop second thoughts about self-termination. After all, the user just needs to enter in their log in information and a captcha to reboot their account. Going back to Facebook really is too easy to resist.

If the user is smart enough to know how to delete their account, Facebook also does a decent job of making termination seem like it is not worth the user's time. This perception is created through their advertising, their F8 Conferences, and the interviews they give to the media. To avoid Facebook, it would seem that one is rejecting an inevitable aspect of technology. Those who do not accept Facebook may even be seen as backward or too paranoid for even the slightest advancements in technology. This is especially true for the older rejecters of Facebook.

Another illusion that is promoted by Facebook is that membership is essential for a functional life. This idea is encouraged by Facebook infiltrating every aspect of society. The work place, the school, the home, and anywhere else the user may go are becoming dependent on technology that is affiliated with Facebook. If the user wants to communicate with their boss, professor, friend, or family member it might be easier if they do it on Facebook. But that does not mean they must. There are plenty of other ways to communicate if the user wants to leave.

If the user can walk away from the convenient features and gain the understanding that Facebook is not a necessary aspect of life, they are still forced to break communication with a large number of people that they care about. Facebook's statistics show that there were 150 billion friend connections on the network at the end of 2012.[87] That comes out to roughly 130-150 friends per average user, but most users probably have more than that because there are many fake accounts that have fake friends.[88] When the user deletes their account, we can assume that the user will not be able to communicate with most of those people the way they did through Facebook. Friends of the user that live far away or that they simply don't see very often are what Facebook holds as collateral until the user comes to their senses. Either the user stays a member of Facebook, or they disappear from a lot of people's social radar. It is a difficult choice to make.

Based on another survey done by *Pew Internet Research,* 64% of users have taken a break from Facebook and returned within a year. These departures all had reasons to leave Facebook, but they were not enough. Aside from the 4% of users who left because of privacy related concerns, the reasons ranged from growing tired of the network, losing internet access, lack of time, illness, or changed in location.[89] But the important thing to recognize is that the methods Facebook employed to keep users loyal worked. Facebook not only recruits and extract information from users, but they can keep them on the network for extended periods of time and prevent from leaving for too long. Facebook is more than just an information collection machine; it is place that users do not want to leave.

The Cycle

The result of this addiction cycle is that Facebook is a great place to advertise products. User membership, content shared, engagement, and just about every other indicator that can be measured are ridiculously high for Facebook because of this system. People are sharing more information than ever with this site and there is no sign stopping any time soon. From these high numbers, Facebook's stock is rated higher and their ability to generate revenue continues to increase every year.[90]

Because of the encouragement Facebook receives from the market, there is a financial incentive for Facebook's organization to keep users addicted to the network. As we will see throughout this book, the benefits that Facebook achieves from this process are substantial and grand. For the user, however the consequences can far outweigh any direct benefit that Facebook may provide. Sharing massive amounts of information with many casual acquaintances on the internet has its risks. But if this system fits Facebook interests, the user will go along for the ride.

4. Security

There are many things that could happen to a user that would cause them to realize the importance of the information they share on Facebook. Perhaps they apply for a job and become afraid they will not get hired based off their Timeline information. Maybe they try to get out of a bad relationship and grow concerned that their former boyfriend or girlfriend is keeping tabs on them. They might even have concerns over excessive government surveillance by watching the daily news. Whatever it is that causes the alarm bells to sound, a realization will be made that forces the user to think twice about sharing their information with Facebook. When that happens, the user may consider leaving Facebook for good.

The solution to this problem for some users is to just be careful with the information that they share. They believe that if they keep sensitive information to themselves they can avoid any harm that would come from using Facebook. The user could also lie about certain information they give to Facebook such as their address or birthday in order to protect themselves. This method of withholding information allows the user to continue being a Facebook member without worrying too much about future penalties for information sharing.

While this is somewhat of an acceptable strategy, the problem is that a user only knows so much about what information is acceptable for future situations. No one really knows how people they come in contact with later on will look at the information they are sharing in the present. For instance, a user might see their current Facebook activity as portraying a relatively conservative lifestyle, while a future employer may see that activity differently and use it as a reason not to hire the user.

The second problem in the withholding strategy is that the enjoyment that the user receives from Facebook is built around the user sharing lots of truthful information. If Facebook doesn't know who the user's friends are, then the user cannot communicate with them on the network. Facebook also depends on a list of real friends in order to make friend suggestions to the user. So the user can technically withhold information, however Facebook is built to prevent that strategy from being embraced wholeheartedly.

To keep users from embracing the withholding of information strategy, Facebook also gives users several remedies to help them protect their information. Privacy controls, educational materials and encryption are the three major ways that Facebook does this. These remedies help rid the user of feelings of hesitation or paranoia in sharing what they normally might keep private. While this exchange has the appearance of being legitimate, closer examination proves otherwise.

It is important to remember that Facebook, from what we know, has no interest in seeing direct and immediate harm come to the user from sharing information. Facebook needs the user to feel safe so they will return to the site. But at the same time Facebook needs to have a lot of users and a lot of information. There is a balance that must be struck between these two competing desires if Facebook intends to have them both.

Privacy Controls

The basic method of protecting Facebook data is through the privacy controls. Facebook provides these tools to users so that they can have control over how their information is displayed on the network. The controls vary in what they do, but their main focus is on verification of the user's identity and on helping to conceal information they have shared on Facebook. Unlike some of the other security measures that Facebook employs, the controls require some time and energy to be invested in by the user. Because the tools require input, most users will be somewhat familiar with how they function.

The first verification tool that every user interacts with on Facebook is the password feature when they register their account. Every time the user logs in they must give Facebook their password to obtain access to their profile information. And Facebook may also ask the user what device they are using so that they can detect suspicious behavior.[91] If a novel device that is different from the usual machine was used to access the user's account, it could mean that the account was hacked. By asking for a simple piece of information to match with the IP address, Facebook can help prevent different machines from impersonating other users.

Facebook will also ask the user for the answer to a security question that they selected during the registration process to defend against these suspicious devices. An example of this could be "what city were you born in"? If the user can answer the question then they will get access to their account. If they can't answer the question then the user must go to the log in screen and have their password and answer reset through their email.[92]

Along with these simple measures there are also advanced features that the individual can use to verify their identity. For instance the user can put special codes on their account so that when the user logs in from a foreign device Facebook will ask for the code to permit access. Facebook even has this feature for applications that individuals have added to their profile.[93] The only real drawback from this use of additional codes is that it means the user must remember more codes that they are likely to forget, or even worse, write down to remember.

To ensure that the user does not have their account hacked while they are logged in to Facebook, the user can also use the active sessions tool that allows for only one log in from one location at a time. The active session tool also prevents against people from watching what users are doing while online.[94] And if all else fails, the user can have notifications sent to their phone every time someone logs in to their account.[95] This might become a major annoyance, but in the end, it does serve the purpose of keeping the user's account safe.

After putting in all this effort to ensure who the user is who they say they are, Facebook moves on to the second goal of helping the user conceal information. Because users share so much information with Facebook it is important that they believe they can hide it whenever they want to. Without this ability, users would be much more cautious in the information that they share. This would result in Facebook collecting far less information. But Facebook will not allow for such doubt to creep into the mind of the user.

For every single piece of information that the user can give, Facebook provides users with the ability to adjust that information so that only certain people on the friends list can see it. This applies for posts, comments, videos, application updates... everything.[96] But remember that Facebook is not erasing this information, they are only hiding it. Facebook can still see every piece of information regardless of what the user does until they permanently leave. That is why they give users so much power in hiding what they share. It does not really affect Facebook in the long run.

Facebook even goes so far as to let users hide their entire profile for a period of time. The user has the option of deactivating their profile information from the public's viewing until they decide to log back in. A reason for temporary deactivation could be that the user does not want anyone to see their information temporarily, but they also do not want to lose that information either. Whatever the reason for deactivation, the user's profile will be inaccessible without having their password.[97]

The result of these privacy options is not a total failure on Facebook's part. Security problems can be prevented by the user if they are diligent in the application of these tools. And there are critical weaknesses in these controls as we will see in later chapters, but the tools still achieve what Facebook has created them for. They give the user the impression that they have control over their information when they clearly do not.

This illusion of control allows for excessive sharing and usage to continue without concern. Now the user can hide the posts they do not want others to see. They can put special alerts on their account when people log in. If someone else logs in for them, the user can see their location based on the IP address Facebook tracks.[98] This provides the appearance of a formidable defense of sensitive information.

Unfortunately, it is also a defense that most users do not even make use of. A study by MacAfee and Evalueserve suggest that 24% of Americans are not confident in their ability to use privacy controls.[99] And another study by *Consumer Reports* estimated that 25% of users do not use the privacy features at all.[100] This is incredibly telling when we see how often the privacy controls are pointed to as a reason for why the excessive sharing of information on Facebook is okay.

And even if the user does embrace these privacy controls, Facebook still sees everything that the user shares on the network anyway. There is no button that prevents Facebook from seeing certain aspects of the user profile. Facebook gets it all and Facebook sees it all until the user decides to delete their account. Because of this crucial flaw, the privacy features are not really privacy features but distractions meant to make the user feel safe.

Education

To find Facebook's educational materials, look at the small type font links located at the bottom of the log in screen. These links will provide information that ranges from how the site works, to the advertising features available, all the way to information on how developers can build applications for the site. This book will look at all of these topics, but for right now we will concentrate on the information related to privacy.

There are two major aspects of the information on privacy: informed consent and intelligent usage. By informed consent, we mean that Facebook tells the user in their policy documents all the information that they collect on the network and how that information may be used. By intelligent usage, we mean that Facebook provides information on how the user can share information on the site while protecting themselves and their peers.

The informed consent materials are best represented by the data use policy. The policy enumerates for the user in small 8-point font every piece of information that Facebook collects and how that information may be used.[101] By giving up some its own privacy, Facebook helps to achieve the appearance of visibility and honesty. The language of the policy, like any legal contract, makes the situation that users are placed in seem unimportant. Ideas about losing rights to information or lack of liability for Facebook are put in bland language that makes the words seem innocuous and not worth reading. This makes the document difficult for the average person to read and understand, which means that they probably will not read it at all.

If the user is too lazy to read the data use policy, Facebook offers them the choice of downloading all their information so they can see exactly what they are sharing.[102] Usage of the download feature could open the user's eyes to help change their behavior or it may lead to a sense of resignation. Seeing the wealth of information that Facebook already has may cause the user to accept a life without privacy, which in many ways they have no way of refusing if they are on Facebook.

While getting the user to consent to the excessive data collection is rather easy, getting them to use the site intelligently is another matter. Facebook is an excellent place to find people who are not technologically oriented. To address this Facebook provides information in their Help Center and under the Privacy link to tell people about how to remain safe on the network. This kind of information includes not just information about how to use the privacy controls, but also what not to click on or subscribe to while on using Facebook.[103]

After educating the user about what to expect from the network, Facebook asks that users report any profiles that may be exhibiting threatening or suspicious behavior. The reporting feature allows Facebook to identify more problems with the website by using fewer employees.[104] Instead of scanning through millions of profiles, Facebook can just look at the profiles that its users have identified as a problem. By asking for help from the users, Facebook can delete fake profiles that may pose a threat to the site while improving its ad targeting machine.

It is also hoped with education that the user will be wise enough not to infect other users with malware and viruses that are features of Facebook. Education is almost like a vaccination for Facebook users. When they see what to look out for they are guarded against it. Of course most users still fall for the scams that are seen on the Newsfeed and in the message box, but the education is still worth a try.

The intentions and potential effects of this educational strategy are diverse. As with the privacy controls, the educational materials help to make the user feel in control of the situation they are in on Facebook. Reading the privacy policy as well as information in the Help Center about malware could make the user feel that there is nothing to worry about. The average user may not know the implications of sharing their location, IP address, facial image, and name all at once. But because Facebook told them that the information was being collected in the privacy policy, the user may feel that they know what to expect.

With this sense of control, Facebook also gets users to share some of the blame that comes with excessive sharing. Now that the user has access to a wide range of educational materials, it is difficult for them to say they didn't know what was happening with their information. Despite the inadequacy of materials, Facebook gives the user enough information for them to understand what this site really is all about. The problem is that most users do not read the educational materials and that they probably do not know why they should.

As you will notice in the end note section, this book frequently cites Facebook's educational materials for reference. They clarify how Facebook works and they give excellent reasons why the network should not be used. But they also only provide a portion of the story that Facebook wants users need to hear. And the information that is provided is written in in such a way to give the impression that everything is okay. That is the reason why users should turn to other sources information about Facebook. It is simply not enough to trust them; users must get knowledge from other places.

It could also be said that a user should not have to read countless pages worth of information to make an informed decision as to whether they should use a social network. And even after reading those materials and perhaps after reading this book a user could still not know all of the tricks that Facebook might be pulling. Facebook is constantly coming up with new features and changing their policy so as to stifle a quality understanding of the site. It seems that it doesn't really matter how transparent Facebook is with their site because they are engineering the situation for people not to even make an attempt at understanding it.

Encryption

A part of security that is important but should not require any real effort from the user is encryption. By enabling encryption websites can protect their users from people who are trying to monitor their network. But if a user wants to encrypt their Facebook information that responsibility lies on Facebook. The administrators are the ones who must outfit the site with a layer of encryption to prevent eavesdropping from unauthorized individuals. All the user can do is decide whether to turn the encryption on if it is not already on a default setting.[105]

Facebook has had an excuse, as many other websites have had, for not using this encryption in the past several years. Outfitting a site with HTTPS can cause the site to run slower and may even destroy functionality. If you have ever used a banking website or an ecommerce website you may have experienced how long it takes for encrypted pages to load when entering in sensitive data. Some sites can even be "broken" by turning on HTTPS encryption which can destroy functionality.[106] Facebook could avoid HTTPS by telling everyone they were too large and could claim fears of network failure if they implemented the encryption.

This excuse may have worked in the early part of the decade, however as time went on other major sites gave users the option of encrypting their data. The first notable example is

Google who implemented the HTTPS option in 2008. This was not the result of any true sense of responsibility but from pressure put on by journalists and bloggers pointing out the errors in the excuses internet companies were making.[107]

To elaborate, Google told the public that they could not afford to do the encryption and that it would slow down their services. The excuse over cost measures was exposed to be untrue by blogger and ACLU principle Christopher Soghoian who sent a letter to Google CEO Eric Schmidt that was later published in *Wired Magazine*. We could also point out the error in values in that Google as well as Facebook cared more for growth than about security for their users, but we will get to that later.[108]

Following Google and many other notable websites, Facebook began to offer the option of encryption in 2011. This was after seven years of allowing user to enter in sensitive user data unencrypted.[109] The length of time between launch and encryption speaks to how little Facebook cares for the privacy. Had it not been for pressure by the media and competitors, Facebook may not have even bothered with HTTPS yet.

In November of 2012, Facebook finally offered a default encryption setting of mutual HTTPS for North American users that will eventually include all users. A default HTTPS setting means that users will no longer forget to use encryption or neglect it for the sake of speed. When users do forsake the option, they leave other users open to monitoring attacks.[110] So after nine years Facebook has finally ended a hole that they allowed to stay open for the sake of growth.

And despite its benefits, HTTPS is not bulletproof. Like any encryption, HTTPS can be deciphered. If a government agency for instance wanted to look at a specific profile for instance they could crack the encryption.[111] HTTPS can also be circumvented through falsifying an encryption key that allows the hacker to receive information from the client and the server without being blocked.[112] And of course encryption won't even come into play if someone just guesses the password or infiltrates the user's network. At the end of the day encryption is just something Facebook was supposed to do, and not something they should now use to defend their excessive collection of data.

Personnel

After the user has done what they can to protect the network's information it is then the job of Facebook's security personnel to take care of business. The security team, headed by former Justice Department employee Joe Sullivan, is tasked with investigating major attacks that are launched against the site every year as well as smaller bugs that might causes users some trouble.[113] While the security team breaks down into many different divisions, we will just refer to them as security for now.

Facebook's security investigates major intrusions by doing things such as monitoring underground internet forums, exchanging information with third parties such as law enforcement, and actively monitoring the network's infrastructure to detect any irregularities in behavior. When they identify specific ways that hackers are exploiting the network, the team will strike back by creating tools that target the hacker's specific strategy.[114] Facebook will also litigate against attackers for compensation or help prosecute attackers for their imprisonment.[115] To commemorate their victories over cybercriminals who cause serious problems the team has a hall of fame called the Scalp Wall which serves to boost morale for the organization.[116]

To take on the job of fighting the smaller hacks, Facebook will outsource the work to white hat hackers to keep the system running smooth. White hats are considered responsible hackers as opposed to black hats who act irresponsibly by exploiting the weaknesses they find in networks for their personal gain. Facebook runs a White Hat program known as Bug Bounty that gives out monetary rewards to hackers who identify bugs in the system.[117] These bugs can leave the network vulnerable to attacks so it is important they be found as soon as possible. By giving incentives to security specialists outside the company, it helps to bring fresh eyes to problems that Facebook may be facing while simply expanding the number of people who are looking at a problem.

This program however does not always go as planned. A good example comes from the recent hack on CEO Mark Zuckerberg's profile. In mid-2013 a hacker who found a bug in Facebook that allowed him to make posts to other users' Timelines contacted the White Hat Program to collect his reward. This hacker was ignored by Facebook so he decided to hack Mark Zuckerberg's account and demonstrate the flaw. The hack attracted headlines and made the Whitehat program look silly because they ignored a serious flaw that needed to be addressed. To deal with the embarrassment, the security team made a post on their page detailing the incident with the hacker and what they were going to do about the problem. They did not pay the hacker however.[118]

Facebook's Security page is established to give out alerts and tips to users so that they do infect other users on the network. But in addition to the role that it plays in education, the page also helps boost Facebook's reputation by clearing the air when a problem surfaces in the media. And it also helps create the impression that Facebook is being diligent in defending the privacy of their users by showing off their hard work through the page. As of August 21, 2013, that page has 7 million likes and roughly 15,000 comments. It is difficult to say how effective it is at protecting privacy, but it is giving off an impression of safety to many people.[119]

Off the main security page a user can also go to the AV Marketplace to download protections viruses that might surface on the site. Through the Marketplace Facebook partners with security firms such as Total Defense, Avira, and Kaspersky Labs to provide users with free anti-virus software so they can keep the site clean These software packages usually have hundreds of thousands of likes and in some cases over 3 million which show how much users are aware of them.[120]

Facebook's security personnel represent how far they will go with protecting user information. And this is not for nigh either. They do get major victories in the fight against cybercrime. A recent report by *Business Insider* showed that Facebook has very low levels of spam, something to the order of 5%.[121] In a recent case Facebook won approximately $826 million dollars in damages from over 30 plaintiffs that were charged in the case. And perhaps their greatest victory came in 2012 over the Koobface virus that had plagued the network for three years until they managed to put it into a state of remission.[122] After looking at everything that Facebook has done we cannot say that an effort is not being made here. But that really isn't the problem here.

Sad Reality

While these efforts by Facebook are not to be dismissed entirely, there is however a much simpler solution to the anxiety that a user feels with sharing information. Facebook could just take in less information from the user. They could forsake asking for such things as personal history or name of high school. They wouldn't necessarily have to cut out everything, but they could reduce what they collect so that users retain a degree of privacy.

Or even if Facebook still wanted to take in massive amounts of data, they could choose to delete that data after a certain amount of time. Six months could be a reasonable cutoff date for information that users post but forget to delete from their account.   And that would not have to include all the user's information either. Name and birthday would remain, but information about the user's hiking trip two years ago is something that could easily go.

What also should be admitted is that certain types of information are only valuable for so long. Pictures of a person from three years ago for example may depict the user differently from who they are today. Therefore, if Facebook allows their users to permanently delete their photos, it won't really matter in a larger sense. And if the user should want to keep their photos for a longer time they can just store them on their computer. This would not necessarily make the photo safer as it does put more control in the hands of the user.

To protect the user better Facebook could also make the network less open and more protected compared to its current form. Ending the promotion of excessive friending is one recommendation that could help secure the network. There are so many people on the average friends list that it makes it impossible to truly protect someone's data no matter how hard they try. All it takes is one infiltrator to get access to a friend's account and they are in the user's network.

The last key recommendation that could be made is a return to an era of online anonymity where users have screen names instead of real names. Regardless of the risks that this brings with sexual predators, the average user should not have to risk their security online because of the mistakes that other websites have made in the past. Returning to anonymity would end the direct targeting that is made possible when Facebook matches a name to a face. In some ways having a screen name could be as helpful as having a password in preventing people from gaining information about who the user is.

Facebook will most likely never implement these kinds of strategies to protect their users. Doing so would require Facebook to sacrifice information that they use for ad targeting. Making changes to information sharing could also scare off users who feel the site puts them in danger. Or it could just displease certain users who like having everybody know everything about them. While changing their policy of excessive collection could result in less money and users, it would make the users safer which should be more important than anything else.

But aside from ignoring a more effective way at running the website, the solutions that Facebook has provided users are not full proof by any means. The privacy controls leave the user exposed not only to Facebook and the advertisers that use the site, but also to the user's entire friends list. The educational materials provide the most sanitized version possible of what users should know about Facebook and the internet. HTTPS encryption can be circumvented with a moderate degree of effort. And even the security division is not exactly the greatest cyber security outfit in the world. Perhaps the reason why Facebook provides so much is because each aspect of security provides so little compared to how much they need to protect.

What is also unfortunate is that when we consider the encouragements to tell the truth, the lack of proper security features, and the desire to communicate with one's peers, it becomes almost worthless for a user to bother protecting their data. The Facebook experience has not only accomplished excessive information collection, but it has made the user realize they shouldn't care about their data when it is taken from them.

Wearing down user's expectations of privacy helps not just Facebook's bottom line, but it reinforces a societal norm of openness. This norm encourages individuals not to worry about what information they share online. If everyone has lots of information available people may tend to think that it is okay. If someone does have apprehensions, they could fall victim to the burnout that users experience with the controls. The individual is surrounded by people who do not care about their information and the individual faces an uphill battle trying to secure it.

What makes this situation most difficult is that on some level Facebook seems to believe that they are treating their users fairly. By providing users with a great services and security Facebook believes that they are balancing the evil they commit with their excessive collection. On the surface, this is a legitimate deal. But as we will see in the following chapters, Facebook's actions are not correct or square by any means.

5. Advertising

In order sell products, a company needs to have information about the audience that they are selling their products to. Having a picture of who the audience is allows advertisers to create promotional material that speak to the consumer instead of just at them. It is also important that the company build a relationship with their audience while they are advertising their product. By creating a relationship with the consumer, the company can keep the consumer coming back to them without having to repeatedly advertise a specific product. This essentially is the nature of brand marketing.

One of the ways that businesses can do brand marketing is through Facebook. The billion plus users that Facebook has within its servers gives businesses a chance to see and connect with a massive audience unlike ever before. Instead of interrupting what the consumer is doing through TV commercials and radio ads, the company can engage the consumer through ads placed within a social context that are less distracting. This is like the way product placement works in television shows and movies. The consumer sees the ad, but because it is put in a social context the individual does not try to ignore it.

A Brief Description of the Process

Businesses conduct advertising on Facebook by creating a page for their brand or product. A page will allow the business to post information for users to see and it will also give them a chance to advertise on the Newsfeed. Every time a person likes the Facebook page of someone's business, that like is displayed on someone's Newsfeed. Therefore, almost every commercial or sign you see these days will provide a link to their Facebook page. If they get one person to like their page it could mean that a hundred more people will see their name on a Newsfeed. When the ad is clicked on again, the process will repeat itself.[123]

To help promote their Page's distribution, businesses will often provide incentives to users who like their page. When a user likes the page of a restaurant for instance, the user may receive updates on special deals and information about new additions to the menu. The other incentive for liking the page is the user wants their friends to know their interests. Someone who likes a show such as the Walking Dead will be telling their friends that they are fan of survival horror television. It might also make the user feel cool for being known as a fan of a popular television show.

After setting up their Page, the next step for the business is to start creating advertisements to be featured on the network. The purpose of the ad will be to lure users into the company's Facebook Page or external website. Once the user is there it is hoped they will read information about the company or perhaps decide to make a purchase. This is similar to the way that most advertising is done on the internet. You bait users into clicking on the ad, and you try to get them to buy something. It is simple, but lucrative if done correctly.

Where Facebook differentiates itself however is with its ability to accurately target advertisements to specific users. Businesses can choose which advertisements are shown to whom by setting demographic specifications on their ad. Because Facebook has so much information available on users, businesses are more likely to reach the people that they want.[124] This innovation changes advertising from speaking at the masses to speaking to the individual.

When setting the target demographic, the business has five specifications it can choose from. They include location, age range, gender, interests, education, and connections.[125] The specification for connections refers to people that are connected to the page in some way. This could be through liking the page or through being friends with someone who has liked the page.

These settings allow for the targeting to be exact or generalized which in turn allows for more customization. Targeting users by age range for instance gives the advertiser multiple ranges to pick from instead of just one specific age group.

Along with setting demographic specifications, it is the job of the advertiser to decide whether to go with a cost per click or a cost per impression pay range.[126] With cost per click Facebook gets a percentage for every click that the advertisement receives. With cost per impression, Facebook gets a percentage for every time the advertisement appears on the Newsfeed. To prevent the payment system from getting out of control, administrators can set a budget for how much they intend to spend on advertisements. Once the spending limit for the day is up, the advertisement will stop appearing.[127]

After the advertisement has been crafted by the company's creative department and the specification have been set, the ad will then be shown on the side of or inside of the Newsfeed depending on where the company wants it.[128] The performance of the ad will later be generated in a report for the advertiser to see. This information will typically be presented in a dashboard format with charts and graphs that provide visualizations in addition to raw data. The readout will contain numbers such as the budget for the ad, the number of impressions, the social percentage, and the number of clicks it received along with the average cost per click.[129] Social percentage refers to the percentage of impressions where the advertisement was shown with a social context.[130]

While that process mostly sums up how Facebook advertising works, it is also important to highlight the guidelines that ads must follow to be featured on the network. These guidelines must be followed or else the advertisement will be erased.[131] The rationality behind this effort is to protect the integrity of the site as a quality place to advertise. Facebook wants their users to be comfortable with what they see on the network so they will be encouraged to return to the network. Preventing the proliferation of graphic or insulting ads is just one of the ways that Facebook does this.

Advertisements are also forbidden from using spyware or "adware" that allows for the infiltration of the user's system.[132] The rule against adware is put in place for the same reason as the prevention of obscene material. Facebook wants users to feel comfortable with what they are taking part in. Think of it like a gang leader who forbids violent crime in his territory but permits drug dealing and gambling. When advertisers alienate users and harm their computers, negative attention gets called to the network. When advertisers play by the rules and only do subtle targeting of users such as emotional appeals and tracking of information, then everyone can make a lot of money.

In the case of application advertising however, the rules are somewhat different. Applications cannot use ad targeting for the advertisements that they display on their application. They can only use targeting specifications for advertising the application itself to other users. That is where the controversy lies with applications because each one has a distinct way of using information to promote itself. To understand how the application uses data an individual would have to become familiar with a different policy for each separate application.[133]

While users may be burdened with understanding information about what they are taking part in, companies can be burdened by the information that their advertisements and applications collect. To handle this information the companies will buy services that specialize in Customer Relationship Management or CRM.[134] CRM's are similar to what Facebook Insights provides, but they are more advanced and cover a variety of networks A CRM essentially monitors social media for other companies and helps analyze what is collected. After the data is analyzed, the CRM will then give the company a report of what people are saying about their brand. This readout will also appear as a dashboard that includes a variety of marketing indicators such as how often the brand name was mentioned, what type of attitude people had about the brand, what websites the conversations took place on, and what percentage the brand held in the conversation.[135]

The business of monitoring what internet users do and analyzing the data from it has become a major trend in the tech world. Companies such as Oracle, Microsoft, Salesforce, and IBM are just some of the major companies that do this market analysis that depends on companies like Facebook. Modern social networking has given these corporations a window into the social life of the internet user. Without that window, it could be assumed that the CRM's would have to start analyzing less meaningful data sources that are not as centralized as Facebook.

In addition to the companies that are taking advantage of this data, other websites have also taken up the Facebook brand of advertising. Facebook has set a standard that encourages websites to gain as many users as they can while collecting as much information about them as they can. So, Facebook has raised not only the quality of social marketing but also the bar for what internet users will accept. The rest of the internet's data miners owe a debt of gratitude to Facebook for the new standard they have created.

What is not said about this usage of CRM's and Facebook however is that it essentially amounts to customer surveillance. By watching everything that the customer says or does, the CRM can tell the company what decisions they should make next. This is not a revolutionary marketing strategy or a new way of delivering a brand message, it is simply a benefit that comes with spying on the consumer. They are getting information that other companies may not have access to and therefore they have an advantage in the market.

Necessity

The advertising benefits that Facebook brings to companies is slowly becoming a necessity more than an advantage. Companies that choose to ignore Facebook face certain penalties that exist for not going along with the program. This is because the network contains conversations about millions of products that are sold around the world. It is important that a company listen in on those conversations because other potential customers are listening to them as well. A post about a malfunctioning product can go from ten comments, to ten thousand comments in two days. Companies know this, and they know they will be powerless to engage that conversation if they leave Facebook.

To deal with the problem of Facebook, companies will hire CRM's to discover what people are saying before it becomes mainstream conversation. This gives businesses time to prevent complaints and rumors from spreading over the network about their products. And if the company embraces Facebook and has a good CRM on their team, they are in decent shape to meet this challenge. This is not to mention that the CRM's will still help provide insights for intelligent marketing strategies that could bring increased profits in the future.

But as more and more companies use these CRM's, more and more companies have to use them. Monitoring social media has become more of a necessity than an advantage in brand marketing. Companies will have to stay ahead of not just the consumer opinion but their competitors to stay alive.[136] This scenario combined with the danger of consumer gossip serves to thoroughly prevent any companies from abandoning Facebook out of a concern for customer privacy.

A major reason for this lack of discretion is that businesses have far more constraints than individuals do. Businesses must earn a profit, stay relevant, maintain and recruit employees, maintain their customer base, and dozens of other requirements to remain successful. They can't just delete their page on Facebook tomorrow; they must maintain a presence for the well-being of the company.

Along with the business itself, there are also individuals in the business world that depend on Facebook for their reputation. Whether you are just out of college or a district manager, you can never have enough business contacts. A study reported in *The New York Times* found that 92% of companies are now using social media for recruitment on new employees. Facebook was cited as the most popular network for recruiting next to LinkedIn.[137] While the professional still has a degree of liberty to leave Facebook, that option is starting to disappear on a recruitment level because of its increased acceptance as a recruiting tool.

And for some people once they get hired they may have to keep their account. There could be many understandable reasons for this such as the sharing of information between employees and management. Another reason could be that Facebook serves as a chemistry builder for the workplace environment.[138] Some work places even value their employees based on their business contacts. So the idea that someone can just quit after they get hired isn't too realistic an idea.

The Facebook obligation is no less true for people in show business. If the celebrity wants to be famous they need to have their name recognized. Being a member of Facebook is a way for the celebrity to tell the world who they are when they are not on camera. It can also be used for celebrities to promote where they are going and when fans can see them. For example, a comedian or musician could promote their tour dates on Facebook. Writers can promote their book signings. Actors can plug their movies. Because of its ability to facilitate interaction with many people, celebrities take a gamble when they forsake Facebook.

Facebook has created for themselves a niche in the business environment. Brands depend on Facebook to survive now; it is no longer just about gaining an edge on the competition.[139] Because Facebook is a trend in future technology, companies that shun it will also be hiding from the future. Those that embrace it are given advantages that allow them to win the day in the marketplace. In a way businesses are given an offer they can't refuse with Facebook. Either they take the advantage of the network or they suffer the consequences of ignoring it.

Cattle

After looking at the way advertising is done on Facebook, it becomes clear that Facebook is not really the product that is being sold. The product is actually the users and their information. The network itself is merely a tool to lure in the users so their information can be voluntarily collected from them. Facebook in a way is like a game preserve for hunting wild animals or a pasture where cattle graze. It is just a way to get everyone in one place so that companies can get their information all at once.

Thinking of users like cattle allows us to gain insights into how Facebook works. If you look back to the security remedies in the previous chapter, you will notice that Facebook is only concerned with what will scare users away. They are not truly concerned with the safety of the users, just like ranchers are not terribly concerned with the ultimate wellbeing of their cattle. Facebook just needs to keep their users from leaving, and that requires a small degree of concern on their part.

Facebook users are also similar to cattle in that they produce something for Facebook the same way that cattle produce something for their owner. We can think of the information that users share perhaps like milk for cows or wool for sheep. Facebook cannot butcher their product; however, they must cultivate it by letting their users share as much as information possible. In the process Facebook also gets eye balls to look at their advertisements for prolonged periods of time.

Users also tend to experience harm because of the cultivation process, much like cattle do. Cows for instance can be abused by workers or perhaps develop diseases because of their living conditions. Facebook users can have their identities stolen by hackers or their computers inflicted by malware. The size of the network drastically increases the chance that harm will come to the user much like factory farms increase chances that harm will come to stockyard animals. But because there is so much money to be made in cultivating their product all at once, Facebook is willing to put their cattle at risk.

Balance

Another example of the negative effects that this type of social networking gives to users is in the customer business relationship. The Federal Trade Commission recognizes that consumers require a certain amount of privacy to prevent predatory business tactics.[140]   Having privacy allows consumers to operate from a position of strength when shopping for a product instead of being placed in a situation of desperation. A business might be tempted to take advantage of customers who they know everything about and that are in dire need of the product the company sells. There is a necessary balance that must be struck between the amount of information shared and withheld by the consumer. Just like there is only so much information the public can know about corporations, there should be a limit to what corporations can know about consumers.

But with Facebook individuals give away their privacy in exchange for the small reward of social connection.   Facebook on the other hand keeps very tight control over the information they release to the public. There is no discussion in the information that Facebook releases about how their algorithms make their selections of who receives what advertisement. The released data doesn't tell us what information is useful for advertising and what information is just for a social experience. There is also absolutely no way of knowing what the corporations who receive aggregated information on users do with that data. Having these educational materials wouldn't fix everything, but at least the equation would be somewhat balanced.

These are only a few of the questions that will not be answered by the information that Facebook releases because ultimately the information is not for users to look at. The information that gets released is primarily for businesses that are hoping to advertise on Facebook. Whatever sense of personal comfort that users might get out of the information so be it. Facebook could also argue that these questions are trade secrets that must be protected for the success of the company. But at the same token it could also be said that these secrets must be released so the user can make a reasonable decision about having a membership to this website.

What makes all this secrecy especially worrisome is that the advertisements Facebook delivers are made with the intention of users eventually buying what they see. It is the users who pay for Facebook by purchasing goods and services advertised on the site. Without the user buying at least some of the products that they see, Facebook would not be able to make a cent off their advertising machine. Users are not only giving up their information, they are paying for Facebook's service as well.

When we establish that there is a certain expectation of what users will eventually do, we should recognize the dangers of excessive advertising combined with social media intelligence. Excess advertising alone can cause its subjects to spend recklessly to gain a sense of fulfillment. Advertisements are made to generate feelings of want and envy in those who see them. The objective of the advertising is to make the viewer buy something they didn't know they needed or wanted. This can cause people to waste money on things they do not need. Advertising creates a hole that the subject is always trying to fill. This is good for companies, but bad for the individual.

This feeling of wanting leads to a culture of consumerism that advertising tries to foster. That type of culture cares mostly for material goods and very little for higher pursuits. By placing people in a culture that cares only for consuming, the people will dwell only on achieving material wealth. This encourages people to focus on the pointless and be manipulated by objects such as money and goods. They will also neglect areas of life such as relationships and spirituality that lead to a greater sense of fulfillment and mental health.

Finally, advertising can ruin the aesthetic nature of what could be a beautiful world. Even without talking about the real world, we can all admit that the internet could be a wonderful place with less advertising. Imagine a world with less pop-up bars and flashing banners. Less junk email that complicates our trip to the digital mail box. And most importantly, less advertisements that are disturbingly close to our own interests and desires.

The system of advertising put in place by Facebook should concern us because it places even more power in the hands of corporations then they had before. With Facebook, they can collect more business intelligence, spread more advertisements, increase their reputations, and make money. While many users may think that they are just connecting with friends and family by using Facebook, in reality they are also fueling corporation's efforts to get stronger and stronger.

Bitter Pill

At a lecture given in Boston called "Advertising and the Perfect Storm", Professor Sut Jhally of the University of Massachusetts discussed the dilemma that advertising places on users who recognize its lack of immaterial value. He noted that most people understand that consumerism is not the most important value in life. The important things in our lives are not material objects Jhally says, but instead the people in our lives who we truly care about. He continued to say however that advertisers understand this fact as well. To respond, advertisers try to combine the things that consumers care about with the things that advertisers want them to buy.[141]

Facebook provides a good example of this with its use of social interaction and advertising. What Facebook has done is that they have managed to combine advertising with the things in life that users care about the most: their social connections. Because of this manipulation of the user's social life, the user is put into a dilemma that forces them to choose between privacy and social acceptance.

By joining a negative thing (advertising) with a positive thing (social interaction) Facebook also makes the negative thing easier to swallow. It is becoming less noticeable. It is not like the commercial that comes after the lead character is done saying their lines on a television show. The Facebook advertisement fits so well into the social landscape that they almost seem to belong there. This is important according to Jhally because most advertisements are instinctively blocked out by most people. There is so much advertising filling up our consciousness that we have to ignore it just to function.[142]

Facebook gives businesses something different with their advertising because the user must look at the ad. No longer is it: "Buy Call of Duty Black Ops 2." Now the advertisement reads: "Just got done playing Black Ops". Advertising is becoming even more interwoven with our social lives than ever were before. As a result, people will be more tempted to embrace the norms that advertising promotes such as consumerism, greed, and envy.

This combination also works because advertising has become a necessary evil of the internet, and of the world. People hate seeing ads everywhere they go, but they understand that it has a purpose. Advertising is what gives us Google search, Twitter feeds, YouTube videos, comedy podcasts, news websites; any place on the internet that gives its product away for free is most likely fueled by advertising. As for right now, advertising is what the internet lives on and until someone develops a better system it will be this way for a while.

The legitimacy of advertising has given Facebook a blank check to take as much information as it wants from the user. It is normal for what Facebook is doing because people equate this collection with necessity. But, Facebook is only taking advantage of the naiveté of the public and their ability to put up with seemingly endless information gathering. Facebook does not need to collect nearly as much information as it does; the public just allows them to.

As we have discussed earlier Facebook could respect the boundaries of the user. They just care more about the success of their site. That doesn't necessarily translate into making a profit. Their strategy is closer to promoting the proliferation of the network. Having a successful advertising machine allows Facebook to attract and store more people. It allows Facebook to grow without running out of capital. Capital in this case being funds as well as good engineers and infrastructure. Success is the name of the game, and Facebook will go at any lengths to gain success.

We should realize after discussing this source of revenue at Facebook that advertising is a major factor in generating the decisions that Facebook makes. Commercial success, not social goals, is what drives Facebook. A Facebook feature is designed to make money for Facebook Incorporated. The money comes from the personal information that Facebook has obtained about their users. By having honest, accurate information, Facebook can help companies tailor advertisements that reach their target audience. If that information is not honest and accurate, then the advertisements are not as effective and Facebook will lose money. And even if the information does meet that requirement, there is still a chance that the person who sees the advertisement will not buy something because of seeing that information.

Always remember that Facebook will constantly be testing the boundaries of what they can ask from users until they are told no. Facebook has transcended the necessary and reasonable amount of information collect by a website from its users. It has an inherent, profit making interest in doing this. Facebook will never tell their users not to share information. They will always take and accept whatever they can get because they know the success of the company is dependent on that information.

If Facebook tells us anything it is not that we should get rid of advertising all together, but that a line must be drawn between what is acceptable and what is not. If we are going to live in a capitalist society, businesses will need a platform to promote their products to the public. While it could certainly be argued that there is too much advertising in society that does not mean we should get rid of it all together. Advertising was here long before Facebook came along. We may even need advertising for the success of a capitalist society, we just don't need Facebook.

6. Weakness

Despite the efforts of Facebook as well as other social networks to secure their systems of information collection, cybercriminals have done an excellent job at utilizing what these networks must offer. The annual Norton Cybercrime Report showed that 1/6 of social network users reported that someone tried to hack into their account and that 4/10 fell victim to cybercrime in 2012.[143] Social networks can be dangerous places if the user and the administrators are not vigilant in their efforts to protect the network's data. Facebook is no exception.

However, any awareness that Facebook is a dangerous place does little to stop user victimizations. Users still continue to share large amounts of information with Facebook as though they have nothing to worry about. Because users often see the threat of cybercrime as remote, very few of them exercise real caution when on Facebook. Not only are privacy controls used sparingly, but billions of pieces of content are shared with Facebook every day.[144] The excessive sharing of information in and of itself is dangerous, and it doesn't help that Facebook encourages with every feature they create.

This heavy volume of information makes Facebook nearly unprotected when combined with its large concentration of users with weak ties to one another. Facebook profiles can easily be impersonated which allows hackers to gain the trust of their targets in an environment that is assumed to be safe. If the hacker can gain the friendship of the user, the privacy controls will begin to lose value. With enough determination, the hacker will eventually find a way into the profile; it just takes some time and effort not to get caught.

Many of the crimes that are connected to Facebook include things such as murder, vandalism, or drug dealing that were solved by looking at Facebook information. These crimes while significant will not be our focus because they usually are not the result of Facebook's excessive collection of data. Instead we will concentrate on the crimes that are such as identity theft, sexual predation, cyber bullying, theft of trade secrets, and cyber terrorism which thrive off the wealth of data that Facebook can provide for potential victims. This is not to suggest that Facebook is the direct cause of these crimes. It is just to say that Facebook makes these crimes so much easier than they were before. This leads to their exploitation by the government which we will cover in later chapters.

Identity Theft

When attacking a profile at the password stage, the brute force technique may be used all though this is not recommended. This type of strategy involves using a piece of software to crack the user's password by entering in repeated attempts until access is granted. Brute force can take a lot of time and faces manual security hindrances so it is not preferred.[145] While in certain cases cracking a person's password can be easy, in other cases simpler, quicker methods can be used.

Social engineering is one alternative that could be attempted. A social engineering strategy refers to a hacker using easily obtainable information about the target to gain access to a secure network. An example of this strategy could be looking for a post-it note with someone's password written on it instead of using a sophisticated program to crack into a person's account. The point of hacking is to find the path of least resistance. Social engineering just applies that way of thinking to people instead of network defenses.[146]

Facebook plays well into this social engineering strategy because it has data such as names of family members, pets, birthdays, past locations, and a number of facts that can be used to guess a password or security question.[147] Facebook can also have more vital information such as email addresses and phone numbers which are important for making a clean steal of someone's identity. When you are trying to take advantage of someone everything they give you is weapon to be used against them.

While collection of left out information could be considered the first part of social engineering, using that information to deceive the target would be the second. To begin this task the hacker should assume a false identity and contact the target to pry information out of them. This can be done through messages and chats, but it can also be accomplished just by becoming someone's friend. Befriending the user gives the hacker access to personal information such as phone number, address, and email information that can be used to intercept more critical information.[148] For instance by having their home address I may be able to stake out their mail box, assuming it doesn't have a lock on it, and wait for bills and important mail to arrive.

Creating a fake profile and gaining a request acceptance can be hard depending on the target. The Norton 2012 Annual Cybercrime Report also found that about 36% of Facebook users accept requests from people they do not know.[149] These people are easy prey, but for other more intelligent users the hacker should employ techniques that give their profile a sense of legitimacy. After all, the credibility that Facebook brings to its users should be embraced by the cybercriminal, not something that is a total obstacle.

The credibility of a friends list is perhaps best acquired by the duplication of someone else's. A good template for this duplication would be a friend located on the edges of the primary target's social circle. This person can be best identified by looking at the targets friend lists if possible, and matching it with other friends list that the user is linked to. After looking at the two or more lists, a name will surface that the target is not yet friends with but who they probably have met at one time or another. It is also important to note that the use of a good proxy server is needed so Facebook cannot track the location of where the hacker is doing their impersonating from. A proxy server will mask the IP address of the hacker to prevent Facebook from tracking down the machine they are using. Once the profile is duplicated whether by manual implementation or software, a request can then be sent to the target hoping to capture their trust.

However, friendship is obtained, once the connection is made certain strategies then become possible. We are most concerned with becoming a friend of the target not only because of the information that is granted to the attacker, but also because the relationship brings with it the chance to push information at the target. Befriending the target allows the hacker to publish information on the target's Newsfeed.[150] From that point the hacker can post their malware and phishing attacks that rely on temptation and visibility, something the Newsfeed is perfect for.

While the hacker can certainly do large amounts of damage by posting a link on the Newsfeed with malicious script that infects the target's computer, for the time being we will focus on just obtaining access to the profile. A befriended hacker could for instance host a web page through a low-cost webhosting service, copy the source code of a Facebook log in screen, and then create a link for it. The link could perhaps have a picture of an attractive woman or a cool looking video that when clicked on asks the user to log back into their profile. After creating this phishing hook, the hacker could post it on the Newsfeed or even send it to the target hoping they will take the bait. If they do, the password will be in the hackers hands without the target knowing what happened to them.[151]

If the hacker should fail to ever become a friend of their target, they could always try their luck with a technique known as "click jacking." Click jacking refers to a hacker creating a fake button on a website and waiting for unsuspecting user to click on the button. The button may really be a link to a page to containing malicious code or malware, which will then infect the computer.[152] Some of the things that this malware can bring could be viruses that cripple the computers functionality, key loggers that track everything the user types, or backdoors that allow the attacker to reenter the user's system whenever they wish.

Instead of breaking into the user's profile, the hacker could just break into the network the target is using and monitor all the communications made on that network. A scary but potent example of this could be the WI-FI networks that we are seeing more and more of in shopping centers and restaurants. These networks are out of the user's control and are typically unsecure by most standards. The 2012 Norton Study also found that 63% of users access social networks through unsecure channels.[153] So it is not too difficult to find unsecure network, but let us say for instance the target is using a network that is secure. The hacker could just set up a Wi-Fi network that the target may be tricked into connecting to because it has a logical sounding name like "WORK" or "LIBRARY" in the area they normally connect in. Might work, might not, but it is always worth a try if the risk of getting caught is low...which it is.

The obstacles that stand in between the hacker and their goals on Facebook are not formidable by any means. Reporting of fake accounts is a task put upon the user to determine who is real and who is artificial.[154] As we have examined, the elimination of anonymity does not make the recognition of the thieves easier, but occasionally harder and more difficult to distinguish from friends and family. Facebook also employs algorithms that supposedly pursue those who create false identities. These algorithms are reinforced by the judgment of humans who make the decision whether to delete the suspected profile.[155] Both of these obstacles can be fooled with enough dedication put forth to forging the account by the hacker.

While this system on its surface would seem ineffective but manageable, it is permanently crippled by Facebook's greed for higher membership numbers. The number of users Facebook has on their site is tied not only with their market value as a company, but also to their self-perception as the greatest social networking site in the world. Were Facebook to take an active role in deleting the accounts of these identity thieves, they would also have to delete portions of their own value. This is decreases their enthusiasm for taking the initiative to protect users.

Deleting fake accounts goes up there with all the other security remedies that Facebook offers its users. The concern shown for safety is always tempered by a drive for more users, more engagement, more revenue...more everything. Their self-obsession with their user numbers makes necessary and strong actions against identity thieves unthinkable by those who manage Facebook. Numbers like engagement and revenue will always mean more to them than the cost bore by the user who loses their identity but who makes up only a small fraction of the total users on the site.

And even if Facebook did show the necessary concern for their users and delete the fake profiles that surround them, the deletion is not a death sentence. Deleted profiles can quickly be replaced by more fake profiles that are registered through fake IP addresses and from fake locations that get past Facebook's guard. The cold hard truth is as inescapable as the night is dark. Facebook, like most social networks, is difficult to secure which at times can make it dangerous to use.

Cyber Bullying

A topic that doesn't necessarily require hacking but still affects many people on Facebook is cyber bullying. Various studies suggest that anywhere from a quarter to a half of all adolescents and teens were cyber bullied at one point in their life.[156] And because there are so many kids on Facebook, we can assume that a substantial portion of the bullying is taking place there. Despite losing some steam among teenagers, Facebook is still considered by most teens as their favorite social networking website.[157] This raises the question as to what role Facebook plays in bullying that takes place online.

Facebook aids cyber bullies by providing a new method of access to their targets. With Facebook, a bully can have access to their victim's identity whenever they wish through the variety of communications features that are provided. These features can allow for direct harassment through messages or simple mockery through usage of the Newsfeed. No longer must the bully wait for class to start, they can now harass their victim from the edge of their keyboard.

A recommended strategy for victims in this situation is to block the aggressor from contacting them on Facebook.[158] In a study done by the National Child Protection Council they found that over 70% of teens surveyed said that being able to block cyber bullies was the most effective method of prevention. This strategy allowed the user to continue social interaction without having to deal with the bully. But this tactic also requires the victim to conflict with the demands of the aggressor, which may result in angering the bully in real life.

The other major flaw in this situation is that the bully doesn't necessarily need to communicate with the victim to make fun of them. A bully can always just create a fake profile to mock the victim on the network.[159] They could also post embarrassing photos or videos of the victim to the Newsfeed for everyone to see. This could all happen flawlessly unless someone tells the victim this is going on which may be a hopeless considering the victims social situation.

The third solution that Facebook provides for this situation as well as with direct bullying is reporting. Facebook offers users a chance to do this by having a report button located on every post and on every profile. The problem with this strategy is that many users may ignore what is happening or be a part of the problem. Something that most people forget about bullying is that most often it is rather humorous to those who are watching, but not for those who are experiencing.

For the most part, these problems with cyber bullying are some of the same dilemmas that teachers and parents may face in real life with the issue. Bullying happens where children and teenagers are, and it just happens now that most of that age group is on Facebook. Where Facebook separates itself from these other areas of life is that the user is not just accessible on the network, but that they lack the anonymity necessary for avoidance of bullies.

For the child who is victimized by a bully, Facebook is just one more way for the tormentors to pry into their life of fear and shame. Before the victim could skip class or miss lunch to avoid the person who is causing them problems. Now the victim must allow their social identity to be available to the bully at all times. This identity is almost like a virtual punching bag to be used at the bully's discretion.[160]

If the user wishes to avoid the confrontation that comes from Facebook's solutions, the user could delete their profile. This would allow the user to avoid further harassment while disengaging from any action that may threaten the bully. The problem with that strategy is that it gives the bully another victory in the many battles they will fight against the victim. It tells the bully that if they push someone enough they can get the amusement they desire while making the individual do something even more humiliating. And once again the victim will be forced to sit out another part of their life that all their peers get to enjoy.

Sexual Predation

Supporters of Facebook have often pointed to its lack of anonymity as a benefit in deterring and catching sexual predators that operate online. While the chat rooms are still the most dangerous place for a sex crime to begin, social networks are where people are now. According to The Pew Research Center's Internet & American Life Teen-Parent survey, almost 89% of teenagers had a Facebook account in 2011.[161] With a large pool of potential victims, Facebook and other social networks have attracted a large share of sexual predators as well. Another study by the *Journal on Adolescent Health* found that 33% of internet sex crimes involved a social network.[162] So this is something that should cause concern for everyone regardless of whether an improvement has taken place.

The risk of having teenagers on a site like Facebook comes from how truthful they are in the information they give. Pew Internet Research also found that teens will often be honest about: how old they are, the city they live in, the school they go to, and the places they normally visit. They will also upload other sensitive information such as personal photos and videos. These are all pieces of information that could put minors in harm's way without them realizing it.[163]

What makes this problem difficult is the large number of underage users who are on Facebook in violation of the company age policy. A 2012 *Consumer Reports* study found that 5.6 million kids under the age of 14 still had accounts on Facebook. This was after Facebook deleted over 800,000 underage accounts in the past year.[164] While Facebook is trying somewhat, these numbers show either how little they care or how impossible the situation really is to keep underage users off the network.

Anonymity may be dead with Facebook, but the social network has other benefits that it can offer to sexual predators. The ability to run artificial profiles while being undetected is one example. Another is the wealth of information that Facebook can provide on prospective targets. When they combine these two key features, sexual predators can then develop personas that suit the target they are pursuing. The attacker could for instance make their profile picture an image of an attractive person and set their interest and activities as that of their target. This would make starting a relationship with their target easier than if they were messaging them anonymously in a chat room.

The initial interaction could then lead to a grooming phase were the predator attempts to coerce the target into meeting them, or it could just be to obtain information.[165] Facebook profiles can have data on where the target lives, when they go out, who their trusted contacts are, and even what time they typically go to sleep. All that information can be obtained with little effort put forth by the predator. The effect of using social network data when engaging a target is best reflected in the "success" rate that sexual predators have with the medium. The study done by the *Journal of Adolescent Health* found that about 81% of internet initiated sex crimes involving a social networking site led to a face to face meeting between an attacker and a victim. To be fair not all of these instances involved Facebook, but it does reveal what is possible when a criminal uses the modern social networking for reaching targets.[166]

In addition to being a tool for stalking and solicitation, Facebook also gives child pornographers a place to meet with each other in private. Online social networks work very well for these criminals because it gives them the ability to make random encounters with people they may not know in real life. The anonymity from artificial profiles can encourage child pornographers to lower their guard and engage in risk taking behavior such as the sharing of photos and discussing previous crimes. These uses are aided by Facebook's large and diverse user base that spreads across the globe. This means that child pornographers can trade illicit material to each other without having to worry about jurisdictions where there is no extradition.[167]

To expose the proliferation of child pornography on Facebook, investigative journalist Chelsea Schilling created a fake profile and infiltrated some of the worst child pornography groups on Facebook. These groups were easily searchable and required little effort to gain access to. To pass for a pedophile Schilling simply uploaded photos of underage children she obtained online and traded them with other pornographers to gain their trust. After she finished her undercover work she published a story in 2012 detailing her experience to draw awareness to the issue. Schilling would remark throughout the story how little success she had at reporting the sexual predators and child pornography that she met on the network to Facebook.[168]

Another notable investigation into Facebook's role in sexual solicitation was done by former Attorney General of New York Andrew Cuomo in 2007. To test how diligent Facebook was with pursuing sexual predators, Cuomo's office hired investigators to go undercover as users on Facebook who would solicit underage users for sex. The investigators would then call into Facebook to report themselves while pretending to be irate parents of the teens the double agents were pursuing. Facebook responded very poorly according to the Attorney General's report. While they did make efforts to take down inappropriate material posted by the undercover sexual predators, they did nothing to delete their profiles or report them to police.[169]

An explanation for the outcomes in these two cases could be found in Facebook's priorities. The illicit sharing of objectionable material presents a problem for the fake world they create on their network. Having child pornography hurts the image of the network and makes people feel uncomfortable, and it is also easy to address. Reporting users who engage in such behavior however takes more effort and costs Facebook user numbers. The illicit material however only serves to keep sexual predators on the site, so it can be deleted with little hesitation.

As for attacking the fake profiles, Facebook has only recently begun to put that on their agenda. In 2012 Facebook launched an initiative to combat the proliferation of fake profile on their website. It was estimated that there were as many as 83 million fake profiles out of the billion some users.[170] This high number could have been a serious threat the Facebook's reputation had they not disclosed it immediately and done something about it. However, it does beg the question as to what Facebook was doing in the previous eight years while these accounts were taking advantage of people, but for now we will just have to trust that Facebook is doing the right thing.

Theft of Trade Secrets

Another crime that Facebook plays a role in is the theft of secrets that for our purposes includes economic and industrial espionage. Economic espionage is defined as whoever knowingly performs targeting or acquisition of trade secrets to knowingly benefit any foreign government, foreign instrumentality, or foreign agent.[171] Industrial espionage is like economic espionage except that it is done on the behest of corporations instead of foreign governments.[172] Because the United States is an incredibly open society, the theft of trade secrets is a major problem for U.S. corporations and businesses. A report by the FBI stated that there were over $13 billion in losses to the American economy in 2012 as a result of economic espionage.[173] This theft is so great in fact that NSA director General Keith Alexander often refers to it as "the greatest transfer of wealth in human history."[174]

While Facebook is not the sole location for this R&D heist, it does serve as an important role in launching social engineering, phishing, and malware attacks that target employees and corporate databases. As we have covered earlier, social engineering involves targeting the person who has access to data more than the network that contains the data. According to RSA speaker and cyber security expert Ira Winkler, when social engineering is applied directly at employees for the purposes of espionage Facebook is generally used in two ways. Facebook first serves as an intelligence gatherer for the purposes of either obtaining the desired secret through the company's posts, or to obtain information on how to access the secure location where the secret information is held. The second way is as a recruiting tool for spies who want to engage stupid or disgruntled employees.[175]   Once that connection is made it is just a matter of time before the employee lets a key piece of information slip.

This form of espionage is becoming more of a problem for corporations because society is becoming more connected to Facebook. It has been estimated that 75% of all workers check Facebook on their smartphones at least once a day while at work.[176] This is not mention the exorbitant amount of time people spend on Facebook while they are not at work. There are plenty of openings for a spy with some ingenuity to find an employee on Facebook who knows something that they want. The only question is in the amount of skill and determination required.

Along with employees with loose lips, corporations in general are embracing social media for advertising and public relations purposes. These efforts at bringing information to their desired customers or publics can allow for information for the infiltration of networks to leak. Winkler also notes that things such as product development updates and new employee hiring announcements can offer guideposts for the corporate spy looking for some direction. While employees on Facebook are often seen as the weak link that must be mended, the corporation itself has holes because of their organizational use of Facebook.[177]

Because Facebook is such an important aspect of running a business these days, the corporations that use it are put in somewhat of a dilemma. Companies can both ignore Facebook for privacy concerns and risk falling behind the competition in the race for market intelligence or they can embrace Facebook with caution while risking intrusions by those who wish to steal their secrets. This problem shows that excessive information sharing effects not just the employee, but also the employer.   And until Facebook is gone, corporations will most likely have to take the risk of intrusion while informing employees that their jobs depend on correct social media usage.

Cyber Terrorism

The last of the major crimes that Facebook's information collection has a role in is cyber terrorism. This crime refers to using computer networks in a way to perpetrate either online or real-world attacks against innocent civilians. That category can include things such as cyber-attacks that are organized through Facebook groups all the way to bombs that are created based on information that was exchanged using Facebook.[178] There are a lot of places that we could go but let's first start with recruiting.

Facebook gives knowledgeable terrorists an opportunity to introduce angry and perhaps non-violent users into the world of cyber terror. This can apply for hacktivist organizations such as Anonymous that are looking for good hackers as well as online Jihad movements that wish to spread their message. The important role that Facebook plays in this recruiting is that it permits the recruiter to see information about people that haven't spoken with them yet. This gives the recruiter, much like the sexual predator or the corporate spy, the chance to shape their message to fit the individual they wish to convert to their cause. Facebook also allows recruiters to communicate over vast distances with people who sympathize with those who fight the ground war in terrorism but who live too far away to participate.[179]

In addition to the recruiting of prospective warriors, Facebook can also be used to target individuals or locations based on the information users share.[180] An example of this could be the targeting of former veterans of the wars in Afghanistan and Iraq based on their profile information. Such targeting could be accomplished by looking up people who like U.S. military pages and seeing what their interests or backgrounds are. Another example could be scoping out locations such as stores and malls that are frequently checked- into on Facebook. This information could lead not only to the identification of peak times when that location is populated, but also images and videos of what the location looks like in real time.

Aside from the more headline grabbing attacks that occur in real life, Facebook is also instrumental in cyber-attacks that can be perpetrated by individuals as well as states looking to cause havoc.[181] A major attack that was launched against Facebook in 2012 was the Butterfly Botnet that supposedly infiltrated over 11 million computers and stole approximately $850 million. A botnet works by infiltrating computers, taking their vital information, and then using the computer to attack other computers. To defeat the virus Facebook worked closely with law enforcement and supplied users with antivirus software to prevent the virus from spreading.[182]

Another similar attack was the Koobface virus that worked by tempting users into clicking on links that take them to an antivirus software site. Once there, the users would turn over their credit card information thinking it would fix their computer. Instead it made the Koobface gang as they were known very wealthy and supposedly netted them $2 million a year for their three and half year reign.[183] They also managed to infiltrate between 200 and 400 thousand computers until Facebook could take down the server they were running the botnet from.[184]

In addition to attacking users, Facebook can also be used for the targeting of officials who believe they are unshakable even though they have a Facebook account that is anything but that description. As with economic espionage, social engineering attacks can work great against the employees who hold the keys to important infrastructure that civilians depend on to live such as dams and power plants.

This process of recruiting and targeting comes together when terrorists begin to use Facebook for information sharing. Because Facebook allows for private discussion amongst large groups of individuals, things such as planning and logistics can be accomplished quickly and quietly free of charge. While the critic would most likely point out that Facebook's identification features would prevent this from being effective, terrorists who use fake profiles and proxy servers would suggest otherwise. With the correct connections made between the knowledgeable hacker or bomb maker, the necessary steps can be completed by a person who previously never would have access to such information through the normal channels of search engines or forums.[185]

When looking at how Facebook is used by these cyber terrorists, it is important that we recognize what is Facebook's fault and what is not. Just because a terrorist uses a cell phone to blow up an IED on the side of the road does not mean we should abandon the use of cell phones. Facebook in fact is a lot like the cellphone in that it allows individuals to communicate privately where ever they can go that has service. Facebook is also no different from a lot of other technologies and other social networks in that they allow for people to come together despite geographic separations. The fault lies in how Facebook is similar to these previous forms of communication and how it is different. Recognizing this difference is important to prevent us from dwelling on just any social problem that Facebook might be tied to.

The difference is that Facebook allows bad people to access too much information on too many people too easily. It makes attacking people incredibly simple when you have all or at least most of the information that you need put in one easily accessible place like Facebook. This isn't about blaming technology for the evil of mankind; it is using common sense in daily life. Losing control of one's information leads to victimization.

To Err is Human

After looking at these cybercrimes that Facebook has played a role in, it becomes clear that Facebook is a bold step in the wrong direction for information technology. The frictionless sharing that users are forced to partake in can have serious problems that previous websites and technologies may have experienced but never on such a scale grand. These crimes are not the result of bringing people together so much as it is Facebook's desire to destroy privacy and anonymity for the sake of their advertising revenue and corporate legacy.

This after effect is only worsened by the fact that Facebook promotes an illusion of security in a place where users should be afraid to share anything. The internet has always been a place where these crimes such as hacking and cyber stalking could occur. The bad thing about Facebook is that they made it easier for these crimes to be committed while telling the user they shouldn't be afraid of sharing copious amounts of information about themselves. It is understandable why Facebook did this. Motives such as greed and amorality are easy to comprehend; they are just not something that should be accepted by society.

The failure on Facebook's part to protect users or at least make them aware of the threats they face does give us some insight into what Facebook is as a network. The crimes that are committed on Facebook are not the result of bad privacy features or a careless administration. It is the very nature of Facebook in combination with the indiscretion of the criminal that is to blame for these crimes. With the amount of information that is available and the ease which it can be had, who can blame he identity thief for going to Facebook to get what they want? It is almost too tempting for some advertiser to resist, are we really going to expect some hacker to exercise anymore self-restraint than we would a marketer or public relations analyst?

This is not to say that users should not be responsible for the hardship they bring about by sharing too much information, it is only to examine the effect that Facebook has had on cybercrime. The business model that Facebook has chosen makes users dumber online then they naturally should be. Instead of educating them effectively on how to deal with these threats, Facebook keeps them in the dark to play with privacy toys. This effectively ensures that the argument of safe Facebook use through learning will never come true.

And perhaps Facebook is even afraid of having users learn properly how to share information with Facebook. Maybe they are afraid that if the user gains a proper understanding of how dangerous the site really is they will leave? Or even to a lesser extent they will share less information. Unfortunately for Facebook those are the only two solutions to this problem. Either users leave or they share drastically less information about themselves. Facebook certainly wants neither, so the user is told only very little about these threats if anything at all.

7. Network

Facebook is an excellent tool for criminal investigations both online and in the real world because Facebook can provide a lot of information on suspects free of charge.[186] This cooperation is necessary to prevent the network from becoming merely a place for criminals to exploit naïve internet users. Should Facebook go the way of MySpace with criminal activity it would draw negative attention which could lead to regulation and rejection. Facebook does not want that so they make a point of cooperating with law enforcement agencies to the fullest extent. The cooperation gives the appearance that Facebook is doing everything they can to keep their users safe while at the same time creating an environment for total government surveillance.

Law Enforcement

To protect the network, Facebook's security team does everything they can to thwart hackers like the Koobface gang that we talked about earlier. But understand that Facebook's security can only do so much to protect its large network. They must also cooperate with law enforcement entities like the FBI to help track down cybercriminals who are causing problems.

The length of time that this cooperation has gone on has led to the construction of a relationship between Facebook and government.

Out of that relationship, two important things happen. The first is that tax payer money and government employees are being used to protect the network. While this is true for all internet companies somewhat, it is troubling in Facebook's case because they cause a large degree of their problems by how much information they collect. And at the same time, they cause users problems by putting their information at risk while expecting the government to protect users from the criminals that the information attracts.

The second major result of this relationship is that Facebook and government essentially share information to help thwart the cyber criminals that are on the network. These criminals can be hackers or sexual predators or anyone else who the government might be interested in. The sharing of information about criminals on the network is important because much of the information that Facebook shares with government on its users does not have to do with cyber criminals. A lot of the information that the government collects on Facebook is for unrelated real world criminal investigations.[187]

When conducting a criminal investigation that involves an internet user, the first place that an investigator should go to for evidence is the third parties that store the user's information. These third parties can include entities such as websites, internet service providers, or even email providers. According to the work of law professor Orin S. Kerr, the reason why an investigator goes to third parties first is because they typically require the least amount of documentation to obtain user data. They are also far less likely to destroy evidence compared to the suspect who would have the information stored on their computer. Instead the third party has the information that law enforcement wants without the risk or effort that goes with getting it from the suspect.[188]

Because Facebook is used by so many people, it has become a well-known place for criminal investigators to obtain information on their suspects. According to a 2013 study done by Lexis Nexus, 80% of local and 72% of state police departments use Facebook for their criminal investigations.[189] Also significant is that as early as 2009, Facebook was receiving 10 to 20 information requests from police agencies a day.[190] This high volume of requests has led to Facebook placing guidelines on their site instructing police how to go about requesting information.[191] So using Facebook is not just some new way of catching criminals, it is now a routine part of police work.

For an officer to obtain user information, they must meet certain requirements that are dependent on what they wish to know about the user. If they are seeking basic information (name, length of service, credit card information, email address and a recent login/logout IP address), they only need a subpoena. If they wish to get general records of communication such as message headers and IP addresses the officer will need a court order. To obtain user content that Facebook has stored such as messages, photos, videos, posts, and location information the investigator must have a search warrant.[192] The ascending order of requirements is somewhat misleading when we realize that all Facebook information can be used to incriminate someone in a crime. Setting dividers between these categories of data only gives people the impression that protection exists.

Facebook has also recently added another requirement to their list: National Security Letters. These letters, which are often used by the FBI and NSA, are distributed by federal agencies to force third party service providers to turn over desired communications without any dispute. The receiver of the letter cannot complain, they cannot ask why, and they cannot tell anyone about the information that is requested of them.[193] Under Facebook's guidelines, if they receive an NSL they will only turn over the name of the user along with the length of the time they used the network.[194] This declaration to protect user data from such unaccountable authorities may seem disingenuous but keep in mind that NSL's were recently declared unconstitutional by a federal judge.[195] So Facebook is at least drawing the line somewhere.

Once an investigator has one of these four legally required permission slips to access the user's information, the next step is for the investigator to give Facebook certain documentation to specify who they are and who their target is. This data includes: what law enforcement agency they work for, their badge number, their name, their phone number, a request time, who they want information on (A Facebook User ID number, profile name, profile URL, birthday, and email address), and the time of user activity.[196] That information would not be hard for an officer to obtain seeing as most of it could be found on the affidavit they filled out for the warrant.

Now if the police officer cannot get the necessary documentation, there are of course faster ways that the profile data can be obtained. Because police officers can have Facebook profiles, they can always use their own profile to collect intelligence on people in their town or area.[197] This could be as simple as just having a friend's list of 150 friends and using their connections to explore their social networks. The officer would be limited to just those 150 people for their news feed information, but they would have access to a large amount of profile data that would help them identify suspects for real world observation.

We are assuming here that the officer does not just create a fake, undercover profile to collect Facebook information. Having a fake profile would allow the officer to target certain suspects for surveillance that set their profiles to private to prevent outsiders from seeing their lives. The officer could do this by using the variety of social engineering attacks discussed in the previous chapter. While having multiple profiles is banned by Facebook, most police departments do not seem to care about this rule as evidenced by many of them putting the technique in their department handbooks.[198]

These strategies assume that the officer is not prepared to break the law to get the suspect's profile information. If the officer could gain access to the suspect's profile the information would be more detailed compared to the outside view a friend connection would give them. The evidence obtained from any illegal means would not be admissible in court barring any extenuating circumstances, but it would provide valuable insight into the lives of suspects. Police departments are also starting to make social media training a priority which could lead to hacking becoming a skill like that of lock picking or enhanced interrogation techniques.[199]

This development is troublesome when we also consider the use of Facebook for public surveillance in addition to targeted investigation. Police departments see Facebook as a cost-efficient way to keep an eye on the citizens in their jurisdiction. This tactic begins first by creating a department Facebook page. When people like or befriend the page the police department will receive updates on activity and alerts in the area. In exchange for this information, the police department will be able to see Newsfeeds and profiles of people that have liked the page. Along with informing users, the alerts are also like fishing hooks that tempt people into revealing information about crimes they may know of that involve people they have met or things they have seen. All the department must do is make a post, and then watch the comment thread to see what people say.[200]

Another way for departments to obtain information is for local residents to directly give it to them. Police community pages often encourage users to report suspicious activity through posting information and content to the department's page. This method of information gathering is beneficial for the department because it is direct and voluntary. The Department doesn't have to do anything except monitor what information comes in. That task can be formidable, which we will cover later in the text.

Not only can the local police agency use Facebook pages for surveillance, but they can also manage their image as well. Much like corporations, police departments can create posts and distribute content to help give off a positive image to the local community. The Facebook Law Enforcement Guide book even provides information on how police departments can increase visits to their page and boost engagement.[201] This manipulation of image may be necessary as law enforcements moves closer to a total information awareness form of policing and away from a community focused strategy.

Altogether the use of Facebook for law enforcement purposes represents an expansion of the area that police previously occupied in our lives. Before we saw them walking on patrol or driving down the street, now they are online and can communicate with us at any time whenever they wish. And at the same time, the user can communicate with police in new ways by sending in pictures and video that may help with arrests. Facebook is bringing the public and police closer together at an increasingly fast pace.

Unfortunately, Facebook also separates the community and the police by lowering the amount of interaction that is needed for an exchange of information. Instead of calling 911 or going downtown to the police station, the user can just make a comment on the police department's page. And instead of having to go out into the community and associate with the local population, the police officer can just get information about suspects from monitoring Facebook.

The result of this increase of connection with a removal of real contact is a smarter police that is distanced from the people they are sworn to protect. That is a bad combination when we consider how concern for reputation and ability to gather information is effected by police misconduct and brutality. Facebook will not entirely rid police of their reputation concerns, but it will allow for an increase in bad behavior without as much worry of angering the local residents as time goes on.

Intelligence Gathering

While police certainly benefit from what Facebook can provide, government intelligence agencies also have much to gain as well. By collecting information on a subject, it is hoped that the gatherer can make the intelligence customer smarter. This is done by answering questions that the policymaker might have, by providing them with warnings regarding current situations, and by shaping the way they look at strategy. Because they are in a sense smarter it is hoped they will make good decisions when the time comes.[202]

This effort to improve the intelligence of American policymakers has brought with it an attention to social media. The wealth of information that social media has available on billions of internet users as well as other countries makes it an irresistible target for intelligence gatherers. And of all the sites that make up the social media target, Facebook is the largest. They have the most users, the most content, the most engagement, and the most reach. While it is certainly not the only major network to look for information on people, it is certainly the best one.

If members of the American intelligence community wish to access Facebook's information, they could of course employ all the strategies that any law enforcement official would engage in. It could even be assumed that a federal agent would be better at these tactics than the average sheriff's deputy. But there are also illicit methods that intelligence agencies can employ which would be out of reach for the local police department.

When it comes to Facebook intelligence gathering the National Security Agency should be our major focus because they gather most of the intelligence for the United States. This is because they are responsible for the interception of electronic communications which is by far the most plentiful sources of intelligence.[203] In contrast the CIA handles human intelligence that deals with spy networks and tactical operations.[204] The National Reconnaissance Office deals with taking care of those satellites that are used to collect certain forms of electronic signals in outer space. The National Geospatial Intelligence Agency handles the pictures that those satellites take.[205] Once these agencies collect the information that they specialize in, it is then expected that they share it with other members of the community who need it.[206]

In collecting this data, the NSA has a variety of strategies that they can use. The official way is for them to obtain legal documentation for the information they need from a federal judge. But from what members of the intelligence community have been telling us this form of collection is going out of style. According to several whistleblowers from both the NSA and one from the telecommunications industry, ISPs have allowed the NSA to build secret rooms at their switching stations that give them the ability to copy all the communications that go through those stations. This data amounts to billions upon billions of individual bits being collected every second. That data includes not just Facebook posts and pictures, but also everything else that is being done on the internet. Google searches, emails, typed URLs, all of it is just be fed into collection devices operated by the NSA.[207]

It is also been alleged by NSA whistleblower Edward Snowden that Facebook and other Silicon Valley companies are giving the NSA direct access to their servers.[208] This has been denied by Facebook's management who says they comply with law by turning over information not access.[209] But if it turns out that Facebook is lying, it doesn't really change anything as far as ability to obtain information. Having direct access to the servers would just speed up the collection process. They are getting it all either way.

Along with the direct infiltration of the network, the NSA has also been known to hire former employees of the companies they wish to tap into. Employing former technicians allows the NSA to reverse engineer network systems so they can get access to information without having to go through the actual company to get the data. This has been done with many Silicon Valley companies that include Facebook. Former Facebook Chief of Security Max Kelly now works at the NSA after having worked at Facebook for four years.[210] His former position could help not only with surveillance but also with understanding Facebook's role to withstand cyber-attacks, which in a way would legitimize his existence at the NSA.[211]

Despite how unconstitutional this might sound, the NSA does not feel this this is surveillance, they only consider it interception. To them, this data is not illegally collected until it is looked at by a pair of human eyes. Understand that most of this data is just collected and stored by machines that sort the data. So when Congress asks the Director of the NSA Keith Alexander or the Director of National Intelligence James Clapper if any illegal collection is going on, they can simply say that no Americans are being illegally surveilled. This excuse is protected by the fact that the NSA cannot go through all the data they are able to collect at once. They must pick in choose what they wish to look at as of the current state of technology. But as technology advances this excuse could certainly become unworkable.[212]

Along with the wholesale surveillance that the NSA has done, other smaller but still powerful agencies like the FBI and CIA among others have admitted to monitoring social media.[213] These admissions come from press releases that are given to the media because they are technically not illegal. When these smaller agencies say they are monitoring sites like Facebook and Twitter they are referring to the publicly available information that they can easily get access to.[214] This type of data collection is called open source intelligence and is gained a lot of steam in recent years because of the amount of publicly available big data.

Industry

The intelligence community has turned to private industry to outsource the work of analyzing the wealth of information that they are collecting. There are many advantages to using industry instead of government to conduct surveillance. Usage of contractors can help make government appear smaller and more efficient to those who lack understanding of what is going on. Contractors also do not have to abide by the same regulations nor answer to the same bodies as a government agency would. This allows for contractors to act in ways that a government agency would have to worry about answering to Congress for. The situation is however tempered somewhat if the company is publicly traded. This means the company will be held to a standard higher of transparency compared to their private competitors.[215] So in a way there are oversight tradeoffs with privatization.

But aside from whatever obstacles regulations may present, the market appears to help make intelligence analysis more powerful. Because they are not on a government budget contractors tend to pay their employees better and as a result they get better people than an agency would. The contractors will also recruit directly out of intelligence agencies such as the NSA or CIA to get the necessary government knowledge that the company needs. This makes the government agency almost a sort of farm team for the contractors. The lack of regulations in this area of recruitment also helps to make the revolving door between government and industry work very nicely.[216]

When discussing Facebook and the intelligence industry, there are six contractors that deserve our focus. These companies are not the largest contractors out there, but they all hold connections to Facebook which will be illuminated more later on. Some of them also are exclusively used for social media intelligence which can be very revealing. For right now we will just focus on what these six companies do and how they can use social media to help governments discover important information.

A good example of a company that is doing impressive work for the government is Palantir Technologies. Palantir is a Silicon Valley based company in Palo Alto California. The company was started by its CEO Alexander Karp, along with present Chairman of the Board Peter Thiel.[217] They currently employ 550 people that are scattered throughout offices in California, England, and Virginia, the company was started in 2004, the same year as Facebook.[218]

The way Palantir works is that it takes in large data sets, it integrates them, and then it creates visualizations based off the level of authorization the analyst has. The finished product is typically an interface that may be a graph or chart about the individual that the analyst is trying to focus in on.[219] Making these visualizations is important because it allows for an organization such as a police department to make sense of all the data they have access to on the individuals they are investigating. This is like Facebook's Open Graph that tries to map out an entire individual's life based off their connections on the network.

Another company that analyzes social networks a bit differently is Visible Technologies. Visible Technologies was founded in January of 2005 and is headquartered in Bellevue, Washington.[220] Unlike Palantir, Visible Technologies was not started with the intention of serving the intelligence industry. Their specialty is monitoring social media websites such as Facebook or Twitter to help companies as well as agencies make better decisions. Their software works much like a CRM would by providing the user with alerts and updates on what social media users are saying online.[221]

A third company that deserves our attention is Recorded Future. Recorded Future was started in 2001 and is headquartered in Cambridge, Massachusetts.[222] Their software works by harvesting texts from websites and then analyzing that text for valuable information. They then re-analyze the data several times to detect anomalies in the results and then start to draw conclusions. The finished product of this system is a visual interface that shows the user what events are likely to happen in the future.[223]

Attensity is another one of the social media monitoring company headquartered in Palo Alto, California. They also have offices in Virginia, Germany, the United Kingdom, and Belgium. Attensity markets four products: Pipeline, Command Center, Analyze, and Respond. This product line up is very similar to other companies. Pipeline is a tool for gathering large quantities of intelligence and eliminating irrelevant results. Command Center is a way to monitor conversations that are circulating about specific brands or topics. Analyze is a tool for processing collected information and turning it into visualizations. Respond is largely a social network manager platform that allows the business to handle questions and send out messages over several networks at once.[224] Collect, observe, analyze, visualize, and manage. Same old tricks put on display.

The fifth company that should be discussed is Quid. The Quid product works by capturing data, structuring it, and creating visualizations based upon that information. The big draw with Quid is that they create 3D visualizations which allow the analyst to really immerse themselves in the data. They also provide expert analysts in addition to the software that they sell which allows for a more total intelligence outsourcing experience. This is most likely needed because the Quid software does not look like something that the average bureaucrat could understand.[225]

The last company that should also be highlighted is BBN Technologies, which is owned by its parent company Raytheon. BBN does a wide variety of work both the military and intelligence communities. But they also have translation and web monitoring technologies that work well with analyzing information from Facebook.[226] Raytheon happens to be one of the most influential intelligence contractors in Congress and may be a force in preventing Congressional action on this issue.[227]

The list that has been presented does not encapsulate all the companies that would analyze the sort of material that Facebook collects. It is also not the case that the software these companies sell is being used only for manipulation of Facebook data. The people who buy this software do not necessarily have to tell the world what they do with it. All we know is their products are designed to handle the type of information that Facebook has, and because of that they deserve our attention. If there are companies that are going to help the intelligence agencies that receive social media data do their work, these companies are it.

Law Enforcement 2.0

What prevents most of intelligence from being put into action is that there is a hesitancy to share information in the intelligence community. One of the chief criticisms made by the 9/11 Commission's Report on the intelligence community was that lack of intelligence sharing led to the 9/11 terrorist attacks. [228]While a lot has changed in the community since the attacks, there is still good reason to believe that sharing is still not where it needs to be. This is evidenced by numerous expert recommendations that frequently call for more sharing almost 13 years after 9/11.

There are also several reasons why we should expect this hoarding of intelligence would occur. One concern is that if the intelligence is shared too much, it will leak out into the public sphere. Leaks obviously have been a real problem in recent years which have exacerbated the fear of sharing information. Another reason is that intelligence can be used as a bargaining chip when one agency needs something from another.[229] But perhaps the simplest reason is that intelligence agencies tend to have long standing disagreements over the way intelligence should be used. These keep information from being utilized effectively, and therefore serve as a check on the abuses by the intelligence community. [230]

This problem that is often pointed to in discussions of intelligence analysis has not been ignored however. Starting in 2003, the federal government began building Joint Terrorism Task Force centers or JTTFC's to stimulate information sharing between federal government agencies like the FBI and CIA. In addition to implementing a horizontal approach, the federal government has also constructed what are known as "fusion centers" to stimulate sharing between federal government agencies and state and local law enforcement agencies.[231] As of a 2012 report done by the Senate Intelligence Committee, there are 78 different fusion centers inside the United States for the purposes of conducting surveillance to aid in law enforcement and anti-terrorism activities.[232]

These centers work by aggregating the data they receive from various government agencies and outside sources. From this aggregated data, trends and networks will emerge that the center will then focus in on. Understand that the point for the centers is not to follow any one individual as much as it is to build awareness of an entire geographic area.[233] The fusion centers are almost like intelligence agencies for police departments that cannot spend the resources to do such work. This creates a window for illegally obtained information to seep its way into the justice system much like it does the policymaking process at the federal level.

What makes this even more troubling is that the Department of Homeland Security has been recorded as saying that they will be engaging in the monitoring of social media along with the other members of the intelligence community. This is being done to cultivate a situational awareness for government agencies in the time surrounding a terrorist attack or natural disaster. By gathering up posts, tweets, and uploads from a targeted area, the DHS plans to orchestrate an effective response based off the information from people experiencing the event. The DHS even hopes one day to be able to prevent such attacks from occurring just by following the collected data.[234]

When we combine the help that local and state police agencies receive from the fusion centers with the help they can receive from intelligence analysis software, it seems that we have a new era of policing. This era may include digital mass surveillance and analytical software to handle police work in addition to having police patrol the streets through their cars and on their feet. No longer will Americans just have to worry about the abuses of the NSA, but now they will have to worry about their local police department watching everything they do if they were not already.

This emphasis on the capabilities of local and state agencies is important because most of the regulation that Americans experience is at a state and local level. The stronger these agencies get, the more the restrictions that Americans will experience on a daily basis. And while some might say thee fusion centers are needed to fight terrorism, the fusion centers are mainly being used to go after drug dealers that have no connections to terrorism at all.[235] Also consider the fact that crime rates have been decreasing in this country for years and do not require the zealous response that comes with mass intelligence driven police work.[236]

The effect of this network that has formed around the monitoring of social media is an overall tighter web of surveillance for the American citizen. By giving information to Facebook, Facebook users help to strengthen this network. It is their information, their personal lives, that is being used to power this machine. After seeing this information no Facebook user can deny what they are participating in. They are sanctioning their own surveillance for the sake of meager social and economic benefits.

8. Analysis

The data that Facebook has collected is far more powerful than it could ever appear on its surface. Within the mountains of information there are hidden insights to be derived on Facebook's users and the social networks that they belong to. But to find these insights, analysis must be done. This analysis while time consuming can be incredibly valuable at uncovering truths about the targeted person or their network. When the correct requirements are met and the proper analysis is done, information that would normally be invisible can become a solid object.

Fortunately for the intelligence community, Facebook is perfect for this task. The network has plenty of information and that information can be analyzed in a number of ways. It is almost as though Facebook was designed for what the government has been using it for. Facebook is not just a good source of information, it is almost perfect. And if you want evidence, just look at the benefits of using Facebook for intelligence analysis.

Benefits

It is important to understand that Facebook wants their data to be easy for their customers to analyze. With good analysis, companies can make good marketing decisions regarding their products and advertisements. When companies make good decisions, they make Facebook more money. So there is a good incentive to make the network simple and understandable for the observer.

The result of that incentive is that Facebook is an excellent data source for intelligence analysis. One of the best things about Facebook in this regard is that it has plenty of data and it is always trying to get more. A source needs to have a lot of data for the analyst to detect patterns from which important insights can be derived.[237] It is also important for the data source to collect as much information as it can because it is difficult to tell what the right information is. The rule of thumb is that you can never have enough information so get it while you can.

While having lots of information is important, it can be difficult to make use of it if that information is diluted with worthless data. Facebook prevents this by having a simplistic design that is good for separating out worthless information. Notice there are no annoying glitter tags and songs that play when you visit someone's profile. A Facebook profile is just information that pertains to the user and their network. While there are some distractions such as notifications and background photos, Facebook's content standards typically keep things like that to a minimum.

Along with a design that cuts out the junk, Facebook also creates features that force the user to put their information in order. The Timeline feature is an excellent example of this. Everything the user wants to share is in a somewhat neat chronological format for an analyst or an algorithm to run through. All the user's friends, likes, and interests, are put on lists for the observer to read through. Every action that the user takes has a time and date and sometimes a location next to it. Facebook is incredibly efficient with what it does by making a point of not getting lost in its own information.

Having data available in text form is also very important for analysis because it allows a machine to go through it faster. Information about the user such as friendships, planned events, discussions of past gatherings, and numerous other pieces of data are not only brought to Facebook but are given to Facebook in text that an algorithm can go through it quickly. Yes, Facebook has information that is slightly more difficult for analysis such as photos and videos, but for data that Facebook brings in they are doing a good job at keeping it simple and machine readable.

To compensate for whatever gaps that exist with regards to data quality, Facebook has excellent algorithms that can go through the data very quickly. An algorithm is a mathematical equation that allows software to search through data for a desired value. It is important that algorithms be very complex to ignore the irrelevant values and retrieve the important ones in large data sets.[238] Facebook's search algorithm is a useful tool for analysts because it allows them to be specific about what returns they want from the Open Graph. Along with whatever software they might have at their disposal, the analyst can use Graph Search to find individuals based off their actions instead of their identities. This is important when you are looking for suspects who fit a profile that you are interested in tracking down.

The last and most important quality of Facebook as a data source is that its information is accurate. The social norms that exist in society serve to encourage honesty on the network for a large part. Facebook is also designed so that if the user wants to receive utility from its features they must be honest. A *Consumer Reports* survey found that only 25% of people lie to protect their identities on Facebook.[239] Those lies usually only make up parts of the information the person shares which means that those lies can be filtered out with algorithms in intelligence analysis software designed to sort out the meaningless data.

The benefits that Facebook brings to its analysis are just a few things that should be looked for in a good data source. While Facebook is certainly not perfect in meeting all the requirements necessary for analysis, they do a fairly good job for a civilian designed intelligence gathering machine. It gets a lot of information, it is well organized, constantly updated, it uses powerful algorithms to locate data, and it's a fairly accurate at getting information out of people. Facebook is a pretty good find for an intelligence analyst looking to track suspects for free.

Analyzing the Data

Facebook is compatible with a wide range of analysis disciplines that include behavioral analysis, social networks analysis, geographic modeling, and event modeling. Facebook is not limited to just one thing, it offers many things for those who are willing to consider the data. Facebook has this range of possibilities because of its design and the truckloads of information that the design yields for the observer.

The first form of analysis for someone to engage in with Facebook data is profiling. With this type of refinement, the analyst tries to place the target into a category of people that exist in society. To do that the analyst will use the detailed profile information source like Facebook provides on its users as the basis for putting the individual into a specific category. That determination will be made by looking at the person's self-image, how they form ideas, their relationship with authority figures, and their ability to express self-control.[240]   With these aspects of an individual's personality, they can then make assumptions about behavior and activities that the user might engage in off Facebook.[241]

When we look at the information that Facebook profiles can contain the analyst has much of their work completed for them. A person's self-image can be determined by looking at the profile picture, their posts, their interests, and the comments that they make to other people. Their thought process can be understood by what games they play and how successful they are, how they talk on the newsfeed and in private conversation, and in how they make use of privacy controls.

The determination of relationship with authority can be a little bit more difficult than the first two. Posts that pertain to criminal or deviant behavior could be a starting place. Communication between parents or relative authority figures could occur but that is not always something to lean on. The analyst could also look at workplace and school history to look for patterns of either obedience or insubordination. The user's perception of authority can be discovered but it takes work and probably some outside knowledge of psychology to make a good conclusion.

The last critical aspect of profiling is for the analyst to determine the target's ability for self-control.[242] That could also be heavily related to relationship with authority based on what the user posts to the newsfeed. Aside from just posts that they may be embarrassed about, the user could post information about dietary, exercise, study, or work habits that could tell the analyst about their discipline. Once again, the school and workplace history might also come into play to see how well they behaved in different situations. And if the analyst is lucky enough the user might also have evidence of a relationship history on Facebook that would reveal any indiscretions that may have occurred.

While understanding the individual is important, it also necessary to remember that individuals make up larger constructs known as networks. To understand these networks the analyst will engage in what is known as social network analysis or link analysis. This kind of refinement requires that the analyst document all the relationships that exist within the network into a graph or matrix format.[243] By using these forms of documentation, the analyst can develop inferences about the individual that wouldn't be as obvious in a text or any other visualization.

The comments and private messages that the individual exchanges with his or her connections are very revealing about how the network functions. It can for instance identify groups within the network called "cliques" that are closer to each other than the rest of the individuals in the network.[244] If it is a work group the network could reveal a hierarchy where some users are more respected or powerful than others. The level of activity that takes place on that network says how talkative its members are as well as how close they are with one another.

Facebook's Social Graph API is designed with this form of analysis in mind. The Social Graph is a tool that allows developers and users to search through Facebook based on the connections between users on the network. These connections reveal what people might be interested in based off their associations with other people.[245] From examining the relationships that exist between users the analyst can discover information that behavioral analysis with individual profiles simply cannot see.

In addition to their Social Graph that tracks relationships, Facebook has what is known as the Open Graph which tracks all the user's connections to the world   This includes not just people but objects as they are known such as pages the user has visited, places they have gone, and applications that they have downloaded. In intelligence analysis, this type of graph construction is referred to as general network modeling and according to author Robert Clarke is perhaps the most useful graph for analysis because it encapsulates all the information available about an individual.[246]

This idea of general network modeling can be used to form the basis for a broader construct known as human terrain mapping. By taking Facebook's Open Graph and putting that data on top of a map, the analyst can essentially give the graph real world substance. This would require a reconfiguration of the graph's nodes along with a minimization of certain attributes but when completed it would be a very resourceful tool for understanding the targeted geographic area.[247]

To aid in the construction of such a model that one might see on Google Maps or Google Earth, the analyst must also take in other information aside from objects such as individuals and natural and man-made structures. It is important to understand that there are events which can affect the individual's, networks, and geography for a given area. Facebook is excellent for understanding the impact of events because it can capture a large amount of information that could be associated with a major incident.

Take for instance an earthquake. In the event of an earthquake people in the area would upload videos and pictures of what happened. They would make posts about what they were doing before, during, and after the earthquake occurred. Users might even send each other messages to make sure they were okay. While this information might seem incidental for one user, when we combine it over an entire geographic area it can be incredibly revealing at how that event impacted the local region.

This kind of analysis through Facebook is not exclusive to just the major news stories either. Remember there are also parties, reunions, weddings, and dinners that people invite each other to while on Facebook. People who are going to that event can even write about their expectations on the event page to say how much they are looking forward to the event. The page will also contain a list of the people who planned on attending the event, as well as a list of people who weren't sure and those who knew they weren't going. It is little things like these that help to provide a whole picture of the individual that Facebook is always aiming for.

Looking at these different facets of a person's life (behavior, associations, environment, and events) the analyst can then begin attempting the ultimate goal of intelligence analysis: prediction. Anticipating what the target will do next is what allows the analyst to make or suggest the correct action for maximum advantage. While prediction is very important, it is also very difficult. Prediction is rooted in the understanding of the factors that can affect the way a series of events will play out and Facebook can certainly not list them all. [248]

But nevertheless, Facebook is still a good place to look when pondering what the target's future will look like. Take for example the ability to use Facebook to predict an election outcome for a small town. The individuals in that town will make posts that indicate what their political views are. Facebook may have information about their social and economic backgrounds as well. Interactions over networks can indicate who the influential users will vote for and who is likely to follow them. When we combine this intelligence with outside information such as polls taken in the area and past election results, we may be able to predict the winner to of the election.

You can exchange this example for a few other events that a person may wish to predict. Will they all come through as expected? No. But perfection is not what the analyst is trying to achieve here. They are trying to make a prediction that has the greatest chance of coming true. It is a numbers game, and Facebook has plenty of numbers to use.

Weaknesses in Facebook Analysis

While Facebook can be a powerful tool for understanding people, it of course has its flaws. Keep in mind that a lot of the analysis that occurs through Facebook is automated for both advertisers and the intelligence community. The computers that look at the information have difficulty understanding things that might be obvious to the human observer. And at the same time humans are limited in what they can do in refining the data themselves, so as a result accuracy is lost in what may be reported from Facebook.

A good demonstration of how Facebook fails in accuracy is in the millions of fake profiles that fill the website.[249] The second major flaw comes with the artificial social environment that Facebook has created to boost engagement on the network. While these failures in certain ways help Facebook collect more information by attracting more users, they still serve as a detriment to analysis. A way this problem will be mitigated is with the increasing dependence of society on Facebook which will in turn promote the ability of Facebook to demand more authenticity from its users.

Another problem with data mining in conjunction with social media analysis is that it faces the danger of creating false relationships between nodes. Just because two nodes are in the same social network does not necessarily mean they discuss whatever the analyst is trying to investigate. Even pure data mining that searches for keywords is forced to assume that the user means what they are saying. These types of problems can be overcome with collecting the right kind of information, but that is not always an option.[250]

These false relationships can be even more difficult to see if the analyst develops tunnel vision with regards to their work. This occurs when gathered information looks so comprehensive that it drowns out other ideas. Having created a visualization or report from this information, the analyst then becomes unable to see relationships that may exist outside of their analysis. By committing themselves too heavily to the image they have created, they have limited their vision of the situation.[251] It is up to the analyst to keep an open mind, but that requires using other sources and methods in conjunction with Facebook.

Another reason why tunnel vision can be a problem is that Facebook has trouble in detecting change. Understanding change is a big problem that comes with focusing too heavily on the graph or matrix that one is looking at.[252]   For instance, Facebook information can reveal when two close friends have stopped talking to each other. This can be shown by a drop off in communication between the two nodes. But Facebook would have no idea however if distant friends became angry at each other. Because Facebook cannot document every social interaction, the analyst just must go with the information that is given. This can lead to assumptions which are sometimes wrong.

It could be assumed that without these obstacles we would see more effects from Facebook in our daily life. The task for Facebook and its monitors will be to diminish these problems while maintaining the level of user engagement that exists on the network. A likely answer to this dilemma will come from advances in technology that make things like artificialness and tunnel vision easier to prevent. When that happens, analysis of Facebook could achieve a state of perfection like that of the network's ability to collect data. But as for now the obstacles still stand in the way of a complete understanding of the user and their networks.

Integration

A method that decreases some of the risks associated with using Facebook for analysis is its combination with databases outside of the network.   This technique of combining information from one source with that of another source is known as data integration.[253] By doing this companies and agencies can increase the value of seemingly worthless information into quality material to be used for analysis.   For instance, information such as annual income and local population would have a limited set of uses under normal circumstance. But if this data were to be integrated with the family tree and friend list information on Facebook, it would become more valuable for advertising or however the analyst wanted to make money from it.

The practice of data integration is disturbing when we realize that Facebook is only one of numerous data store houses that exists in this world. There are also hospitals, competing social networks, e-commerce sites, and police organizations that all have information that could be enriched by combining it with Facebook data. This data would be difficult to obtain for the average internet hacker, but for a researcher, intelligence agency, or multinational corporation, they could already have this data lying around.

Facebook currently has exclusive partnerships with four data aggregation companies that include Blue Kai, Epsilon, Acxiom and Data Logix. These companies all collect lots of publicly available data for the purposes of helping companies market their products. Facebook is in a partnership with these companies so they will give Facebook's advertisers access to their wide range of aggregated data.[254] The expectation being that more information will allow advertisers and Facebook to make more money. The other result is that Facebook is much larger for corporations that use these data aggregators than it is to everyone else.

Once the integrated master data sets have been properly constructed, they would be able to break through the anonymization features that sites like Facebook use to protect their members while sharing their data. Typically, when a site has anonymized data, they will share information that would be valuable for their customers, universities, ad agencies, etc. while leaving out what they consider personal identifiable information or (PII). With data integration however, the analyst can discern the identities that the information belongs to by matching up the anonymized information with other sources that could include help to identify patterns in data.[255]

While this might sound like only a theoretical situation, understand that this been done numerous times by researchers around the country as well as various hackers looking to debunk the myth of anonymized information. These analysts have helped deanonymize information using sources that include: Facebook, Twitter, Netflix, and even information from hospital databases. The threat from data integration is real, and it transforms the impact that Facebook could have with regards to big data analytics substantially.[256]

To handle the mega databases that can be created by aggregating Facebook with other data, government agencies will turn to the social media intelligence contractors like the ones discussed earlier. As we have seen Facebook on its own is an excellent intelligence gathering program. But to overcome the flaws that it has, agencies will use software like Palantir or Recorded Future that takes Facebook and combines it's with other important data sources.[257] The value of the software is determined by how much data it can handle and the type of interface that it gives to the analyst.

As time goes on the abilities of analysts to aggregate and integrate huge data sources like Facebook will also become even more powerful in the years ahead. Advances in developing technologies such as quantum computing, cloud computing, and big data analytics will continue to make it easier to form master datasets that know everything about everyone in that dataset. As of right now these are the hottest fields for a graduate with a degree related to information technology to go into.[258] It would seem that the future is bright for spying on people through social networks like Facebook.

What this is heading towards is the creation of databases that can erase any attempt at privacy made by a user or the company they associate with. Companies like Facebook will be able to gather and distribute their anonymized data sets while certain organizations will be able to reveal all the identities in that data set without having to get permission from those identities. Facebook can claim it is respecting privacy while the government or corporate data aggregator can have an entire map of an individual's life. Because Facebook is technically "trying their best," they will get away with aiding people who may try to take advantage of the user.

Amidst all this number crunching and user tracking no one has confronted the question of the ethical or legal implications of analyzing Facebook. Throughout their existence, Facebook has been criticized by privacy and civil liberties groups who say that the site is a tool of Big Brother. While this criticism is often brought up in the media it is rarely discussed in detail. To address this lack of investigative reporting the next two chapters will examine just what these groups might be complaining about.

9. The Law

While the executive branch is an essential part of government, it is to be the most feared aspect of government as well. The reasons for this have been demonstrated throughout the history of the United States. Executive agencies have a tremendous amount of power to do what they like if the rest of the government stands by and watches. It is the role of the legislature and the judiciary to not sit idle in this regard. They have a responsibility to ensure that the executive branch runs efficiently and effectively while not trampling on the rights of the people.

The legislature and the judiciary could end this total surveillance if they wanted to just through using the law. Congress could hold hearings, pass legislation, and restrict funding to counteract this activity. The judiciary could rule against claims of state secrecy and demand the information that the intelligence community has about this issue be made public. It is this power that causes the intelligence community as well as Facebook to be careful about the things they do and the moves they make.

, the other branches of government have not made any real effort to stop the executive branch or Facebook from doing what it likes until recently. Instead the legislature has been crafting laws that remove the rights of internet users. The bills that are being sponsored by the legislature aid the executive in their activity as do the rulings made by the judiciary. They also aid in protecting industry from cyber-attacks that may harm their business. None of this effort does anything to protect the user from the problems that Facebook has created.

Current Situation

The ability of law enforcement to monitor what happens on Facebook is governed by an extensive set of legal codes that have been developed over the past 50 years. Under the Stored Communications Act the police can obtain basic Facebook information with just a subpoena or communications information with a court order. To obtain the rest of the information, law enforcement just needs a search warrant under the Fourth Amendment in accordance with state laws when they apply. [259]

This ability collect data is derived from legal precedent that has been shaped in the criminal justice system. In 1967, the Supreme Court held in Katz v. United States that a person does have a reasonable expectation of privacy when they go into a phone booth to make a telephone call. Because of this expectation, the government needs a warrant to wiretap a phone booth. But that expectation of privacy is determined by the action that the person takes to keep their communication private (going into a booth and closing the door), and that society recognizes that the person has an expectation of privacy (people expect phone booth conversations to be private).[260] As to be expected, the judiciary has recognized very little expectation of privacy over the internet despite efforts made by users that may signal an intention to preserve confidentiality.

The reason for this lack of recognition comes from the ruling in Smith v. Maryland (1979) which held that when an individual gives information to a third party they lose their expectation of privacy. This is extremely problematic for internet users because most communications on the internet are done using third parties. According to the IACP Center for Social Media, both Katz and Smith allowed for a string of rulings that would destroy the expectation of privacy on the internet such as Commonwealth v. Madigan, U.S. v. Maxwell, U.S. v. Charbonneau, and Ohio v. Lerner, Courtright v, Madigan and Guest v. Leis. These ruling say that a person who uses email, chat rooms, or Newsfeeds that make use of a third party have little expectation of privacy which means there will be little need for a warrant to get the information, and they can instead settle for subpoena or a court order.[261]

While these laws and rulings are disagreeable in certain respects, they do offer some protection for the data of Facebook users. And the reason they exist is only because of a legal system that promotes and challenges what law enforcement does on a daily basis. That system can be oppressive at times, but because it has checks built into it the public accepts its power over them. Otherwise no one would ever share information with Facebook or even consent to their imprisonment for that matter. Laws serve to protect the system while at the same time protecting the people.

The intelligence community however does not have to worry about a legal system with extensive legal protections getting in the way. They operate by a different set of rules that are less concerned with imprisonment of U.S. citizens than they are with influencing policy making and preventing major threats to the public. Because of the different mission, the check of public awareness and legal trials is lessened to a larger extent. Instead, government agencies only need to get permission to monitor a target's communications.[262] The only check after this comes from congressional intelligence committees that approve their budget and hold hearings for reported misconduct.[263]

The permission that federal agencies get to monitor targets on American citizens on U.S. soil comes from warrants issued by the Foreign Intelligence Surveillance Court or FISC.[264] This Court was created in 1978 to put restraints on the intelligence community following the findings of the Church Committee in 1975. Chaired by Frank Church, a Democratic Senator from Idaho, the committee found gross abuses by agencies such as the FBI, CIA, and NSA. In order to save the intelligence community while allowing them to regulating their ability to conduct surveillance, the FISC was formed. The FISC meets in secret and approves of the warrants for surveillance that allow for lawful interception when the intelligence community chooses to follow the law.[265]

In addition to a lack of legal ramifications, there is also a lack of oversight to combat this problem. Because much of the information that is relevant to regulating these agencies is considered classified, the committees that oversee these agencies have to meet in closed session. This means that there is little public pressure put on legislatures who tolerate extreme surveillance. Operating in closed session also opens up the possibility of pressure being put on legislatures through fear tactics made by overzealous intelligence officials. This failure is ironic seeing as both the House and Senate Select Intelligence Committees were created in the 1970s because of the abuses that were uncovered in the Church Committee hearings.[266]

The result of this system of regulation, for lack of better word, is that Facebook can be used by the government to conduct investigations and surveillance of internet users. While the tactics discussed in previous chapters such as creating undercover profiles and vacuuming data from internet service providers may seem unacceptable, the system of regulation gives the impression that things are okay. Therefore, Facebook can say that they are not doing anything wrong when they share information with these agencies. Certainly, better informed individuals can see through that claim, but most people do not know enough about the system to disagree.

Aggravation

To the outside observer this system might seem somewhat stable for the time being. After all there is a degree of checks and balances combined with public ignorance that makes it difficult for someone in Congress to generate significant opposition to the issue. But it seems that what government agencies have achieved with regards to information gathering from private companies is not enough. They want more and there are members of Congress who are fighting to get them even more by hyping the threat of criminal use of the internet.

As a result, there has been a constant stream of intelligence sharing legislation being proposed in Congress. These bills are being pushed fervently and if enacted will give law enforcement and the intelligence community even more power over the internet. One such bill is the Cyber Intelligence Sharing and Protection Act or CISPA as it is known. Introduced by Representative Michael Rogers (R-Georgia) and Representative Dutch Ruppersberger (D - Maryland), CISPA if passed would promote sharing between online corporations and law enforcement agencies.[267] The law would essentially decriminalize actions where a corporation shares private online information about its users with the government.[268] Passing of this law would prevent legal action to be taken against Facebook for something they already routinely do.

CISPA has been passed in the House over the concern for cyber-attacks and economic espionage from foreign countries as well as "hacktivist" organizations. Over the past four years there have been numerous attacks against corporations such as Facebook, LinkedIn, Google and other internet companies.[269] The government has also been attacked, but those attacks have not succeeded as well as the corporate attacks have. While protecting government and military infrastructure is a concern, it is more corporate interest that is driving CISPA.[270]

Another related bill that would give the government power to access information obtained by corporations is the Cyber Security Act of 2012. Proposed by Senator Joe Lieberman and Representative Susan Collins, the cyber security act would give intelligence organizations greater capability at isolating cyber threats and collecting information on those threats.[271] The bill failed to make it out of committee but it still represents an attitude in Congress that is willing to surrender control of the internet out of fear of cybercrime and cyber warfare.[272]

Along with using cyber threats to move legislation, politicians are also using pedophilia to obtain more information from internet users. An information sharing bill worth looking at is the Protecting Children from Internet Pornographers Act that was proposed by Texas Representative Lamar Smith in May of 2011. The Act would require communications providers to store for one year the data they have on their customers. This requirement would prevent any suit from being filed against the service provider after the user has deleted their information. The data retention policy would also allow for the subpoenaing of records for non- registered sex offenders to lower the standard for information sharing.[273]

While some bills hope to create new laws, others simply hope to amend pre-existing ones. In 1994 when the Communications Assistance Law Enforcement Act was first passed, it was mandated that all telecommunications networks have access points inserted into them specifically for law enforcement evidence collection. These "backdoors" as they were called would allow investigators to tap into phone conversations as long as they have a warrant to do so. The law however did not mandate that computer networks be made with backdoors, and that is now a source of controversy.[274]

CALEA is now receiving this attention because of issues such as "going dark", as well as criminal activity that take place on social networks. Going Dark refers to the inability of agencies such as the FBI to see into networks that may be used by criminals and terrorists to transmit information.[275] CALEA would give the intelligence and law enforcement communities' access to social networks like Facebook and Twitter for whenever a court gives them a warrant to do so. No longer would they have to wait on the company to turn over the data. The consequence would be legal and nearly unrestricted access to the networks by the intelligence community.

As a last resort to defend against cyber-attacks, Senator Susan Collins of Maine proposed a bill that would allow the government to pull the plug on internet communications altogether. This bill was written for the sake of combatting internet viruses before they take down serious infrastructure that is vulnerable to the attack. But it could also be used against civil unrest that may be sparked by internet usage like what happened in the Arab Spring.[276] Pulling the plug on the internet may seem outlandish but it needs to be addressed when discussing such ideas as civil unrest in America. If the government wanted to they could pull the plug just like Egypt did when things got out of hand, the only question now is whether they could do it legally.

While there are legitimate causes behind these bills, they all serve to protect and strengthen the abuses of internet information collection by the executive branch. And what makes these bills out of place is that not only do government agencies already have a wealth of power to collect information for investigations and surveillance, but that whistleblowers have come forward to tell Congress as well as the public that those powers are being abused. Numerous whistleblowers from the government such as Thomas Tamm, William Binney, Kirk Weibe, Thomas Drake, Barbra McNamara, Russell Tice, and Edward Snowden along with AT&T whistleblower Mark Klein have come forward in the years after 9/11 to bring public attention to warrantless surveillance.[277] Notable journalists such as James Bamford, Amy Goodman, Chris Hedges, James Risen, Dana Priest, William Arkin, Siobhan Gorman, and Seymour Hersh among many others have written books or articles or have conducted lengthy interviews on this issue.[278] It is hard to believe that Congress did not know these abuses were going on while writing their bills for less privacy of internet users.

And it is also difficult to believe that Facebook did not understand what they were doing amidst all this surveillance. Since 2004 Facebook has been collecting as much information on internet users as they can get their hands on. Not only should Facebook have known what was going on from the whistleblowers and the journalists, but they also should have known because of the volume of information requests they received for user's information. Facebook recently revealed that they received over 9, 000 requests for data in 2012.[279] They are just as complicit in what has been going on as Congress has been. For them to argue otherwise is disingenuous at best.

Reaction

The lack of protective legislation for Internet users calls for a different approach by the concerned members of the public. One of the ways that people have been resisting what is going on is through lawsuits. Numerous lawsuits have been filed against corporations that are providing the intelligence community access to the internet, as well as against intelligence agencies that user the information.

A case that demonstrates this is Hepting v. AT&T which was filed in 2006. The plaintiffs in Hepting alleged that there was an illegal wiretapping room being set up inside an AT&T switching station. Despite the testimony of AT&T whistleblower Mark Klein as well as numerous reports that the wiretapping was going on, the case was thrown out for lack of standing. This was the result of FISA legislation being passed that gave telecommunications companies the immunity from any cooperation with government in investigating terrorism.[280]

In the case of Jewel v. NSA, a group of plaintiffs backed by the Electronic Frontier Foundation filed suit against the NSA alleging an illegal wiretapping program that had been conducted since 2001. That case is currently in the appellate stage after being dismissed in district court for lack of standing. Where the telecommunication companies have been given immunity with FISA, the NSA has claimed the state secrets privilege. The NSA argues that they do not have to defend themselves from any allegations because all the alleged activity is classified material. Not even Congress let alone the 9th Circuit Court of Appeals can access the information in question.[281] Other cases with a similar result were ACLU v. NSA and Clapper v Amnesty International, which made it to the Supreme Court.[282]

While preventing the NSA from accessing data illegally has gained plenty of attention, the application of using social media to prosecute cases is becoming more and more common. A good case that demonstrates the lowering of the walls between social media and the police is Harris v. New York. Malcolm Harris was an Occupy Wall Street protestor who wrote about his experience at Occupy on Twitter. When he was arrested for disorderly conduct, the prosecutor tried to subpoena his Twitter records. Harris had already deleted his Twitter account, but Twitter still had the record of his/tweets. Twitter tried to resist the subpoena, but they eventually agreed to turn over Harris's tweets after being faced with a fine for not complying. Harris later pled guilty and was sentenced to a brief jail sentence and community service.[283]

The Harris case is important because if the police can subpoena personal information from Twitter, they can do it to other social media companies like Facebook. This would lower the bar for the documentation that the police would need to obtain to get someone's account information. While a search warrant would require probable cause and the written consent of a judge, a subpoena would only require the authority of an officer of the court such as the prosecutor and a reasonable relation to the case at hand.

Along with lowering of the barrier for legal documentation, we are also seeing the use of legal documentation to mislead Facebook users. In United States v. Drew, an appeals court held that violating the terms of service for website to conduct police work is not a criminally punishable offense.[284] This is in contradiction to the prohibition that is placed on users who may create duplicate profiles of themselves. The government it appears is above the rules when it comes to undercover work.

While these cases are excellent examples of where the judicial branch has failed to protect American citizens from the corruption of the executive branch, they are not entirely the source of this problem. The courts are designed to interpret laws that are created by the legislative and executive branches. There is not much they can do if the law is designed to circumvent the constitution as well the judiciary. It could also be that the people appointed to these courts were selected because they would vote for the government on issues like this. It is the American government's weakest branch, and it should surprise no one that it has been defeated.

In addition to the public's efforts against the intelligence community, certain regulatory agencies have also taken legal action against Facebook. One such group is the Federal Trade Commission or FTC. The FTC is an independent regulatory agency that was established in 1903 to break up the monopolies which dominated the American marketplace in the early 20th century.[285] There were many reasons why they were given this mission, but an example that applies nicely with Facebook is the prevention of deception.

A power that the FTC has in combating deception is that they can file lawsuits against companies who fail to comply with what are agreed upon acceptable business practices. Such was the case of In re Facebook Internet Tracking Litigation. This class action suit was filed against Facebook in May of 2012. The plaintiffs in that case alleged that Facebook illegally tracked their browsing habits by not erasing cookies they placed on user's browsers. Instead Facebook simply disabled them to allow for more data collection without the consent of the Plaintiffs. This action was in violation of the Stored Communications Act, the Right to Privacy act, and several California Penal codes that forbid such activity. There were a combined 21 parties in the class action suing for $15 billion that is still awaiting trial.[286]

In another case several interest groups filed a complaint against Facebook to the FTC in 2007. This led to an investigation and them making several recommendations on Aug 10, 2012. One of the recommendation was that Facebook would be barred from making representations about the "privacy or security" of consumers' personal information. These recommendations also say that Facebook needs to 1) get consent for what they do, 2) they must ask for approval when making changes to privacy policy, 3) Facebook must protect users account data for 30 days following the deletion of the users account, 4) must enact a program to focus on privacy, 5) Facebook must be audited by independent agencies, 6) Facebook will be regulated by the Federal Trade Commission for 20 years.[287]

Along with what the FTC has done, there has also been direct congressional action against Facebook. Senator Al Franken of Minnesota convened a committee in July of 2012 to look into Facebook's facial recognition capabilities. The committee called into question the current laws governing facial recognition. Keep in mind that there is no 4th Amendment protection against facial recognition, and with the current state of technology legislative action could be considered long overdue. The committee pointed out legislative failures while it highlighted the current state of technology in allowing corporations to intrude on privacy.[288] It didn't serve to regulate Facebook as much as to cause awareness about the world that is being created.

Another Congressional attempt at Facebook was also made by John D. Rockefeller IV. Rockefeller, who is chairman of the Senate Commerce, Science, and Transportation committee, requested in November of 2012 that data aggregators turn over information related to ad targeting and Facebook. Of the nine companies that Rockefeller requested information from; three of them were in exclusive data sharing agreements with Facebook for ad targeting purposes. These Facebook connected companies were Datalogix, Epsilon, and Acxiom. The fourth company in the exclusive agreement, Blue Kai, was not addressed by Rockefeller.[289]

In addition to legal action that the government has taken, private citizens have also been using the court system against Facebook as well. A major class action lawsuit that was recently decided was In re Facebook Privacy Litigation. In that case the plaintiffs alleged that Facebook intentionally and knowingly transmitted personal information about Plaintiffs to third-party advertisers without their consent. In November of 2011, the case was dismissed for: failure to state a claim under the wiretap or store communications act, failure to state a claim under the California penal code, and failure to state a claim under breach of contract.[290]

Another good to look at when examining Facebook's durability is the famous Beacon case of Lane v. Facebook. The court held ruled on March 17, 2010 that the Beacon feature was an invasion of privacy and was to be taken down. The plaintiff Shawn Lane received $15,000 in compensation from Facebook and his codefendants also received smaller amounts. With the settlement Facebook agreed to give $9 million to start a group that would help guarantee privacy on the network.[291]

With the Lane case, we see a clear violation of user privacy that was met with a meager punishment considering the number of users the activity affected. This is not to mention that the sum of $9 million does nothing to teach Facebook the price of invading privacy. And along with these failed cases they are outnumbered by the numerous cases that can be dealt with by simply examining the privacy policy outlined earlier in the chapter. Suing Facebook for invading privacy doesn't really work because users are essentially consenting to the invasion.

An example that fits this case profile is Cohen v. Facebook. The Plaintiffs in Cohen contended that Facebook "used their names and profile pictures to promote the Friend Finder service without their knowledge or consent and, at least in the case of some of them, despite the fact that they have not actually ever used the service."[292] The case dismissed on June 28, 2011 because the terms of service informed the user that Facebook could do what they liked with their information. The court also dismissed because there was no cognizable injury.[293]

Something also very basic that people just can't seem to understand is that Facebook can terminate the accounts of whoever they would like. In the case of Young v. Facebook, the plaintiff Beth Young sued Facebook for a violation of her civil rights when her account was deleted for political statements she had made. The U.S. District Court dismissed the case on May 17, 2011 because her claims did not make significant connection between the alleged violation and state law. Her other claims of breach of contract, negligence, and fraud were also thrown out for the same deficiency.[294]

And finally, Facebook can do what they like with the information that users have given them. In the case of Fraley v. Facebook, the plaintiffs alleged that Facebook used their information for the shared stories portion of the site to generate revenue. The plaintiffs complained against this practice because Facebook provided neither consent nor compensation for the information that users provided. Case was dismissed on December 16, 2011 because the plaintiffs were asking for an unjust enrichment of their claim.[295] Unjust enrichment is when the plaintiff asks for compensation that they do not deserve.

While Facebook is given somewhat free reign to collect what they like, the outside world is using Facebook for the discipline of subordinates. In the case of Tatro v. University of Minnesota a mortuary student failed a class because of posts on Facebook about a body she was working along with comments relating to violent fantasy about her ex-boyfriend. The Minnesota Supreme Court ruled on June 20, 2012 that because Tatro was enrolled in the program she had consented to the conditions that allowed the university to regulate her conduct.[296]

A similar case that dealt with the workplace instead of school was Sumien v. CareFlite. In this case two EMTs were fired for making a comment on Facebook about a patient. The plaintiff sued saying that his employer intruded upon their seclusion by looking at comments he was not aware were visible. Sumien also argued against his employer for firing him over a discussion that took place outside of work. The court ruled this argument irrelevant to the claim of intrusion. Sumien also argued that his right for freedom of discussion was greater than any issue for. This claim was also deemed irrelevant to the intrusion claim. Case was dismissed on July 5, 2012 following summary judgment.[297]

Despite what these organizations and individuals have done to combat Facebook through government institutions, these are only small steps compared to what need to be taken. While the Congressional hearings only scratch the surface, the court cases are doomed to fail from the beginning. The rules will simply not allow outside forces to destroy or change this network to protect those who use it. And the people who have built this intelligence apparatus will not tolerate its destruction either.

Defending the System

What protects this system from external threats like lawsuits and ambitious senators is lobbying. And in the area of intelligence gathering much of the work has been outsourced, so a lot of lobbying can be done. Intelligence community officials regularly associate with contractors as well as policymakers on threats that the country faces. This means that the contractor has a chance to talk to major players in how the surveillance state is handled. Because of the contractor's position, surveillance may tend to slant heavily towards a profit-making interest rather than any interest in protecting the public.

Influencing the intelligence community official can be done in many ways, the most prolific of which is the revolving door. How this works is that a person will go into an intelligence agency like the Defense Intelligence Agency and work there for a few years. They will then leave and go on to work for an intelligence contractor like SAIC or Raytheon. Having established contacts in the company as well as in the agency they worked for, the individual will then have an inside track into negotiating contracts. This makes them an asset in their company.

But along with having a social relationship established, the infiltrator can also make bargains with their contacts in the targeted agency for a heavy push in intelligence gathering. This could be an outright bribe, or it could be the promise of a position at a company after the task is completed. Because this section of industry operates on rules of secrecy, it is subject to limited government oversight that can be easily influenced by a knowledgeable, well-spoken analyst.[298]

We should also recognize that there is a political card that can be played by the politician who promotes intelligence gathering. Following 9/11 this became a major tool to get things done. Even now politicians still use the War on Terror to promote their causes, and they still make sure to acknowledge it in case someone questions their patriotism. When we combine the political pageantry with influence from industry, it seems unlikely that the system of surveillance will fix itself.

The final source for influence is the campaign contributions that are made by intelligence contractors like Raytheon which shape the focus of Congress. Raytheon as you may remember is the owner of BBN technologies, an intelligence contracting firm that does work with web monitoring technology. Raytheon is also rated number 1# for companies in electronic defense contracting who lobby Congress by OpenSecrets.org. Closely following Raytheon were General Dynamics and SAIC who also have interests in seeing increased surveillance take place. As of right now the other social media monitoring companies are still too small to make a real push in Washington so they can get by through benefiting from what the larger companies do.[299] But the same cannot be said for the social media companies that have been doing the collection. In addition to fighting off court cases and strategically crafting their policies to absolve themselves of responsibility, Facebook is also lobbying Washington for relaxed regulation. To do this they recently formed a political action committee known as FB PAC which stands for Facebook political action committee.[300] A political action committee is a way for an interest group or corporation to give money to election campaigns. By forming this committee Facebook is making it clear that they do not plan on changing, they plan on forcing the country to adapt to what they want.

Facebook's influence in Washington is as far reaching as it is strategic. Among Silicon Valley companies, Facebook is ranked 6th in campaign finance donations by OpenSecrets.org with a total congressional contribution of $265,000 for 2012. Facebook has distributed this money evenly on both sides of the political aisle to secure position more than ideology.[301] Right now it appears Facebook just wants to ward off investigations and aggressive legislation.

This strategy is evidenced by who FB PAC has donated money to in the 2012 election cycle. Of the Senate Commerce, Transportation and Science committee, Facebook has given contributions to 14 of the 18 members of the committee. Of the Senate Judiciary committee, Facebook has given contributions to 13 of the 18 members of the committee. And in total, 48 of the 100 members of the Senate have received some form of contribution from Facebook.[302]

In the House of Representatives, we can also see Facebook's strategy put on display. Facebook has donated to 25 of the House's Energy and Commerce Committee's 40 members. Of the House's Oversight and Investigations Committee, Facebook has given money to five of the 40 members. And in total Facebook has donated in some amount to 60 of their 435 members.[303]

While these donations only range from 1,000 to 10,000 dollars per candidate, the effect they have on the situation can be substantial.[304] Donations give Facebook access to the Congress member for further discussion of issues of interest. This give Facebook a chance to argue their case for why they do the things they do. They also give the congress person an incentive to listen closely because they usually need all the campaign contributions they can get.

The result does not necessarily have to be favorable legislation like CISPA that serves to protect the network. The influence could simply be used to prevent a serious investigation into Facebook from happening. Or it may be used to block legislation that would regulate Facebook more closely than it already is. The money that Facebook is spending can go a long way if it is used correctly.

It is also worth noting that while Facebook's first donations may be small, if the candidate responds to their plea they may receive more in the future. This financial incentive applies not just for Facebook, but also for other Silicon Valley companies who may have similar concerns. Corporations such as Google, Oracle, and Microsoft also give donations to many of the same candidates that Facebook does to ward off federal regulation.[305] When candidates make sure to vote against regulating the Valley, the small donations can add up into significant amounts that are needed for their campaigns.

But aside from direct actions that they take, Facebook also benefits from the apathetic environment in the United States. There are not enough calls for regulation of Facebook in the public at large to force Congress to act. Most of the attention is directed towards the NSA which has received some protests and calls for regulation in the media. But Facebook has over 166 million users in the United States who despite the occasional angry post have not posed much of a threat to the way Facebook does things. Until the users demonstrate their frustration with this site, the government will continue to ignore the problem or pretend like it doesn't exist while they concentrate on other issues.

Along with protecting themselves politically, Facebook also does an excellent job of protecting their business through their policies as well. Facebook manages to avoid the FTC label of using deceptive business practices by putting up policy documents that enumerate exactly what they do with the data that users give them.[306] While most users do not read these documents and the documents provide little user protection, Facebook is technically telling them how the site functions. This allows for Facebook to avoid regulation while engaging in activity that would warrant it.

These policies serve to keep Facebook out of trouble, but they also technically constrain Facebook from doing things they would normally do without a concern. To prevent this from becoming a significant problem, Facebook changes their policy frequently to suit their needs. As of this writing the current privacy policy is operating under the December 11, 2012 guidelines. By the time this work is published Facebook will have most likely changed their policy again to suit the features they developed. In total Facebook has changed their privacy policy at least four times in the past five years.[307]

Now that the public has been made aware of what is going on by the leak with Edward Snowden, there is opportunity for Congress and the president to control the issue instead of some regulatory agency or a citizen group who may have more zeal. Congress has recently floated several bills that seek to regulate warrantless wiretapping by the intelligence community. The most recent bill that sought to restrict the collection of phone records failed, but there are more bills which aim to provide transparency and oversight to the process. Increasing standards for collection, changing the way FISA judges are appointed, the appointment of a public defender on the FISC, and an effort for more declassification are all ideas that are being supported now by Congress.[308]

President Barack Obama has also stated that he intends to provide reforms to make the public feel safer about the collection that is going on. At a press conference on August 9, 2013, Obama laid out a plan to work with Congress to provide more oversight for phone and internet surveillance. He also declared that he would: establish a public defender for the FISC, make the system more transparent, and create an external review board for the process. It is funny how Obama and Congress have such similar ideas on how to fix the situation. While it is assumed by the public that these reforms will lead to a scaling back in surveillance, it is never said openly which leaves room for its continuation or even its expansion.[309]

There are also cases that are in the court system as of this writing which seek to end the domestic spying program.[310] These cases represent the unyielding determination of citizens groups like the ACLU and the EFF to end what the NSA is doing. It is difficult to say whether federal judges will allow the cases to be heard considering the rulings in Clapper and the other spying cases. But the struggle should not be given up, not by an inch, because surrender is far worse than failure.

10. Mission Creep

A term that is often discussed when criticizing data mining and modern forms of intelligence gathering is mission creep. This idea refers to a mission that has expanded past its intended objective into unexpected or perhaps illegal territory. When we are discussing government use of Facebook to collect information, we should admit that mission creep is a serious possibility. With the capabilities that the NSA among other agencies has at its disposal, the government may one day use Facebook's data to expand their control over the world. When that day comes it will certainly bring unparalleled power to whoever controls the intelligence apparatus at that point in time. [311] This power as we have seen would be unchecked and without restraint.

While some critics might suggest that surveillance is not the boogeyman that people make it out to be, it should be noted that surveillance is not the end but the beginning of the road to authoritarianism. There are reasons why governments monitor their citizens other than just looking for terrorists who may cause the public harm. Unrestricted surveillance brings with it benefits for the regime that chooses to embrace it. It is these benefits that should draw our concern when we examine what Facebook is capable of being used for.

Censorship

A frequently used counterargument against the flaws of Facebook is that it allows people to discuss and debate issues in an open forum. While this may be taken for granted in democratic countries, it is a blessing in nations like Egypt or Columbia where freedom of speech is not the order of the day. Facebook for the most part lives up to this benefit. People can talk freely about issues that interest them even though they may offend other users. But with this digital liberty, there are also many factors that could infringe on free speech in this environment.

The first is that government surveillance taking place on the internet could serve to control what commenters of government say on Facebook. These people may feel apprehensive about making disparaging remarks towards their government while knowing they are being watched. That fear may be real or imagined, but the effect is what counts. People could shy away from saying what is true in favor of what is acceptable because they think state authorities are watching. The result is an undermining of the discussion environment that Facebook is known for.

In addition to the threat of retribution, there are many copyright laws and treaties that have been proposed in recent years which would serve to cut back on freedom of expression through Facebook. Bills such as the Stop Online Piracy Act and the Protect IP Act were created with the intention of stopping internet piracy with little concern for restricting information sharing over sites like Google or Facebook.[312] Other bills that are less strict such as OPEN achieve the goals of Hollywood movie studios while still preventing information from being exchanged freely.[313] And while these bills and their clone versions may not get passed, international trade agreements like the Anti-Counterfeiting Trade Agreement and the Trans Pacific Partnership may force websites to police their networks from any copyrighted information that they feel they own.[314]

These laws, should they be defeated, may be substituted for stricter content policies on Facebook that accomplish similar objectives. Facebook already has stringent bans on sexual images, expressions of self-harm, as well as violent speech which serve to depress the discussion to a certain extent.[315] But with a government pressuring Facebook there could be even greater restrictions placed on the network. If there is a critic who should question whether Facebook would enforce supposable restrictions, they should consider Facebook's stance regarding China which will be covered in later chapters.

It has also been shown that people engage in self-censorship already because of the large number of friends they communicate with on the Newsfeed. When users make a post or comment they show concern for the large audience that may see that content. This self-censoring could be done simply to avoid offending anyone that might take issue with what the users says. Racial jokes are a good example of something that doesn't make it to the Newsfeed out of fear for offending a Facebook friend or acquaintance. Self-censorship also could be done to avoid criticism from others that the user is not yet ready to take in.[316] It is one thing to make a statement amongst a small group of people, but an entire friends list can be another story.

Outside of just protecting personal relationships, fear of honest self-expression could stem from a concern over sharing personal beliefs with untrustworthy acquaintances. With the large number of "friends" that see the activity of the user, there is also a chance that one of those "friends" will use that information against them. In case after case, it wasn't the boss or the professor who saw what someone put on Facebook, it was the student or coworker that reported it to them. Users have surrounded themselves with acquaintances that may or may not have their best interests at heart. All it takes is one person who disagrees with what someone thinks to tell the appropriate authority to cause trouble for them.

The point that is to be made here is that it wouldn't take much to corrupt the discussion environment on Facebook. Just through making their surveillance capabilities known and getting copyright legislation passed the government could benefit greatly in the form of decreased political activity on the network. They don't need to ban content everywhere; they just need to ban content where it is frequently shared under the guise of protecting the internet users as well as the marketplace. Accidental or on purpose, the mission seems to have strayed from its true objective.

Confusion

In the minds of its users and advocates, Facebook is a chance for the individual to have a voice in a world that ignores most of those who wish to speak. The mainstream media has failed to produce quality journalism and discussion and because of that social media is one of the places where people are going to for information. Compared to mainstream journalism, social media brings with it the benefit of being more free from corporate control and adaptable to the issues of the modern world. But with these kinds of benefits there are also flaws such as the environment and format that detract from what Facebook offers.

A part of the problem is that the information that is shared and discussed on Facebook does not have the accountability that other sources have. Facebook does not screen for inaccurate information. What people post on Facebook is up to them if they do not violate the content policy.[317] That discretion creates a category of acceptable material that has within it both the true and the false. Because the truth is somewhat restricted, the limitless depth of the false has the advantage.

This amount of false information can become a problem when we think about how good Facebook is at disseminating information. By having a thorough understanding of social network analysis, an analyst could spread propaganda very quickly throughout the network. Understanding the points in a network that have the highest influence is important for making messages spread quickly. An excellent tool to use for this would-be Facebook's Open Graph which helps to identify individuals that command a large audience.[318]

That influential person could then be sent or shown a piece of content that says something sensational enough to warrant a click. From that click, the misinformation game starts again. Some people will know better than to like a status that says a celebrity died, but others will quickly like it or make their own status. Before the news media knows anything, half the network will be saying that Will Smith is dead.

Most will admit that a celebrity death hoax is certainly not a tragedy, but it does show us just how quickly an idea can be repeated by users who don't know any better. If it is shocking enough, people will act before they think. Instead of researching the post they will comment on it without second thought. After it has gained enough steam the idea will be corrected by someone either on the network or in the media. How long it will take for that correction to be made and how serious the misinformation is will determine the impact the message has. It is not a matter of whether someone has the right to yell fire in a crowded theater, but whether people will know not to start a stampede when that happens.

This capability to target users is a real problem because Facebook is designed to impair the judgment of the user when they see advertisements. The rating system, the recommendation system, and the Newsfeed can give false credibility to information that would normally be dismissed if the user saw it somewhere else. Not to mention that a good analysis of the network would identify people who tend to believe things the minute they see them.

The confusion that misinformation spawns could be the result of uninformed users making speculation, but it could also be the intentional work of a third party with nefarious purposes. In a 2011 article, *The Guardian* reported about a piece of software developed by the Air Force known as Persona Management that is designed to exploit social networking by creating multiple artificial online personas. These personas are managed much like a CRM would manage the multiple profiles of businesses. By using the software, the controller can impersonate a variety of internet users and send out messages over a numerous of networks. This tool was originally developed for a misinformation strategy in the Iraq and Afghanistan regions known as Operation Earnest Voice. The objective of the operation was to combat enemy propaganda through understanding and turning the misinformation against itself.[319]

Persona Management can also be used to gather information about networks without having to ask for a legal request from Facebook. By creating fake personas, the agent can simply infiltrate targeted networks and listen in on conversations through the Newsfeed. If they wanted to be more proactive they could also solicit information through messaging.[320] This would strengthen the ability of the controller to tailor their messages to those they are targeting much the way a company's social media manager would.

The state of confusion that could be created on Facebook would be even more devastating to the public at large because of the decreased reliability of the mainstream media. People are beginning to turn to alternative forms of news such as citizen journalism that have found a place on Facebook. While citizen journalism does provide a different point of view, it could be easily utilized to spread propaganda that leaves users not knowing where to turn for information.

Manipulation

The result of this surveillance and social control is the proliferation of whatever idea the controller of the machine should desire. Facebook is pushing its users toward a passive way of thinking that encourages acceptance of a desired idea. This is not an estimation of the possibilities of what Facebook can do; this is what Facebook was designed to do. Whether the goal is the marketing of a product or the marketing of a candidate does not matter. A Facebook user will do as it they are told if it they are told correctly.

An example of this influence machine being put into action is the 2008 Presidential Election. Using target advertising and the help of thousands of volunteers, the Democratic campaign utilized Facebook to influence voters for the election of Barack Obama. The network was great for sending advertisements to targeted users that were likely to donate money and join the cause of getting Obama elected. It is even believed by some that Facebook was the deciding factor in the election because the Obama campaign donated so much time and resources into it while the McCain Campaign donated so few. [321]

The role that Facebook played 2008 is very interesting when we consider how few people used Facebook then as compared to now. Facebook had 18.4 million American users in 2008; in the 2012 election they had over 160 million.[322] Also interesting is a study of the campaign by *Pew Internet Research* which showed that only 10% of Americans surveyed engaged in political activity on social networks in 2008.[323] These numbers cast some doubt on the Facebook election hype but they also lead us to believe that Facebook would have a much larger impact in subsequent elections.

Whether Facebook was as critical as some proponents make it to be is up for dispute, but it is without a doubt a major force in present elections. Subsequent campaigns in Presidential as well as Congressional races show an unwavering belief in social media that can be attributed to the 2008 campaign. Social media is a must for the politician hoping to get their name and views in the mind of the voters. Those who forsake it run the same risk that businesses and celebrities do.[324]

Another powerful example of the influence that Facebook and social media can generate is the Kony 2012 movement. Kony 2012 is a human rights campaign started by the group Invisible Children which aims to shed light on the issue of child soldiers in Uganda. In 2012, "Kony" was one of the most shared posts on Facebook.[325] This heavy volume of posts was the result of an aggressive social media campaign kick started from a YouTube video entitled after the movement. The video sought to describe Invisible Children's goal of catching warlord Joseph Kony and it currently has 98 million hits as of August 2013.[326]

The last phenomenon that should be discussed is Gangnam Style. At the #5 spot of top Facebook posts for 2012 was the meme Gangnam Style made popular by the Korean rapper PSY and his Gangnam Style music video.[327] This video has over a billion views on YouTube which makes it one of most shared music videos ever.[328] While some might consider the video entertaining, it is also a good demonstration of what consumers will embrace with Facebook. The idea is not that Gangnam Style is the best video ever; it is just that it is something everyone should be engaged in which is why people are watching it and promoting it.

What these social media hits show us is that Facebook is incredibly powerful at shaping perception. Facebook can make its users embrace an idea whether it is a political candidate, a social movement, or a catchy video. There are certainly limits to what can be pushed onto the network but those limits are not too substantial. The real hurdle is finding what people like and what it will take to influence them. But that only means that the idea needs to be shaped, not so much that it must be changed completely.

History has also given us examples of where we are sure the government used propaganda through what were perceived legitimate channels of communication. On a broadcast of Russia Today, contributor to the program and investigative journalist Wayne Madsen noted that Radio Swann was used in 1960 during the Bay of Pigs operations to spread propaganda on island before the invasion. Madsen even compared that incident with the use of Twitter during the Libya revolution of today. And he would also note the use of Radio Free Europe, Radio Liberty and Radio Free Asia by the CIA to coopt any revolutions that would arise in their corresponding areas.[329]

The discrediting of Radio Free Europe and Radio Liberty, as well as the Congress for Cultural Freedom and the Ford Foundation was also discussed in an *Untold History of the United States* by Oliver Stone and Peter Kuznick. According to their work, that campaign of propaganda was a part of a much larger effort to influence American citizens. Not only did the CIA infiltrate media sources, but they also co-opted professors, students, and civil rights activists to help spread propaganda and disinformation throughout the public. [330] What these alternative narratives of American history show us is that spreading propaganda is not out of the question for the government to do. This is not to suggest that PSY is really a CIA operative, it is just to say that Facebook would work nicely in whatever agenda the government is hoping to further.

Selection

And of course, there are always those people who are not easily distracted. These are the kind of people that make up the contrarians and the dissenters of the internet discussion boards and forums. While they are not always right, they are difficult to control because they know how to think for themselves. Authoritarian governments have little use for these people and they always seek out ways to persecute them when the time comes.

While in the real world or on certain parts of the internet these people can hide in anonymity, on Facebook there is nowhere to hide. A government looking to stifle a movement like Occupy Wall Street or 9/11 Truth could monitor their Facebook pages to see how to target them. Successful monitoring could lead to the discovery of incriminating information. It could also allow the government to plan disinformation campaigns against these movements based on their leader's social media lives. If all else should fail an oppressive regime could use Facebook information to harass the members in the real world.

If this sounds like an extreme scenario, consider that this happened on a systematic basis during the 1950s through the 70's with the FBI's counterintelligence program or COINTELPRO. During this era, the FBI surveilled and harassed groups such as the Communist Party, the Black Panther Party, the Feminist Movement, the American Indian Movement, and several others that sought to speak out against their oppression. This war against subversive groups wasted much of the intelligence community's resources and eventually led to the investigations by the Church Committee.[331] All this activity was done by the government that is monitoring and analyzing information obtained from Facebook right now.

A way that this surveillance can be so terrifying is the concern for not just legal persecution but also of blackmail. This is a tactic that the intelligence community has made use of in the 20th century to achieve a variety of objectives. Famous FBI director J. Edgar Hoover was known for maintaining detailed records on public officials, activists, and celebrities to preserve his hold on power. He is even alleged to have blackmailed John F. Kennedy and Martin Luther King, both for their marital indiscretions as well Kennedy's relationship with former a publicist for Adolf Hitler.[332] There is little to see what good this use of surveillance did for the rest of society other than allowing Hoover to remain at his post for close to 50 years.[333]

Another potent example worth remembering is Operation Phoenix that took place during the Vietnam War. Phoenix was essentially an assassination program run by the CIA whose main objective was to kill suspected communists living in South Vietnam. This was done to eliminate any opposition for the American backed regime, over 20,000 Vietnamese civilians were killed for having suspected ties to communism. No hearing, no Congressional approval, just execution.[334]

Even now the government targets people through methods such as the terrorist watch list. As of 2009 there were over a million people that been placed on the list for being under suspicion of terrorist activity.[335] A critic could say that there are not one million terrorists out there waiting to attack, and they could also point to the numerous well-known, assumed to be innocent famous people that are the list. Notable names on that have been on the list include the late politician Ted Kennedy, actor/activist Mark Ruffalo, and CNN reporter Drew Griffin.[336] What these people did to get on the list is not known because that information is kept secret from the American public.

Aside from the watch list operated by the FBI's Terrorist Screening Center, Facebook could also serve to help target individuals and groups that the government deems subversive or suspects of terrorism.[337]An example could be organizations such as the Tea Party that have pages on Facebook which tend to attract people who want to show their displeasure with the way things are. These pages are effectively creating lists of people to watch out for. While we can only speculate on how those Pages are being used, given recent revelations regarding the IRS and Tea Party, it would be foolish to think they are being ignored entirely.[338]

For those of you that follow these movements, it should be no surprise that people are arrested because of their association with protest movements on Facebook. By simply looking at attendance lists for protest events, police departments can identify suspects who they saw being disruptive in person. This would be further aided if the activists posted pictures of themselves at the movement. Facebook may help these protest movements to a degree, but it hurts them just as much if not more so by helping them consent to their own surveillance.

It is this threat to personal security that makes weighing the benefits of what protestors get from Facebook that much more important. It is not as though these people are making business decisions that might hurt the sale of a product based on the decision to use Facebook; these people are putting their cause and their freedom on the line by using Facebook to plan political action.

People in these movements should recognize however that there is a tradeoff to be made with using Facebook. Occupy Wall Street protestors knew about this trade which is why they tried to create their own version of Facebook to allow for news updates and communication during their protests.[339] While the project failed, it does show what the members of that movement felt about the so-called tool of the revolution.

Because of their cautious thinking, members of the movement also set up their own website called OccupyWallSt.org. The website serves as a news update of what goes on with Occupy by providing visitors with content describing current and upcoming plans. Visitors also have available to them information regarding protest tactics and a forum to discuss that information. Unfortunately, that website does have Facebook social plugins, so that means Facebook sees everything that goes on with the site anyway.[340]

What makes things difficult is that even if the groups would decide to avoid using Facebook to get their message out, people would still use the site to talk about their activities. A movement such at Occupy or the Tea Party is too big to make a strict order against anything really. People who happen to be activists are going to use the site, and they are going to reveal information about themselves by being members of the site. Facebook will always find a way inside of a secret if it is big enough.

By looking to this false solution, users are playing into the hands of governments and corporations that want to identify who they are online. This is normally not too dangerous for an average Facebook user that is cautious about what information they share. But for an activist who goes against the existing social order it can be a huge mistake. They can't target you if they don't know who you are.

Not What Was Intended

At a lecture entitled the "Audacity of Despair", television show producer and former journalist David Simon spoke on the problems facing modern journalism. While Simon did not discuss government influence, he did note that we cannot substitute Facebook or all social media for that matter as a replacement for real journalism. The solution to the problem of a mediocre media he said is not as easy as just turning to social networking for reporting. Simon even suggested that fixing journalism involves breaking up monopolies that have been allowed to destroy the news channels and fill them with corporate advertisements.[341] From what Simon tells us, it appears that Facebook is not up to the job of replacing professional journalism and it never will be.

The reasons that Simon gives for this conclusion is that citizen journalism is not a profession. A journalist needs to be paid to do the job and paid to do it well. That person also needs to also have someone else check over their work to make sure it is accurate and objective. With the benefits that Simon notes with paid journalism, this author would argue that they also prevent a government from abusing the medium like they would on a social media platform.

And while Facebook may not be designed for genuine journalistic participation, there are other alternatives out there that make efforts to mitigate the flaws previously outlined. Websites such as *Digital Journal*, *Ground Report*, and *Huffington Post* are news sources with standards that encourage quality citizen journalism and discussion from the user. If a citizen journalist decides to submit to one of these sites, the content is vetted by an editor on staff.[342] This is good because at least a pair of eyes have seen the material to make sure it is not blatantly false.

Another good quality of designated citizen journalism is that the people who visit are there for citizen journalism. By having a place specifically for political and current event discussion, the site cut down on the trolls who like to ruin things. That would be an impossible task for Facebook but an achievable one for a citizen journalism site.

The problem of fake submissions and rude visitors can also be addressed on a citizen journalism site with content policies that show concern for misinformation and fostering quality discussion. While these sites also have prohibitions against certain forms of speech such as pornography, they at least do it in for the sake of journalistic integrity and not hiding users from the terrors of the real world. The problem of misinformation is also checked against with a registration process and the editor screening system.[343] These obstacles can of course be beaten, but at least an effort is being made that does yield some results.

With the improved screening system that citizen journalism sites ask of their content, a degree of credibility is also given to the material. If the content is featured on the site's page it means that it has at least followed the guidelines of good journalism held by the editor who will look at the material. These guidelines are generally posted on the site to improve the quality of submissions. By setting a standard for what material the site will accept, visitors will view better content and the reporter gains more credibility for future work on and off the site.

When we combine the gifts of citizen journalism with professional journalism, the public is given a greater spectrum of issues while maintaining the quality of content. There is no reason why everyone shouldn't be able to participate in the conversation about issues that are affecting them while consuming information about those issues. But that participation needs to have a standard that Facebook simply cannot provide.

Part II

\

11. Centralization

There are many places that need to be examined when answering the question of how Facebook got here. The first place to look is in the social networks that came before Facebook. These networks are responsible for conditioning users to accept Facebook's level of information collection. Without these past networks, Facebook would just be breaking the ice for someone else to do what they are doing now.

After looking at this material it is clear that Facebook was a predictable event. This prediction would not have to be made by some gifted social media analyst; it could have been made by an average social network user during the dawn of the internet. The technology that is needed to create a Facebook has been around for a while, the utilization and the financial backing of that technology is what has changed.

Early Social Networks

Before Facebook there were plenty of online social networks that did part of what Facebook does today. However, none of these sites collected as much information or had as many people using them as Facebook does. This can be blamed on several failures such as scaling, timing, popularity, and originality that played an impact on why these networks lost their steam. These significant errors helped to show Facebook what to do and what not to do in running a social network.

In the dark ages of the internet there were a lot of decentralized social networks. These were networks that did not rely on one single server for everyone to access their information off. Instead they might use a peer to peer structure that would have the users of the network function as the servers as well the clients that accessed the information.[344] Prominent examples that made use of this form of networking were Internet Relay Chat and Usenet. While these sites had privacy and security flaws as well, they prevented the centralized collection of data that law enforcement and advertisers thrive off today. Ironically enough, that very benefit from using social networks is a reason why they can never be fully implemented a Facebook size scale.

The real change in the internet came with not so much the end of decentralized networks but the rise of centralized networks. These were networks where everyone that used a service was connected to the same server which stored all their information in one place. Centralized networking relies on the client-server model as it is known. The clients are the users and the servers are the collectors of the data.[345] Client server networking is more profitable than decentralized networking because it allows for advertising to be developed from the information that is collected.[346] As a result it is also more useful for law enforcement evidence gathering.[347]

What also makes things difficult with this system is that collection as well as inspection of the data that these centralized networks receive is important for their functioning. In his influential lecture entitled "Freedom in the Cloud", Professor Eben Moglen notes that by their nature centralized networks must collect logs of their data to maintain the sites performance. Because they are the receivers of so much data that could affect their system, the centralized networks must intrude on privacy to handle their massive size.[348] This is a clever way for networks to say that they do not want to spy, but they have to.

To examine some of the centralized networks that made an impact on the internet we should first look at America Online. First founded in 1983 under the name Video Control

Corporation, AOL was one of the largest social networking sites with over 30 million members at its height.[349] AOL had a lot of potential because of the number of services it offered which included search, email, chat, shopping, and watchable content. While the search capability was open to the public the communication features required registration to use. Even today the company still collects a large amount of data but it is not nearly as successful as it once was.

Another company that is quite similar to AOL is Yahoo!. Yahoo! also offered a wide variety of services that gave it a one stop shop type feel. It had search capability, email, instant messaging, a desktop feature, as well news and other media available on the site. Registration was also required for use of the communication features. Since its founding in 1995, the company has gone through ups and downs but still has strength with its communications features as of today.[350]

The third major social network of this time was Match.com. First launched in 1995 by Gary Kremen, Match.com was one the first of numerous dating websites that promised to help people find a mate. It is still alive and kicking today and is available in 24 countries under the ownership of parent company IAC.[351] They own famous websites such College Humor, Dictionary.com, Vimeo, Ask.com, the Daily Beast, about.com, and over 150 other brands.[352]

For those unfamiliar, Match works by the user filling out a brief series of questions much like the typical classified ad. Required information includes: gender, name, birthday, password, email, location, username. Then the engine will ask for information on your desired mate. Zodiac sign, interests, desired gender and age, location preferred. After you fill out the desired information, Match will then start giving suggestions on people you may like to meet. Along with the recommendations they provide, Match.com also allows the users to browse through profiles of people they would like to talk with. The service costs about $24 a month, but the offer a free subscription for new subscribers that lasts up to a month.[353]

Following Yahoo! and Match.com, the Microsoft Network or MSN also launched in 1996.[354] MSN was well known for its Hotmail feature as well search ability and instant messaging. Something that people may not remember is that MSN was also an internet service provider in the beginning which gave it a substantial amount of information about users.[355] Today MSN is still a major website but it is now most well-known for its media channel MSNBC.

This generation of websites represents the first significant attempts at mass collection of data on internet users. They were not extraordinarily successful because no one had absolute dominance in the market like a Facebook would. They also didn't have the game mechanics that Facebook had employed to keep people coming back for more. There was no Farmville that made the user come back to feed their crops, and there was no Newsfeed that users had to check in on. But we should also acknowledge that this was before mobile cell phones and the reduced desk top prices that we see today. The era is almost like baseball before steroids.

Also significant is that social networking was only a part of what these companies did. Along with allowing users to communicate with each other, these sites focused heavily on other aspects such as news coverage, e-commerce, their search engines, and in MSN's case providing internet service. They tried to do too much and because of that they weren't great at anything. In contrast, Facebook focuses on doing one really well, while doing everything else good enough and letting application developers take care of the rest.

The last crucial factor for the downturn of these sites is the time they came from. The heyday of these sites saw penetration of the internet far less than what we see today. Even now there are only about 2.5 billion users.[356] These websites took what they could from who they could, but there just weren't that many people to take from. This may also be the reason why they got away with expanding into so many areas. It wasn't seen as serious a thing for Yahoo![357]t o have email, search, and messaging all in one when they only had 30 million users. While Facebook is also able to get away with this now, every expansion brings with it privacy concerns that Facebook is trying to shy away from.

Along with collecting information these companies controlled avenues of information as well. With their search engines and news updates, they could influence the way internet users explored the web and the information they received from it. These companies were very powerful. And were it not for their lack of size and dominance this book would probably be about a modern version of one of them.

SixDegrees

The centralization of social networks did not end with these internet giants, but it instead inspired more centralization with other networks such as SixDegrees.com. Founded in 1997 by Andrew Weinrich, SixDegrees is regarded by many as one of the first the modern day social networks. It worked by having people create profiles of themselves for other people to look at and interact with. But for a person to join they needed to have a friend invite them first. This would be done through email and it would help keep fake profiles from populating the site.[358]

Once the user was invited into the system and registered they could then begin communication with other people. Communication was done through a message board, much like the Newsfeed. SixDegrees users could also interact with each other through a live chat feature that allowed for more personal communication.[359] At this stage in the evolution of social networking we can see a very primitive form of Facebook within SixDegrees if we try.

While SixDegrees was very innovative in its approach to social networking, it had a major flaw which was a concern for privacy. They did not try to collect every single piece of data that users would be willing to give.[360] Instead they just stuck with the typical banner ads that you would see on the average webpage. Despite the nobility of their approach, the lack of ad targeting with the combined financial costs of running a social network led to the company's collapse in 2001.[361]

In addition to the lack of a quality advertising model, SixDegrees just didn't arrive at the right time. The public and the industry were simply not ready yet for what SixDegrees wanted to do. An idea such as having a profile that was updated regularly was something treated as a novelty. By today's standards that idea would be readily acceptable, but back then it was seen as hassle that was simply not worth the effort.

Friendster

Following the burst of the .com bubble at the beginning of the 21st Century , there was a period of time where no one wanted to invest in internet companies, much less ones that dealt with social networking.[362] It wasn't until Friendster, started in 2002 by Jonathan Abrams, that a new brand of social networking came on the scene.[363] Friendster took the social networking aspect from SixDegrees and refined it to be more about the user instead of the content. It is not just a major inspiration for social networking, but a powerful factor in the way that Facebook developed in general.

We can see the inspiration when we look at how close the original version of Facebook was to Friendster. Ideas of photo sharing, profiles, exaggerated friends lists, and a Newsfeed were all part of Friendster's information collection game. These ideas allowed Friendster to achieve a tremendous amount of growth in a very brief period, just like Facebook.[364] But of these features that Friendster gave to Facebook, the destruction of anonymity was the most important.

Friendster revolutionized online communication by forcing people to establish a public identity while using the service. This went beyond the registration aspect that forced users to tell the website who they were. Now people with Friendster accounts would have to tell everyone who they were on the network. In an interview with notable tech journalist Jason Calcanis, Abrams remarked that the idea came out of desire to eliminate fake profiles while being able to do ad targeting.[365] Facebook benefited greatly from this move because it conditioned users into losing the anonymity they had previously enjoyed with other services.

While Friendster served as a model for what Facebook would become, they also faced several problems that showed Facebook which steps to take. One error made by Friendster was that the company had too much influence from venture capitalists who didn't understand social networking.[366] Friendster was a revolutionary company that wouldn't work by using the rules of the old social networks that had come before. This was similar mistake made by SixDegrees. Entrepreneurs often go into the business thinking they can do things differently, but venture capitalists and the market itself can be quick to correct the assumption.

In David Kirkpatrick's *The Facebook Effect*, he notes that Mark Zuckerberg knew of this problem as all young CEOs today should. He made sure to choose good venture capitalists who provided excellent guidance but who also didn't try to make the company theirs.[367] This is a tendency venture capitalist have because there is so much of their money riding on the success of the company. The trick is for the entrepreneur to find investors who will show concern for the company while not getting in the way.

A second problem that Friendster had to deal with was scaling. In the internet industry, scaling refers to how a website handles the growth that it can achieve. Friendster had gained tremendous growth in a brief period during the 2003-2006 eras, but they didn't have the servers or the expertise to keep up with the site traffic from it. This led to several shutdowns and delays which then hindered growth in the user base.[368] The problem of scaling is something that needs to be addressed in any social network, and when a network has growth and traffic like Friendster it can be a major fiasco that causes users to go elsewhere.

Friendster's failure to scale is perhaps one of the most important lessons that Facebook learned as a startup company. They showed Facebook the disastrous results of trying to scale up instead of out with their social network. This meant that they would put all the information that they collected on one major server which required a lot of money and effort.[369] Instead of this strategy, Facebook scaled out as it is known by distributing their information over numerous servers in numerous places.[370] Had Facebook tried to scale up, they would have eventually realized they needed to scale out. This would have harmed user growth too much by then to make a difference.

The third major mistake that Friendster made was audience. While Friendster had a growing user base at its peak, a lot of those users were from the Philippines. This meant that if American advertisers bought space on Friendster, their ads were being seen buy people who would never buy their products. It is very problematic to build an advertising revenue stream off of a machine that doesn't get people to buy products.[371]

Facebook on the other hand went after American college students exclusively in the beginning. Unlike the social networking Filipinos, American college students were seen as an untapped market in advertising. According to author Kirkpatrick, an employee of Facebook investor Accel Partners would note that college students tended to shun mediums such as television and radio that served as delivery systems for advertisements. Facebook in a sense offered a lucrative window into the college student market which may be what led to them getting the revenue and investment it needed to continue its building stages.[372]

The last lesson that Facebook could have learned from Friendster is in leadership. Friendster had very unstable leadership during its reign. From 2003 to 2009 Friendster had six CEOs in six years. These CEOs all had different ideas for what they wanted to do which led to a change of direction every time one left.[373] While Facebook has also changed leadership positions over the years, Zuckerberg has always been there to steady the ship. Facebook's investors could have brought in some Silicon Valley CEO to run the company, but instead they showed Zuckerberg what to do and he became a strong leader and a model for other companies.

Despite all the mistakes Friendster made, they might have been able to overcome them were it not for the competition that they faced. Around the time that Friendster was fixing its server problems and going through a string of CEOs, MySpace and Facebook were also giving people alternatives. Friendster in a sense was fighting a war on two fronts that they could not sustain. Eventually they capitulated to the forces of the market.

As of today, the site is now out of the hands of its visionary founder Jonathan Abrams and it has focused away from the social networking model we see today. The site is now centered on social gaming since the last time it re-launched in 2011.[374] Most of the patents they held for their social networking features like friend connections are now in the hands of Facebook.[375] They also recently deleted all of the information relating to the old social network such as pictures and posts_[376]. The idea that inspired Facebook and countless other social networks is now only a shadow of its former self.

MySpace

The other contributor to Facebook's image is MySpace. First founded by Chris DeWolfe and Tom Anderson in 2003, MySpace was one of the largest social networks ever with over 200 million members at its height.[377] It was also like Friendster in that it had photo sharing and profiles, but its customization is where it really separated itself from everyone else.

MySpace allowed users to create their own webpages by allowing the inclusion of foreign HTML codes into the user's page. From these HTML codes, there came a dizzying array of backgrounds, games, and glitter tags for the user to play with. This customization in combination with the communication features gave users a reason to come back to the site. In a way, the HTML codes became like a competition for users to create the coolest profile out there.

A part of creating a great profile was giving the visitor good music to listen to while they examined the users page. MySpace became a center for amateur artists as well as superstars who wanted to promote their new music in a place where everyone would listen.[378] Along with musicians there were also comedians such as Dane Cook who achieved a wide following through dedicated MySpace usage.[379] Eventually MySpace would become known for movie trailers and clips to help generate hype for upcoming premiers.

For a while it appears MySpace would hold dominance forever. But as with Friendster, there were still kinks to be ironed out of the social networking model. The attractions that lured users in also helped to clog the site with viruses and worthless content. MySpace had become a sprawling mess that had turned users off by the time Facebook came along.

This problem of organization along with the infusion of sexual predators caused MySpace to have a bad reputation with advertisers and investors. As we have seen with

Friendster, failure to have a promising revenue stream can cause a loss of interest in a site real fast. Not to mention that being known as a site for stalkers because of shows like *To Catch a Predator* doesn't do much to attract additional investment and users.[380]

This association with sexual predators is largely the result of MySpace not allowing but embracing fake profiles on their network. There is a happy medium between authenticity and anonymity that must be established by centralized social network. MySpace allowed users to go to the far end of both extremes by being inauthentic while being anonymous. To shed this image MySpace would cooperate heavily with law enforcement to help catch criminals on their site.[381] They even gave the information about requested profiles away for free when other companies such as Microsoft or Verizon were charging money.[382]

As Facebook learned from Friendster to reject anonymity, they also learned from MySpace to cooperate. Until recently Facebook did little to fight fake profiles and instead used a strategy that made every effort to give information to law enforcement. Facebook has guides posted on their website showing how officers can go through the process. There is even a communications policy specialist who works at Facebook to help the government get the information that it needs.[383] What makes Facebook benefit from this relationship is that they started cooperating from the beginning whereas MySpace only acted until attention was getting called to the site.[384]

Facebook has also benefited from leadership where MySpace has failed. Something that should be remembered from Julia Angwin's history of the site called *Stealing MySpace* (2009) is that before founding MySpace executives Chris DeWolfe and Tom Anderson previously worked as spam emailers in a marketing company known as eUniverse. The people they had around them at MySpace were more geared toward trick marketing techniques than they were for developing a great website.[385] Facebook on the other hand has had an engineering mindset from the beginning because it was run by engineers. One of Zuckerberg's running jokes is that they like to have an engineer for every million users.[386] Facebook didn't focus on cheap tactics to get ad clicks, they just made a great website and that led to a lot of ad revenue.

And the last and largest contribution that MySpace has given to Facebook is its role as a societal barrier breaker. Because MySpace was the first modern major social networking site, they had to deal with many of the counterarguments against social networking before Facebook even got recognized. MySpace had to face issues such as privacy, the objectification of users, sexual predators, and several other social networking complaints. This is important because Facebook wouldn't be able to do the things it does now if had to deal with those counterarguments when they were fresh. People of course still care about those issues, it is just that those people have become outnumbered by those who do not to care at all.

Contribution

What becomes clear after looking at these websites that have come and gone is that Facebook really began in the early 1990's and is still continuing today. All of these companies whether it is Yahoo! or MySpace or Friendster have slowly been eroding at the average user's expectation of privacy. This is not to suggest deliberate intent by any of these previous companies; it is just to examine their effect on the internet.

And when we think about it some of these companies were also quite privacy conscious while being privacy intrusive. SixDegrees for instance only allowed invited members to join their network.[387] Yahoo! and AOL allowed their users to have screen names when they spoke to each other. MySpace even allowed people to be whoever they wanted to be as long as they weren't a sexual predator. The users tolerated these companies because they made such gestures. But as always, they abused their positions much like Facebook has.

We could blame a lot of things for the road that social networking has gone down, but the major cause is monetization. Companies such as SixDegrees who refused to embrace a total corporate internet model were unable to survive while those who accepted the model such as MySpace could thrive. All the while most people have not even heard of services like IRC or Usenet that shied away from absolute centralization. A company faces a dilemma when choosing between a privacy conscious business model and an advertising focused business model. If money is the reason why the entrepreneur started the website, well then, that choice will be very easy.

This dilemma that websites are confronted with was discussed last year at a re:publica conference in Hamburg, Germany. At the conference were two notable privacy advocates Jacob Appelbaum and Dmitry Kleiner. Toward the end of the talk they were posed with a very challenging comment regarding the aspect of advertising and social networking. A man in the audience commented that if someone wants to start a social network they can either ask for money---- which no one will do-- or they can collect user data which everyone knows about which then makes it okay. After hearing these words, several people in the crowd cried out in disagreement.[388]

Kleiner responded to the man by saying that the average internet user has no choice in the matter of using a pay network or a collection based network. The man agreed by saying that business models that ask people to pay for a social platform will not work which is why they are not good to use. After hearing this Jacob Appelbaum simply replied: "Maybe the point is that society doesn't need to be focused around business as the only thing that matters and the only measure of what is good". Following this the crowd applauded.[389]

The ideas that both Appelbaum and Kleiner highlight are very important. The reason why we have centralized, information collection based networks is because it works for corporations. This is not because users love this form of networking so much, but because as Kleiner notes, centralized networking is all that they can choose from.[390] The recent peer to peer social networks such Diaspora, Friendica, or GNUNet could never hope to achieve the level of investment necessary to serve many people. This is because corporations do not want an internet without information based ad targeting and because internet users have become apathetic to their own privacy.

As we head forward through this discussion of how Facebook began we should remember that there were alternatives to networks like Facebook decades ago. In another interview Kleiner would note that many people forget that a peer to peer network like Usenet was started in 1980 way before the web even began.[391] Creating alternatives to Facebook has nothing to do with technology; it has to do with the will to abandon it. Right now, there are networks that work off peer to peer models that rob the surveillance state of everything it wants from the internet. Those networks have been around for a long time, we just haven't truly needed them until now.

12. Genuis*

Now we come to the issue of how Facebook began. The focus of this chapter will be on Mark Elliot Zuckerberg, the founder and current Chief Executive Officer of Facebook. There have been numerous portrayals of Zuckerberg in the media which detail his creation of Facebook along with the success he achieved not long afterward. While these stories are revealing, they tend to omit who Zuckerberg is as a person. They focus too heavily on his oddness, or his brilliance, and they neglect the actions that he took to create Facebook.

It should be admitted that understanding Zuckerberg will not explain all of Facebook. There are numerous influences that have shaped this website. Factors such as economics, venture capital, and the leadership of Facebook have all helped to shape the social network in their own way. But what cannot be escaped is that the original version that inspired the Facebook we see today came from Mark Zuckerberg. That is fact is significant and that is why we should look at how Zuckerberg came to start this site.

Before Harvard

Mark Zuckerberg was born on May 14, 1984 in White Plains, New York. Not long after he was born Zuckerberg's parents moved him to Dobbs Ferry where they still live today. His parents are Edward Zuckerberg, a dentist, and Karen Zuckerberg a former psychiatrist. Karen Zuckerberg stopped practicing psychiatry after several years to take care of the Mark and his siblings. As a child Mark Zuckerberg and his family would live in the area above Edward Zuckerberg's dental office.[392] In addition to providing convenience, the combined living/working area gave Mark an opportunity to use his computer skills for a good cause.

Throughout his childhood Mark would make numerous computer programs that served as a testament to his genius. One early creation of Zuckerberg's was a communication system that linked his home to his father's dental office. The program known as Zucknet would notify Dr. Zuckerberg at his computer in the upstairs living area when an appointment signed in with his secretary at the office. Mark made this program when he was twelve years old.[393]

Along with making communication easier, Mark was also skilled at creating computer games to amuse himself. These games would be based on ideas he received from his friends or from board games that he enjoyed such as Risk. He even made a computer strategy game where he faced off against Julius Caesar. Little toys like the computer games would give Zuckerberg enjoyment while allowing him to hone his programming skills.[394]

As he would get older however Zuckerberg would need more intellectual stimulation than just games. In his early teens Mark's parents hired a private computer tutor to teach him once a week. This served to help Zuckerberg further progress in a discipline he was already very adept at. The tutor even commented that it was difficult to keep up with the young child prodigy. Later on Mark would even attend a community college course to hone his computer programming skills. As to be expected he was the youngest person in the class by far.[395]

Aside from his skill with computers, Mark was an excellent all-around student. While attending Ardsley High School in New York he won several prizes in math, physics and astronomy. He was also a member of the debate team with a specialty in history and politics. Due to his success at Ardsley Mark was be able to leave the public school system and later transfer into Phillips Exeter Academy in the fall of his junior year. The transfer to Exeter would allow Zuckerberg to reach an elevated status among American high school students and can be attributed to his acceptance into Harvard later on. In a Harvard Crimson article Mark would remark that Exeter attracted him because of their quality Latin program and his plans to study classic literature in college.[396]

The transfer out of Ardsley would also allow Zuckerberg to escape the bullying that he experienced as a young teenager. He was reportedly seen by fellow students as a loner that seemed out of place despite his avid participation in school activities.[397] Plenty of intelligent high school students have the chance to attend better institutions then what geography gives them, but they stay because of attachments or because of financial constraints. Zuckerberg had neither which may explain why he deliberately sought out a prestigious school located two states away from his home. It was a way out for him as well as a way up.

Located in Exeter, New Hampshire, Phillips Exeter Academy is one of the most well-known preparatory high schools in the country.[398] Some of its notable alumni include: Gore Vidal, Daniel Webster, Jay Rockefeller, and Robert Todd Lincoln.[399] Despite his self-description as a nerd, Zuckerberg was also captain of the schools fencing team.[400] He continued to do well academically at Exeter as well, showing proficiency in drama and classic literature as well as learning French, Hebrew, Latin and ancient Greek. Mark would later remark in an interview for *The New Yorker* that he chose to learn dead languages because he was terrible at speaking in accents.[401]

While at Exeter, Mark lived with future Facebook employee Adam D'Angelo. D'Angelo by most accounts was also a programming prodigy and according to Zuckerberg was even more skilled at programing then he was.[402] Together they both created a file sharing program known as Synapse for Zuckerberg's senior project. Similar to Pandora Radio or Napster, Synapse created playlists for the user that would predict what music they wanted to listen to. The idea for this program came out of Zuckerberg's frustration with having to tell his computer directly what he wanted to listen to when he was busy doing something else.[403]

To some this might seem like a simple little project that a couple of high school kids made, but in reality it was highly valued program. AOL, Microsoft, and WinAmp offered to buy Synapse from Zuckerberg in 2002.[404] According to author Ben Mezrich, the boys received offers for somewhere between a million dollars or two million dollars. Zuckerberg turned down the purchase because he wanted to go to college and not go to work straight out of high school.

After getting a taste of college life, the boys would attempt to renew the deal but the companies had already moved on.[405]

The creation of Synapse marks a major point in Mark life. It shows the desire to create programs that makes decisions for the user based on personal information. Synapse was a program that thought for the person using it.[406] This type of creativity would later play a role in the development of projects Zuckerberg would complete while at Harvard. The rejection of Synapse that Zuckerberg experienced also may have taught him a lesson on timing. Victory doesn't wait for the victors, they take it.

In the spring of 2002 Mark graduated from Exeter after being accepted into Harvard.[407] Exeter for those who are not familiar is a feeding school for Harvard. Having a good prep school on your transcript is important if you are not a Harvard legacy, which close to 30% of their applicants that get accepted are.[408] Without his brilliance that allowed him to leave the public school system and gain entry to Exeter, Zuckerberg may not have made it to Harvard. While Zuckerberg would not stay there too long, Harvard is important to his character arc for a number of events that would happen to him while he was there.

Harvard

At this moment in his life Zuckerberg had reached a level of academic excellence that few students ever achieve. But academics play very little into the story as we see it unfold. The real things to focus on are Zuckerberg's skill as a programmer and the connections he would make the school to further his ambitions. These two factors are what allowed Facebook to become more than an idea inside of a gifted mind.

At Harvard Zuckerberg lived in the Kirkland House dormitory with three other students. Friend Chris Hughes was his roommate, while Dustin Moskovitz and Billy Olson were his suitemates. They lived in room H33 on the third floor. As a freshman, he would later pledge at the Alpha Epsilon Phi Fraternity, a well-known Jewish fraternity. Zuckerberg's fraternity nickname was Slayer by the way.[409]

While at Harvard, Zuckerberg double majored psychology and computer science. By most accounts he was not a very social person. This is to be expected by his current communication habits as well as past behavior, but it has been contradicted by those who point to his girlfriend and now wife Priscilla Chan. Zuckerberg reportedly met Priscilla at a fraternity party in his sophomore year at Harvard. Priscilla is often used as a badge of coolness for Zuckerberg. Her existence says that Zuckerberg might be awkward but at least he had a girlfriend in college. They also met before Facebook so that is another bonus for him.[410]

During his sophomore year at Harvard, Mark wrote a new program called Course Match. Course Match was designed to help users find other people who had similar class schedules. The program worked quite well and became a hit on campus. This bolstered Zuckerberg's reputation to a higher status prior to what it was when he had first arrived at Harvard. He was already known by many as an excellent coder, but making programs that people actually used really moved the bar for him.[411]

Later that October Zuckerberg would create Facemash which helped rate people's attractiveness. Facemash was accomplished by hacking into the online facebook of Harvard's dormitory houses and downloading their data to his computer. The pictures, which were taken on the first day of orientation, were then uploaded to the site. Essentially people would compare two photos and be asked to determine which one was more attractive. Zuckerberg ran the site from his computer and detailed how the project developed on a blog he maintained throughout the night.[412]

Zuckerberg's computer would later crash because of the traffic it experienced from Facemash.[413] It turned out he had made a very addicting site. Whether he had a natural ability to do this or he had picked it up from his psychology studies is uncertain. But without a doubt he learned how to get people hooked on his work. Computer crash or not, Zuckerberg was good at what he did.

About three days later the Harvard computer service department tracked down Zuckerberg. After the site had been in operation for a few hours, numerous complaints were made to the university which shut down Zuckerberg's internet access. Several of the school's feminist groups claimed the site was harmful to the image of women. The feminists may have had a point seeing as Facemash compared some of the female students to farm animals.[414]

Inspiration

Following Face match, Zuckerberg would go on to create theFacebook as it was then referred to at the time. TheFacebook would be Zuckerberg's most important creation and the sum of years of work with computer programming. His creation would also be the result of several other factors which are somewhat controversial depending on the source. We do know however that explanation for the network's blue white color scheme is the result of Zuckerberg's red green color blindness. [415]

We also know that the networks discussed in the previous chapter were major influences Zuckerberg in his creation of Facebook. These networks taught Zuckerberg lessons about engineering and design that he most likely would have failed at without their guidance. Zuckerberg was also a fan of certain features on these sites and would later transform than for his own creation. The away message feature from AOL's Instant Messenger is one example. Zuckerberg would recall in a 2005 Q&A discussion that he enjoyed reading some people's away messages more than actually talking to them through the messenger.[416]

While some sites served to inspire him, Zuckerberg also made sure to avoid other social network models. Dating websites like Match.com were something he was not too fond of. Zuckerberg didn't want theFacebook to have the stigma of creepiness that dating sites had attached to them. Instead theFacebook would have the promise of getting the user a date without being exclusively for dating. In a way it was but it wasn't, and that's what people loved about it. [417]

Also worth considering is that both at Exeter and at Harvard, students were given text based face books that served to identify other students. While he was at Phillips Exeter, the student government even had the school's face book digitized in Zuckerberg's senior year.[418] Along with Exeter, Harvard made frequent promises to digitally centralize the entire database of house face books from campus. Despite reported calls from students to do so, Harvard never did make their own version of Facebook, so Zuckerberg made it himself. [419]

In addition to the ideas he may have come up with on his own, Zuckerberg also turned to his friends and colleagues at Harvard for inspiration. Immediate connections that helped out were his then roommate Chris Hughes and suites mates Dustin Moskovitz, Joe Green, and Billy Olson. They would all provide help in several ways to get the site going. Moskovitz would even help Zuckerberg code despite his lack of training as an economics major. He taught himself the principles of programming when he realized what a big deal theFacebook could be. [420]

A major source of information would also come from a fellow Harvard student Aaron Greenspan. Currently a software engineer, Greenspan also created at the time a social network called houseSystem that allowed people from each dormitory to communicate with one another.

Zuckerberg would often turn to Greenspan for technical and business advice which later led to Greenspan accusing Zuckerberg of stealing ideas. These instant message conversations are documented on Aaron Greenspan's website about his time at Harvard and his relationship with Zuckerberg. [421]

On February 4, 2004 after only two weeks of work, the original version of Facebook would be completed. [422] While the result of Zuckerberg's efforts would bring him fame and fortune, it would also bring him controversy from those who questioned the origins of his ideas. In addition to the accusations made by Aaron Greenspan, a social network team known as Harvard Connection also would allege theft of their intellectual property.

Harvard Connection/ConnectU

Around November of 2003, Zuckerberg was approached by three Harvard students: Tyler and Cameron Winklevoss and Divya Narendra. The group asked Zuckerberg for help with programming their site, the Harvard Connection. They chose Zuckerberg because he was seen as a good programmer on campus partly due to the Facemash incident. Regardless of whatever personality flaw this could have signaled, the Harvard Connection team went to Zuckerberg because they valued him as a coder and they needed to get the work done. Their previous coder had quit to start a new job and neither of them were particularly computer savvy. [423]

Zuckerberg would agree to complete their project, but, he had no intention of ever working on it at all. Through instant messages given to reporter Nicholas Carlson of *Business Insider* from an anonymous source, Zuckerberg stated that he was having a dilemma about what he should do regarding the Harvard Connection. He could have either of helped Harvard Connection with their project, told them that he was too busy, or he could have waited till his project was finished to tell them the site couldn't work. Zuckerberg elected to do the third option. [424] This would give him a major head start and allow Facebook to become the number one social network on campus.

Because of this betrayal, the Harvard Connection, which had by then become ConnectU, filed a lawsuit against theFacebook. After receiving the notice Zuckerberg even worried that he might get kicked out of Harvard for unethical behavior. This was stated in messages between Zuckerberg and the anonymous *Business Insider* source and it destroys any argument that

Zuckerberg gave ConnectU the wrong impression on accident. He meant to mislead them for the purpose of giving himself an advantage.[425]

When the Harvard Crimson decided to write an article on theFacebook/Harvard Connection controversy, they interviewed Zuckerberg to get his side of the story. From all accounts Zuckerberg was cooperative with the Crimson reporters and showed them how theFacebook was different from ConnectU. Following the meeting, the reporters were satisfied with Zuckerberg's explanation and decided not to run the story.[426]

But shortly after this occurred, the Winklevoss twins contacted the Crimson reporters to try to pressure them into writing the story. They even brought up a second allegation of stealing against Zuckerberg to get the reporters re-interested. To continue with the story the reporters would later call Zuckerberg for comment on the second allegation. This simple phone call caused Zuckerberg to take action into his own hands.[427]

Using information obtained from theFacebook, Zuckerberg hacked into the accounts of two Crimson employees and gained access to their email accounts. This was accomplished by looking for Crimson reporters on Facebook and seeing if they had any failed login attempts to their accounts. Because the employees entered their email passwords on accident for their Facebook password, Mark could get access to their accounts.[428]

Despite Marks efforts to spy on the Crimson, the story about the Harvard Connection Facebook debate came out on May 28, 2004. It gave a basic account of the ConnectU team's conception of their site and the story of them asking Zuckerberg to help them make it. It also gave voice to Zuckerberg's argument that the sites were not original ideas and that Friendster served as the basis for what they had done.[429]

It is difficult to see what Zuckerberg accomplished or hoped to accomplish by hacking into the Crimson website. While he did manage to obtain an email that showed the suspicions of the two Crimson reporters, little actionable intelligence was obtained.[430] The smartest thing for him to do would have been nothing. He had nothing to gain and so much to lose by stealing the identity of one his users for his personal vendetta. In a large way, it shows a lack of rationality. It is something you could imagine him doing in a spasm of rage after getting off the phone with the reporters who asked him about another stealing allegation.

Business Insider has also obtained information about how Zuckerberg hacked into the ConnectU system. To accomplish this, he created a fake account for Cameron Winklevosses to manipulate his profile information.[431] Probably not much damage was done to Winklevosses' reputation, but Zuckerberg did put down information with the intention of making Cameron appear snobbish and sexist. This is just another testament to the vindictive nature of Zuckerberg.

While he was in the ConnectU system Zuckerberg also tampered with several other user accounts to make them appear invisible while on the site. This would make them inaccessible to their friends, in turn making them less likely to visit ConnectU again.[432] It wasn't enough that Zuckerberg significantly slowed down the progress of ConnectU by misleading them into thinking that he would work on their site, but he also had to do whatever he could to sabotage their success.

Leaving Harvard

With the head start on ConnectU that Facebook had, the site easily became another Zuckerberg triumph on campus. Over 650 people signed up for Facebook in five days. Within the first month Facebook had almost half of the Harvard student population. It had also gained territory on the surrounding campuses around Harvard as well as other Ivy League schools such as Stanford, Yale, and Columbia. Zuckerberg had picked these elite schools on purpose to see if Facebook could handle the competition.[433]

As the site spread from campus to campus, the Facebook team essentially waged a proliferation campaign on the American college landscape. While some colleges were begging to be let into the Facebook network, others were already occupied with homegrown versions of their own Facebook. These enemy services needed to be eradicated if Facebook was going to conqueror the social networking world.[434]

To defeat these hold outs, the Facebook team would encircle the targeted college with Facebook launches in schools in the surrounding area. In David Kirkpatrick's *The Facebook Effect* he details how this strategy played out. If the targeted colleges wanted to correspond with their friends from other colleges, they would have to join Facebook. The strategy worked and eventually the map was covered with Facebook victories. It was eerily similar to the games of Risk the roommates would play in their dorm room at Kirkland House as well as the games Zuckerberg made on his computer as a child.[435]

In between the situation with the ConnectU people and his proliferation campaign, Zuckerberg was looking for investors in Facebook. He wasn't really looking for a deal per se, he just wanted to know who was interested. It was more about how serious Facebook was then actually turning the product into a company. He would take several meetings but no one had seemed too authentic about their offers. It was in April of 2004 that Zuckerberg took a meeting with future Facebook President Sean Parker.[436]

Parker had made up his mind to find Zuckerberg after seeing the creators name on the Facebook website. It was an opportunity for Parker to make a break into social networking as well as help the young Zuckerberg navigate the troubled waters of being a start-up.[437] To facilitate this relationship Parker traveled to New York City to meet Mark Zuckerberg and Eduardo Savarin in a restaurant to talk about the site. Parker and Zuckerberg became fast friends at the meeting, but no real offer was made. It must be noted that at this time Parker had no money of his own to offer, just suggestions and perhaps connections.

Arrested at the age of 16 by the FBI for hacking into a government computer, Parker is a brilliant programmer as well as business genius to say the least. When he was 18, Parker made a web browser that won him a science fair competition and which also attracted the attention of the CIA. The browser was so great that the CIA offered Parker a job which he supposedly turned down.[438] Incidents like this raise suspicions about Facebook connection to the government, but we will deal with that in other chapters.

Parker would later go on to cofound with Sean Fanning the famous peer to peer file sharing program called Napster in 1998. But after several court decisions had drained the company of funding, Parker went on to fund a site similar to Facebook known as Plaxo. Plaxo was essentially an organization for the user's business connections that was similar to what LinkedIn would later become. Because Parker had developed a poor relationship with the Plaxo investors from the venture capital firm Sequoia, they had him ousted in 2002.[439]

Between his departure from Plaxo and his meeting with Zuckerberg, Parker began seeking social networking sites to invest in. During an interview with David Kirkpatrick, Parker stated that he was "looking to make a play in social networking". In his effort to find a good social network to invest in he specifically went after college social network because they were the only open markets during the time of MySpace and Friendster. He also notes during the interview that college had the benefit of authenticating who the person was through their college email which was not easily forged.[440]

Zuckerberg and Parker broke apart for a brief while after their initial meeting until Zuckerberg decided to move to Palo Alto, California for the summer of 2004. According to Zuckerberg he moved to Palo Alto because he felt it was the necessary place to be in order to get the site going. He also had friends who worked for Electronic Arts that he wanted to hang out with.[441] Nowhere in the public record does he ever mention a quest to find Sean Parker or anyone that Parker mentioned that might be able to help him with his project.

In only a few weeks after moving to Palo Alto, Mark Zuckerberg supposedly ran into Sean Parker while walking down the street. Parker was helping his girlfriend move out of the house they had been living at so she could go back home to her parents. While she had offered for Parker to live with her for a few days, with the move he would be technically homeless. This occurred only two months after Zuckerberg had met Parker in New York.[442]

While catching up with Parker in front of his girlfriend's house, Zuckerberg offered Parker a place to stay. They had plenty of room at the house Zuckerberg and his friends were renting and wouldn't mind the company. Parker accepted. He must have felt lucky after meeting a possible business opportunity and a place to stay on the same day he would have to start finding a new place to live while having no real income.

Allowing Parker to live with him was one of the best decisions Mark Zuckerberg ever made regarding his company. Parker used his connections with angel investors Reid Hoffman and Mark Pincus to convince the other angel investor Peter Thiel to give Zuckerberg a meeting. Thiel had already been equated with Parker during their time together at Plaxo. He had also told Parker if he had ever found a good idea to bring it his way, and this was it.[443]

Thiel is a libertarian venture capitalist that had made his fame running the online payment site PayPal. He is a very interesting character and we will focus on him later in the book. But for right now let us focus on the initial business deal. After meeting with Zuckerberg for about two hours to discuss the website, Thiel gave Facebook an angel investment of 500,000 dollars.[444] This investment while seeming outlandish to an observer is not that strange for a venture investment. Thiel has funded many startup companies for more than that price in the past.[445]

It seems almost implausible to believe that Parker had not told Zuckerberg to move out to California to get things started. Regardless of the claimed motivations of Zuckerberg, they ran into each other on the day Parker was to lose his place to stay in California. An event that he could have seen had coming two months earlier at dinner in New York. Had Parker told Zuckerberg to come out to Palo Alto ahead of time, the question could be raised whether Peter Thiel had given Parker orders to do so.

Worth noting is that Zuckerberg even admits that he had no real business connections in California.[446] It could be suggested that had it not been for meeting Sean Parker on the street, it would have been unlikely Zuckerberg would have met Peter Thiel. Zuckerberg also didn't have the best credentials for what he wanted to do. Not to say anything against being a college dropout that starts a business, but with no degree, no connections, a site in danger of drowning in traffic, no experience in business, and an ownership dispute brewing; it seems safe to say he had a lot going against him.

When you think about Thiel's relationship with Zuckerberg, it also makes one wonder about his relationship with Sean parker. Parker was also in a desperate situation during this time. His first company Napster had been a commercial failure as well as a legal hassle. He had been ousted as president of his other company Plaxo. His small investment in Friendster had also failed.[447] When he met Zuckerberg for the second time in Palo Alto he didn't even have a place to live. He spent the summer sleeping on Zuckerberg's couch.[448] When a person is experiencing the kind of fall from grace the he was experiencing in 2004, it is understandable to think he may have been desperate to end that situation.

Around this same time Zuckerberg was also sued by his former CFO and friend Eduardo Savarin. This was the result of Zuckerberg diluting Savarin's stake in the company from 30% to less than 1% during the angel investment time period. While some accounts differ, this appeared to be done as punishment for Savarin closing the line of credit he allocated for the company. Savarin took this action because he worried about the company's direction and felt left out of a venture he had funded with his own money.[449]

The *Business Insider* messages also give us reasons why Zuckerberg would not just find it advantageous to eliminate his former business partner, but also causes to pursue revenge against him. One particularly telling email demonstrates Zuckerberg's frustration with Saverin over developing a website that would help people create business connections known as Joboozle. Saverin also set up ads for Joboozle to be displayed on Facebook. This angered

Zuckerberg because Saverin was essentially advertising what he considered a rival site on his creation.[450]

Saverin also had failed to secure quality advertising for Facebook as well as lure investors into the site. One of the reasons why Saverin failed as Facebook CFO was that he was also working an internship while trying to complete his business responsibilities. This might seem understandable because Facebook was still a startup that could have easily failed, to Zuckerberg it could have been seen as disloyalty. Facebook slowly became Zuckerberg's dream in 2004, to Saverin it was business opportunity of the many that he had been afforded in his life.[451] He had made money before and he could do it again some other way.

What makes things complicated is that without Saverin there would have been no Facebook. He paid for the servers that allowed the site to reach enough size to attract the eventual the investors.[452] So Saverin was easily worth more to Facebook then Hughes or Moskovitz was just based on their shares alone. It is not to say that they did not work hard, it is just to say that someone else could have completed their work. The same could not be said for Saverin. Like others that would come after him, Saverin had the money that Facebook needed when it needed it.

It could also be suggested that Zuckerberg's actions were not solely influenced by his own quarrel with Saverin. The other godfather that would allow Facebook to receive the funding it needed was Peter Thiel. If he was going to make sure the company achieved great success Thiel would need to have control over Zuckerberg's actions. That would require that Zuckerberg be in control of Facebook.

The instant messages from *Business Insider* also reveal that Thiel showed Zuckerberg how to diminish Savarin's stock so that they could take on other investors without Saverin noticing at first.[453] This would make sense seeing as Thiel was an experienced venture capitalist and Zuckerberg was a programmer with little knowledge of how to run a company. The lack of business knowledge is admitted by Zuckerberg in his interviews, it is shown throughout his correspondence with Aaron Greenspan, and it is demonstrated by his future actions as CEO of Facebook.[454] If someone was pulling his strings, it was most likely the investor/entrepreneur mastermind Thiel.

This is important because we are often given an image in the media of Zuckerberg being a cold, calculating, Vulcan like machine. It is suggested that he is someone who we would expect to be excellent at chess and better at business warfare. Instead the record shows us something else. It shows an impulsive and reckless kid who will do anything for revenge at the slightest undermining of his reputation.

If Zuckerberg were a regular person with a minimal impact on society it would not be up to us to pass judgment on his actions. But he is not a regular person and his actions as founder and CEO of Facebook have serious impacts on society. We should not ignore obvious, glaring signals of who he is and what he has done. This type of behavior tells us exactly how something like Facebook could have come out of the mind of someone like Zuckerberg. Despite his brilliance and ingenuity, Zuckerberg lacks any moral qualms with taking advantage of someone for his own personal gain. We should not expect any different behavior now that he is at the helm of company with personal information on over a billion people.

13. The Money

To start a major social network in Silicon Valley an entrepreneur needs a lot of money. Fortunately for Zuckerberg he had the right company to receive large amounts of money. Facebook was a centralized collection based network that had no real concern for privacy whatsoever. It was perfect for the advertising model that the other social networks had tried but had failed to achieve. With the right amount of cash and skill, Facebook would succeed were the others had failed.

The way that Zuckerberg chose to fund Facebook was through selling equity for his company. He first sold equity to his friend Eduardo Saverin, but that money only got him so far. To pay for everything that Facebook would later become, Zuckerberg would have to obtain investment from the venture capitalists that controlled technology in the Valley.[455] But in selling equity to the venture capitalists, Zuckerberg would give them a significant say in the future of Facebook.

While the venture capitalists do what they do with the intention of making money, the effect of what they do is far greater than what they may realize. This system that has been created between capitalism and technology has led to only technologies of profit gaining a presence in the market. The technology that these capitalists invest in is given a several years to turn a profit, but they must eventually turn a profit and that profit must be substantial. The only role the public has in the process is whether to accept that technology. By using a social network such as Facebook the public is essentially voting for a candidate that was already chosen ahead of time.

In this system, there could be considered a series of gates that must be opened by different venture capitalists. The opening of each gate will determine whether the company will be able to move onto the next round. This prevents the company from wasting the money that they have been given. Not to mention that venture capitalists can only afford to give out so much money to so many companies.

Partitioning funding into rounds also keeps the company on a close leash. To get the rest of the money, the company needs to show that they are headed in the right direction. In the long term, it is best not to take too much money from investors because it gives them more control over the company. The more equity they have, the more say they have in how the company is run.[456] That voice is generally very quiet with the average investor who buys a few hundred shares. But when we are looking at investment firms and mutual funds, the number of shares can be in the millions. That gives these firms a much larger voice than the average shareholder.

Angel Investments

The first investment that was made in Facebook, known as an angel investment, is generally extremely risky. This occurs when the investor or "angel" buys equity from a company that is in the research and development stage of finding their product. The company is referred to at this stage as a start-up. The start-up does not have an official production strategy just yet but they have a clever idea and maybe even a product. Angel investments generally run from 150,000 to 2,000,000 dollars and they have the longest amount of time for return on investment.[457] In the case of Facebook, the angel investment would take eight years before they reached the initial public offering.

Facebook's angel investment, like the many of their other stages, was a pooled investment. Pooled investments have more than one investor in the round. This limits the amount of equity that each investor can obtain, and it also limits their liability. They get a piece of the company without having to sacrifice a lot of money if it fails.[458] Participating in a pooled round of investment also serves as a guide for some companies. By being in an investment with a company that has a good reputation, the investor can feel a little confident that they have picked the right place for their money.

In addition to the initial $500,000 received from Peter Thiel, both LinkedIn founder Reid Hoffman/ and Zynga founder Mark Pincus bought $40,000 worth of equity from Facebook.[459] These three angel investors Thiel, Hoffman, and Pincus are responsible for giving Facebook the lifeblood it needed to become a Silicon Valley startup company. Having an influx of cash would allow for the Facebook team to get a real office and hire actual employees instead of just interns. It would also allow them to purchase more servers to handle the influx of traffic that was going through the site. [460] Because they used the money wisely, Facebook could move onto the next round known as Series A.

Series A

In the Series A round, a company is still relatively young and subject to unforeseeable problems that could squander the investment.[461] This makes the investment risky despite its low cost compared to the other rounds. Even companies that make it far past the Series A round might never see a positive revenue stream. For some reason, however the early round investors of Facebook saw something in the company, and that is why they took the risk of going in when they did.

The round again featured Mark Pincus the venture capitalist from the previous angel investment. Mark Pincus' Zynga platform has benefited greatly from the success of Facebook so it could be assumed he had made plans for such a company in the future. Zynga founded in 2007 is responsible for such great titles as Farmville and Texas Hold'em that serve to keep Facebook users frequently coming back to the network. Along with Zynga, Pincus is also famous for being the CEO the social networking site Tribe.net and being an investor in Path.com.[462] He also started a company known as Freeloader in where Sean Parker worked as an intern when he was 15.[463]

Another investor in the Series A round was Accel Partners who invested in Facebook for $12.7 million.[464] Notable companies that they have invested in include: Carrier IQ, Spotify,

StumbleUpon, as well as Chinese social media giants Tencent and RenRen. Accel was brought into the Facebook investment by partner Jim Breyer.[465] Breyer himself also invested $1 million into Facebook for an ownership of 1% in 2005.[466] Following the Series A round Breyer served on the board of Facebook from 2005 until he stepped down in 2013.[467] During that time he would play a major role in how the company developed into its current form.

Along with having a role in Facebook and Accel, Breyer is also on the board of Wal-Mart, Dell Inc., and Legendary Pictures. He has previously held positions at Marvel Entertainment, Apple Inc., Hewlett-Packard, and BBN Technologies. Breyer is famous in the business world for negotiating the sale of BBN Technologies to Raytheon on the same day that he sold Marvel Entertainment to Disney.[468] BBN Technologies as you may remember is an intelligence contractor who sells web monitoring software.[469] The associations that Breyer made with BBN will be revealing as we progress throughout Facebook's origin. His position at BBN can be attributed to the investment made by Accel in 2004.[470]

Series B

March of 2006 marked the beginning of the Series B funding round for Facebook. Altogether the company would receive 27.5 million dollars in investment from the round. The financial backers would include several major venture capital firms, the most prominent of which was Greylock Partners.[471] Along with investing in Facebook, Greylock has also made notable investments in Cloudera, Instagram, Digg, LinkedIn, Path, Tumblr, Pandora, Groupon, and Full Capture Media.[472] These companies are all associated in some way with social media and cloud technology which Greylock wants to see progress in the future. Angel investor Reid Hoffman is also a partner at Greylock and is responsible for bringing the company into the investment round.[473]

Another company to get in on the action for the Series B round was the Founders Fund. Both former Facebook president Sean Parker and current Facebook board member Peter Thiel are partners at the firm. The Founder's Fund has invested in notable companies such as Spotify, Slide, Path, Yammer, Airtime, Causes, Quid, and Palantir.[474] As you may remember, Quid and Palantir are the social networking analysis companies that were detailed in the seventh chapter of this work. As for the other companies, they mostly focus on social media usage and likely serve reliable sources of revenue for the Fund.

A third firm that participated in the Series B round was Meritech Capital Partners.[475] Founded in 1999 with funding from Accel Partners, Meritech's notable investments include Vonage, Zip Car, and SalesForce. Meritech Capital is also heavily invested in cloud computing and big data companies such as: Box, Cloudera, Greenplum, Riverbed and NetSuite among many others. These industries will be important for the exploitation of Facebook and social media as time goes on.[476]

The last major company for the Series B round was Interpublic Group or IPG. They invested in Facebook for $5 million in 2006 for .4% of the company's stock.[477] IPG is known as one of the world's largest marketing companies. They are basically a conglomeration of numerous advertising firms that encapsulates over 40,000 employees.[478] Their interest in Facebook could stem from the role that Facebook plays in marketing and public relations but a financial incentive could be at stake here as well.

Series C

Facebook's Series C funding began in October of 2007 and featured one of their largest investors, Microsoft. With a valuation of $15 billion, Microsoft invested $240 million in Facebook.[479]The software company has several good reasons for putting hundreds of millions of dollars into a Facebook that in 2007 was still in the growth stage. Buying equity in the company would also secure a position in a social network that if successful would reap billions of dollars for Microsoft.

The money that Microsoft could make from Facebook's success comes not just from equity, but also from businesses that play off what Facebook had done. Microsoft like many of the tech giants has a CRM product that helps brands analyze social media sites like Facebook to gauge customer attitudes.[480] They also have a product called Windows Embedded, which is a wireless communication software product that may depend on Facebook in the future.[481] There is also Microsoft Domain Awareness which is a system that helps police departments monitor entire cities through surveillance cameras and it could one day use Facebook profiles for facial recognition.[482] Microsoft also makes the Bing language translation software that uses Facebook for crowdsourcing.[483] Based on what has been made public, Microsoft has a lot of things that could profit from Facebook and has made a smart investment.

Another important investor in the Series C round was Chinese billionaire Li-Kai Shing. Shing invested $60 million in Facebook with a valuation of $15 billion.[484] He also is one of the richest men in the world and is the richest man in Asia. Along with investing in Facebook, Shing has bought equity in Siri the personal assistant application and Spotify the music application company.[485] Outside of his business prowess Shing is famous for running the Li-Kai Shing Foundation which gives money to healthcare, educational, cultural, and community projects.[486]

And the last investor for this round was the European Founders Fund that invested $15 million dollars into Facebook in 2008.[487] The European Founders Fund has no relation to the American Founder's Fund other than being interested in social media. The EFF is run by the famous Samwer brothers who are investors in LinkedIn as well as the German Facebook clone Studivz.[488] In addition to copying Facebook, the Samwers have also cloned other companies such as eBay and Airbnb to introduce them to the German market.[489] How nice of them.

In addition to allowing investors to purchase equity, startups will also engage in an activity known as debt financing when the need for cash is substantial. Debt financing is a way for companies to raise money for a capital expenditure without having to issue shares. Instead the company will issue bonds or bills that certify they owe an x amount with interest. This form of lending is done for capital expenditures prior to an initial public offering.[490] In Facebook's case, the capital expenditure in question was servers that were needed just after the Series C round.[491]

To raise the money needed for new servers Facebook used Triple Point Capital in May of 2008 to back their debt. Triple Point loaned Facebook $100 million to be paid back at a later date.[492] Along with Facebook, Triple Point has given money to major companies such as: YouTube, Tagged, Chegg, Lockerz, and Slide.[493] There doesn't seem to be any real agenda with Triple Point's loan other than making money off Facebook.

Series D

Facebook's drive for more cash would continue into May of 2009 when they took on an investment from Digital Sky Technologies or DST. The Russian venture capital firm headed by famous venture capitalist Yuri Milner invested $200 million into Facebook. At the time of this investment the valuation for Facebook was at $10 billion.[494] DST has become a major force in

Silicon Valley with their other investments in companies such as Groupon, Zynga, Spotify, and Twitter.[495]

Milner is most notable being the CEO of Mail.ru, a very successful Russian internet company. He also has held notable positions at the World Bank, Alliance Menatep, and New Trinity Investments. Something interesting is that he serves on the board of marketing company Work4Labs with *The Facebook Era* author Clara Shih. *The Facebook Era* is a book that shows people how to use Facebook for marketing purposes. And along with investing millions of dollars into Facebook through DST, Milner also serves on Facebook's investment arm.[496]

While Facebook reportedly had no immediate plans for the money, it did help build a connection between DST and Facebook. It also gave them some breathing room in case they needed to spend more money on servers or acquisitions.[497] The most valuable part of the relationship would be DST bringing in Goldman Sachs for a major investment in 2011.[498] Perhaps coincidentally, Shih also used to work for Goldman Sachs.[499] It seems that you can go far when you know how to social network in your professional life.

Venture Rounds

Following the series rounds, there are other investment rounds that take place in the lead up to the initial public offering. These rounds are referred to as late stage investment or venture rounds and tend to see individual investments over many months instead of pooled investments all at once.[500] The first venture round investors for Facebook was Elevation Partners who invested $120 million in June of 2010.[501] Elevation primarily invests in media and entertainment companies during their later rounds of investment.

Two notable members of Elevation include U2 singer Bono and brother-in-law to Sheryl Sandberg, Mark Bodnick. Facebook is easily their most important investment out of the seven total companies they have put money into. The fact that Bodnick is married to Sheryl Sandberg's sister could be seen as the biggest reason for Facebook to do business with them.[502] Bono is also notable in that he is a well-known proponent of globalization for development of the third world.[503] In later chapters we will examine the importance of Facebook for globalization from a technological standpoint.

A corporation that is not to be ignored or forgotten in the Facebook's venture round investments is Goldman Sachs. In January of 2011, Goldman would invest 450 million dollars in Facebook valuing the company at $50 billion.[504] They would later go on to invest over a billion dollars into Facebook through their foreign. Along with Facebook, Goldman Sachs has also invested in LinkedIn, PayPal, and DropBox to name just few of their many other major tech companies.[505]

Goldman Sachs plays a significant role in understanding Facebook not only because of the money that they have put into it but also how they have managed that money. In the years before their IPO in May of 2012, Facebook received their funding from private investors such as Goldman Sachs who were not subject to stringent regulations. What was controversial however is that Facebook did not list each investor as individuals, but instead listed them as one investor under Goldman Sachs. Under SEC regulations, a privately traded company with more than 500 investors must go public once they reach 500. Had Goldman Sachs listed each investor individually, Facebook would have been far over their legal limit. As to be expected no charges were filed by the SEC regarding this crime. The absurdity was even pointed out on an episode of *The Daily Show with Jon Stewart*.[506]

DST also invested in this round with Goldman Sachs, giving $50 million of their own money. When we factor in the money Goldman Sachs invested from their own funds as well as investments from over sees, this round comes out to about $1.5 billion. This was the largest of all the investment rounds, and it also makes Goldman Sachs the largest single entity to contribute money to Facebook.[507] To receive this much money Facebook must be one of Goldman Sach's favorite technology companies ever.

A third notable late round investor in Facebook was Kleiner, Perkins, Caulfield, & Byers. They invested in Facebook for $38 million for a $52 billion valuation in February of 2011. Their share of Facebook was .073% at the time of purchase.[508] KPCB has also invested in Twitter, Friendster, Spotify, IControl, IFund, iPad, Amazon and Google.[509] CEO of KPCB John Doerr has stated that he sees Facebook as part of Web 3.0 and the future. The firm has started a joint venture fund called sFund. The fund will go to investing in social networking companies and developing the future that Doerr envisions for Silicon Valley.[510]

Another major player in Silicon Valley and investor in Facebook was Andreessen Horowitz, a venture capital firm started by Marc Andreessen and Ben Horowitz. They invested in Facebook for $150 million also in February of 2011.[511] Marc Andreessen is most famous for inventing the Mosaic and Netscape web browsers that were later purchased by Microsoft. In addition to Facebook Andreessen has invested in Zynga, Groupon, Skype, Digg, Twitter, Foursquare, and Instagram.[512] Marc Andreessen is also on Facebook's board of directors which was the result of his firm's investment among other reasons.[513]

The last notable investor in Facebook during the venture rounds was T. Rowe Price. They invested in Facebook for $190.5 million with a share of .6% in March of 2011.[514] T.Rowe Price is an investment firm that also deals in venture capital for tech companies. They have invested in social networking companies like Twitter and Living Social, along with game designer Zynga. Other significant but less important investors of Facebook include Fidelity Investments,[515] General Atlantic, and Western Technology Investments.[516]

The investments made by these companies are significant because they show us how valuable Facebook is considered by corporate America. This money has allowed Facebook to navigate the waters of being a young social network while trying to figure out how to approach growth without harming their product. So while Facebook was once just an idea, it became much more than that because of the money invested in it.

These investment firms also should not be forgotten because of the agendas they brought with their money. Microsoft was one illustrated example but others such as Greylock Partners and Jim Breyer will be worth noting. These forces control the money that gave Facebook life. It would be foolish to think that money didn't come with special interests. No one opens up the technology gate for nothing in Silicon Valley or Wall Street.

The IPO

In May of 2012, Facebook filed its initial public offering or IPO as it is commonly known. Filing the IPO meant that shares of Facebook Incorporated could be traded publicly.[517] This would allow Facebook to take on more investors and thereby acquire more money. But going public also meant that Facebook would have to face tougher scrutiny from the SEC and other regulatory bodies. Facebook could only do investor fraud through Goldman Sachs for so long apparently.

To file their IPO, Facebook needed what is known in finance as an "underwriter" to guide the company through the process. In exchange for a certain fee, the underwriter would help the company set the price of their shares as well as help the company decide how many shares to sell. The underwriter that Facebook chose for this process was the investment firm Morgan

Stanley. They would serve as the lead underwriter while J.P. Morgan Chase and Goldman Sachs would serve as secondary underwriters. At their conclusion of their services for the Facebook IPO, these three companies would split $176 million dollars in fees.[518]

During the underwriting process, Morgan Stanley made estimates on how well Facebook would do as a publicly traded company. A brief time before Facebook was to have their IPO, Morgan Stanley made an estimation that downgraded the worth of the company but they only gave that information to certain hedge fund owners. The rest of the general public was unaware of the downgrade in value at this time. This resulted in Facebook being rated very high before the IPO.[519]

Along with the information withholding by Morgan Stanley, there was also a disruption in the computer system of the NASDAQ Stock Exchange the day trading on Facebook shares began. What happened was that investors who had purchased stock in Facebook and decided to sell it were stuck holding the stock after it had been decreased in value on the first day. The shareholders in this case were basically powerless to do anything or know anything about the stock while they watched it tumble in value.[520]

Both the secret release of information as well as the NASDAQ disaster resulted in a huge decrease in value for Facebook's stock despite being valued at $116 billion the week before. This resulted in what was previously a highly valued and respected company having equity traded lower the ten dollars a share. Facebook's stock fell to such a low price that NASDAQ froze any further sale of shares. This freezing is mandatorily done when there is a massive sell off any stock to prevent any excessive turbulence in the market. Several of Facebook's executives also left the company and the employees were reportedly eager to sell the stock. The devaluation of Facebook's stock price caused many to say that the social bubble had officially been popped.[521]

As of August 18, 2013, Facebook's market price has climbed to $38 since it fell to its lowest point in September of 2012 at $17 a share.[522] Had the destruction of the stock occurred on purpose with the intention of buying it on the cheap at a future date this would be considered short selling. What happens in short selling is that a trader will acquire stock at a high value and sell it with the expectation of the stock to decrease in value. When the stock reaches the very bottom of its decline, the original stock holder will buy the stock back at a very low price with the expectation of it increasing. This process is the reverse of the traditional form of investing known as "going long" where an individual will originally buy the stock at a low value with the expectation of it increasing in value over time.[523]

The reason why short selling may have happened here is that Facebook has a significant role to play in the world that the Valley is trying to create. Facebook is not scheduled to be "replaced" as many of its critics may suggest. Facebook will be here for a while if the plans of the corporations and venture capitalists of Silicon Valley come to fruition. It is not out of line to suggest that people with knowledge of how important Facebook is to the future would try to benefit off its high original stock price. And that future some might even suggest is more important than any short-term profits maybe a few crooked Wall Street traders.

The other important development with the IPO is that Facebook now has to share a lot of its information with public. Facebook did their best to delay that order for as long as they could because they have to maintain the perception of transparency. This means that vital information such as conference calls and financial statements can be accessed by the public that reveal how Facebook works. Because of that release of information more people will come to understand the role that Facebook plays in a surveillance society. Facebook knew this, and it's likely that because of that they avoided the IPO as long as they could.

14. The Valley

Aside from the very idea of the social network itself, the requirements for success as a social networking website are very straightforward. They include: highly trained personnel, adequate facilities, state of the art equipment and smart acquisitions. Facebook has met these needs because they have received the necessary funding to afford them. And funding as we will see is nearly all that matters in developing an idea like Facebook.

During the venture capital process Facebook received over $2.33 billion in venture funding according to Crunchbase.com.[524] With that money Facebook amassed some of the most qualified candidates in the world to run their company. They also started offices all over the globe and leased an illustrious headquarters in Palo Alto, California. To run their network Facebook constructed four enormous data centers each costing tens of millions of dollars in their creation and maintenance.[525] To maintain what they had built, Facebook bought out the competition that stood in their way and in doing acquired valuable assets to add to their arsenal. There are many ways that a company can spend its money (legal fees, penalties, lobbying), but it is this base of infrastructure that makes Facebook such a strong player in today's market.

The Talent

One of the major factors that allow Facebook to be successful is the world class talent that it has attracted.   These recruits allow Facebook to develop their products and maintain one of the world's largest social networks. To give just an idea of what we are talking about here, look at this list of individuals who hold the highest positions at Facebook and some of the qualifications that they possess.

- Founder and CEO of Facebook Mark Zuckerberg attended Harvard University before starting Facebook in 2004.[526]

- Chief Financial Officer David Ebersman worked at Genentech Inc. as its Chief Financial Officer and Executive Vice President. He also holds a bachelor's in economics and international relations from Brown University.[527]

- Chief Operating Officer Sheryl Sandberg earned a bachelor's degree in economics from Harvard and an MBA from Harvard Business School. She is a former Vice President at Google and Chief of Staff for the U.S. Treasury Department.[528]

- Chief Technology Officer Mike Schroepfer holds a bachelors and master's degree from Stanford University. He formerly worked at Mozilla and helped develop Firefox.[529]

- VP of Product Christopher Cox attended Stanford, studying artificial intelligence and symbolic systems.[530]

- VP of Advertising and Global Operations David Fischer has a bachelor's degree in government from Cornell University and a MBA from Stanford University. Before Facebook Fischer was VP of online sales and operations at Google. Before that he served as the deputy chief of staff at the U.S. Treasury during the Clinton years.[531]

- VP of People and Recruiting is Lori Goler. She has a Bachelor's degree from Yale, and an MBA from Harvard Business School and a Master's degree in public policy from the Kennedy School of Government. Before Facebook she was a business strategist for Disney.[532]

- VP of Partnerships Dan Rose went to Harvard and later the University of Michigan before joining Facebook he worked for Amazon.[533]

- VP of General Counsel Ted Ullyot holds a bachelor's degree from Harvard and a law degree from the Chicago School of Law. He has served as counsel for AOL, as chief of staff of the Justice Department, as law clerk for Justice Antonin Scalia and as a deputy assistant to the President.[534]

To give an example of how well these people do, let's look at COO and board member Sheryl Sandberg. She gets paid $340,000 in annual salary plus $50,000 for her board seat, plus a $276,730 bonus for 2012. This goes along with having 17,788,268 class A and 78,332 class B shares in the company. When we factor these numbers together, Sandberg made $26,216,173 at Facebook in 2012. And if for some reason Facebook decided to fire her, she would get paid 75 million dollars in severance pay.[535]

Other very wealthy members of the management team for 2012 include David Ebersman who made $17,543,861, David B. Fischer who made $12,013,232 and Mike Schroepfer who made 20,725,928. CEO Mark Zuckerberg made 1,990,714 in 2012. His number is much smaller because the compensation committee will no longer give him any more equity because he owns so much already. He owns over 60,000,000 shares of Facebook which were valued at $2,276,677,500 when the report was made in 2012.[536]

Along with the executives who help carry out the day to day operations of the site, there is also the board of directors that makes the long-term decisions for the company. We have already displayed two of the board members Sandberg and Zuckerberg, so let's fill in the other six.

- Peter Thiel helped found Pay Pal, the online payment system that was purchased by eBay in 2002. Thiel has also served on the boards of Clarium Capital and the Founder's Fund. Before that he worked for the prestigious New York law firm Sullivan & Cromwell. He also attended Stanford University and Stanford Law School.[537]

- Marc Andreessen was the founder of Netscape, served as Chief Technology Officer of America Online Inc., is now a partner at venture capital firm Andreessen Horowitz, member of the boards of directors of eBay Inc., the Hewlett-Packard Company and several private companies, and he holds a B.S. in computer science from the University of Illinois at Urbana-Champaign.[538]

- Reed Hastings is the CEO and founder of Netflix, a board member at Microsoft and he holds a B.A. in mathematics from Bowdoin College and an M.S.C.S. in computer science from Stanford University.[539]

- Donald E. Graham is the CEO of the Washington Post, is also on the board of the Pulitzer Prize, and he holds an A.B. in English history and literature from Harvard University.[540]

- Erskine Bowles was a former chief of staff for the Clinton administration, also worked for Morgan Stanley, served as Co-Chair of the National Commission on Fiscal Responsibility and Reform, holds a B.S. in business from the University of North Carolina at Chapel Hill and an M.B.A. from Columbia University Graduate School of Business.[541]

- Susan Desmond-Hellmann is a Professor at the University of California, San Francisco (UCSF), a president of product development at Genentech, an associate director of clinical cancer research at Bristol-Myers Squibb Pharmaceutical Research Institute, a member of the board of directors of The Procter & Gamble Company and she holds B.S. in Pre-Med and M.D. from University of Nevada, Reno, and an M.P.H. from U.C. Berkeley.[542]

For the wealth of experience and hard work each member of the board gets $50,000 a year. Members of the board as well as some of the executives also get bonuses for working extra hard.[543] This is usually on top of the stock options that are given to Facebook executives. What also helps their financial success is that they hold positions on other boards as well. As you can see all of these people hold board seats on multiple companies which give them plenty of knowledge about what it is happening in the industry.

And in addition to the major players that were involved in the creation and guidance of Facebook, the company is staffed by numerous highly qualified personnel. To work at Facebook a typical candidate must have years of experience in their field along with having at least bachelor's if not a master's degree.[544] While being a graduate of the most elite schools is not required. Facebook does recruit directly out of those institutions.[545] This is all in addition to the other hands on skills they must develop while working at Facebook in a fast-paced environment.   If there is any testament to how qualified Facebook's employees are, it is not the requirements they must meet but the lack of positions that get filled. As of June 2013, Facebook had posted almost 500 vacant positions to fill on their website.[546] They don't just hire people who can do the job. They hire the best people to do the job and if they can't find those people the position stays vacant.

The dedication that Facebook expresses in finding the best candidates leads to them being one of the strongest internet companies in the world. It also may be responsible for why Facebook has lasted so long compared to other networks of its type. Maybe the reason why Facebook is here and MySpace is only but a shadow of its former self is because Facebook hired the best while MySpace couldn't get the best. Having skilled personnel is not something that everyone can get, but if you want to be Facebook it is non-negotiable.

A Nice Place to Work

To attract the kind of talent that can run a website like Facebook, the company has made the work environment a very pleasant experience for its employees. Facebook is such a good place to work at in fact that Glassdoor.com named it 2013's Number #1 place to work. In addition to that ranking from reviewers, the employees of Facebook also spoke very highly of the company. About 97% of them approved of Mark Zuckerberg as a good CEO.[547] So from what we see this is not the typical corporation that is filled with well-paid but miserable workers. The people who work at Facebook are happy to work there, and that is for many reasons.

Something that was brought up time and again by employees was the amenities that Facebook gives to those who work there. Facebook has several arcades with pool tables and videogames for workers to play with.[548] The cafeteria has food that ranges from snacks to vegan lunches.[549] On the walls of the offices are graffiti artworks done by famous artists such as David Choe.[550] During the summer time people have parties and cookouts on the roof. During the colder months, employees can grab an alcoholic drink at the bar called "Happy Hour" located inside of Facebook.[551] With all of these perks that employees are given it would almost seem like it is too comfortable a place to work.

To help keep work productivity high, Facebook embraces what they call a "hacker culture" which promotes a relaxed but motivational workplace. Around the offices there are motivational signs and posters everywhere. They say phrases like "this journey is 1% finished" and "what would you do if you were not afraid?"[552] There are black boards that line the walls, and white boards that fill the lounges.[553] These are just some of the small things that Facebook does which separate itself from the more business oriented corporations in the valley. Facebook is about doing serious work, but they are more about innovation than business at the end of the day.

Aside from the symbolic aspects of the work environment, the most prevalent reason why people are motivated to work at Facebook was the other people that worked around them. Employees often remarked in the Glassdoor reviews that they felt inspired to work at Facebook because they were surrounded by brilliant people who were the best at what they did.[554] The result was that people worked hard not because of strict managers or tough rules, but because they wanted to achieve something.

A point that should also be said about the employees who make up Facebook is that they are typically young. The average employee age is 28 according to *The New York Times* which cited a report from the Seattle based marketing firm Payscale.[555] The youth of Facebooks employees allows them to get more effort out of workers because their obligations are few and the expected rewards are great. Youth can also be important to have in well trained employees because the young worker is still capable of doing their job without having reached the callousness that comes with middle age. The castles in the sky still seem real when you are young.

By having this type of employee demographic, Facebook makes the non-stop work parties such as the famous Hackathons possible. Hackathons are all-night long programming sessions the encourage employees to think "outside the box" about their work. The Hackathons also serve as a time for socialization among coworkers which boosts the workplace morale somewhat. This offers employees a chance to talk with the executives as well as interns on an even footing.[556]

Something else that could be considered valuable by these Hackathons as well as Facebook's f8 business conferences is that they restore faith in the administration. Having all the employees in one place hearing the boss talk about the exciting future of the company does something for the worker spirit. It reinforces the idea that Facebook isn't just a great place to work but a place that the employee should be proud to work at. Based on what is shown at these conferences and from what is said in the reviews, it seems that Facebook employees are very proud of their workplace.

But if for some reason an employee did have a problem with the way things were done, there is probably very little they could do as a worker to change that. Rising into management level positions is very difficult at Facebook because the management tends not to promote people from within the company. Another frequently posted comment in the Glassdoor reviews were that most of the upper level management positions are people who were brought in from other companies who already have management experience.[557] These people are valuable to Facebook not just because of their expertise but because of their knowledge of the competition. This is something that the low-level employee who works at Facebook for years cannot provide. Fortunately for Facebook however, most employees see the company as a place to work at temporarily and not a place to spend their entire career.

The concern over worker dissatisfaction is also mitigated by the nice salaries that lower and mid-level Facebook employees enjoy. Interns make close to $70,000 dollars a year.[558] Entry level Software Engineers come in at about $100,000 a year.[559] Management positions make about 125,000 to 150,000 a year.[560] So these people get paid very well to do what they do. Not to mention that some workers get paid in stock options that also can be lucrative as many of the executives will tell you.

If none of these perks and gifts help ease the employee's conscience about what they are doing; the employee can decide to blow the whistle on the company. This would require the employee to break the confidentiality contract that they first signed when they joined the company.[561] Despite leaks here and there that show up on the internet, no employee has decided yet to go public about their disgust with some secret the company is keeping hidden from us. This assumes we haven't been told that secret already. Sometimes the truth is out in the open waiting to be seen.

Storage and Maintenance

One of the most critical expenditures that Facebook has made with their money is the servers that house all their data. Without these servers Facebook would never be able to handle the level of traffic they enjoy as the world's largest social network. Failure to meet this requirement is often the reason why companies accept funding from whatever venture capitalist that will buy equity. The company knows that without the servers their idea will quickly suffer a meltdown, so they engage in a risky relationship with a wealthy stranger.

As of this writing Facebook currently has four data centers to house the information that they collect. They are located in: Prineville, Oregon; Forest City, North Carolina; Lulea, Sweden, and Altoona, Iowa. Together they hold all the information that Facebook has obtained on its users during their 9 years of existence. That mass of information comes to over 100 petabytes of data.[562]

In total, the operation of Facebook consumed 532M kWh in 2011. The bulk of that energy consumption comes from storage, but it also come from protecting the servers from overheating. This is because Facebook needs complex cooling systems that constantly keep the air cool and dry inside the data center. Those cooling systems require not just energy to run, but also backup generators in case the main system should fail. The diesel generators run on a 24/7 basis in case that the power for the cooling system fails.[563]

A large part of this energy input comes from how Facebook is run. Barring any outages, Facebook is accessible at any time on any day of the year. It is not available everywhere of course, but it is available somewhere. This means that the network is constantly requiring great amounts of energy to keep things running smoothly.[564] The total amount of pollution emitted from Facebook was roughly 285,000 metric tons of greenhouse gas emissions in 2012.[565] This includes not only the data centers but also the offices, and travel of the employees when taken as a whole.

If Facebook did not store so much information they would not need to use all this energy. Facebook forsakes this concerns with the amount of money they can make keeping the site online. They have even been fined for pollution they cause in the areas that their data centers inhabit.[566] To them, polluting is just the cost of doing business.

However, Facebook is not alone nor are they the largest polluter based out of Silicon Valley. A 2012 *New York Times* article highlighted Facebook's data center pollution as well as other companies such as Google and Yahoo that require large amounts of energy to keep their websites running.[567] This is not to mention that social networking is just one of many industries that cause large amounts pollution. Newspapers are an obvious example that was pointed out in the article with the cost of cutting down trees, printing the paper, and distribution. But the concern for pollution isn't as strong with newspapers because it is an agreed upon need for society. People need newspapers to be informed about their world, but they don't need Facebook just yet.

Aside from being a major source of pollution, Facebook's data centers represent just how far ahead they are compared to their other competitors in their field. Not only does Facebook have a site that people are in love with, they have the capability to store information on over a billion people. Other domestic competitors such as Twitter and Pinterest have only one. MySpace at its peak had four but at that time storage capability is not what it is today.[568] As to be expected Google has the most with 13 data centers spread throughout the Americas, Europe, and Asia, but we will address why they are different shortly.[569]

The Competition

Despite the position of strength that Facebook holds in the market, they still must deal with the competition they face in the Valley and elsewhere. The domestic competition comes in the form of two types of companies the alternatives and the conformists. The alternatives are networks that do things differently than social networks like Facebook would. Examples could include Diaspora or Friendica which use more of a decentralized network format that puts control of information in the hands of the user instead of one corporation. Because of their concern for more privacy or internet freedom, these companies have poor business models by corporate and venture capitalist's standards. The inability to generate mountain sized profits for their investors means that it is unlikely these companies will receive the funding necessary to compete with Facebook.

These companies also stand in opposition to the billions of investment dollars that are being put into cloud computing and big data. This is not exclusive to just the investors of Facebook but to Silicon Valley as a whole. Facebook's style of doing things is a part of the future that the Valley wants to create. The last thing they are going to do is undermine their investment by trying to unseat Facebook with a new alternative.

The conformists to Facebook's style are companies that embrace the information collection business model while still differentiating themselves from Facebook at the same time. These companies do not care about privacy the way decentralized network startups would. They are accepting of what the industry wants from social media and they are willing to do what it takes to please the venture capitalists. Examples could be Twitter, Instagram, or Tumblr to name a few. They are different somewhat from Facebook but because they go along with the plan sort of speak, they can attract the funding necessary to become a real threat.

If Facebook wants to maintain market dominance these conformist companies must either be marginalized or eliminated. To marginalize their opponents Facebook will a launch a feature that is similar to what the competing company specializes in. A photo sharing feature to combat a photo sharing service could be an example. Or an email feature to combat an email services could be another. As a consequence of this maneuver the rival company will have to focus heavily on their specialty to defend their market position.

This may explain why the challengers to Facebook are usually relegated to niche positions within the market. For instance, LinkedIn with 225 million users focuses on professionals, much like Facebook focused on students.[570] Twitter with 550 million users focuses mostly on their micro blogs.[571] Google+ with 359 million users focuses on email.[572] Pinterest with 25 million users is about showing off artistic achievements.[573] Each company has a special unique characteristic that allows them to exist in the market while at the same time limiting them from ever becoming a real threat.

The marginalized existence of these rivals gives certain benefits to Facebook as long as the rivals do not get too big. They give Facebook a legitimate reason to keep changing its site and making it more intrusive. Because there are other sites that are on Facebook's heels, Facebook can say they need to keep updating and making their site better. If they didn't do this, they might go the way of MySpace and become irrelevant. This gives an excuse to make innovations such as Timeline and the Newsfeed that are considered by the media as an update on the network despite being incredibly intrusive to user privacy.

Aside from the larger conformist companies who manage to take a chunk out of Facebook's market, there are also the startups that Facebook has to deal with. What Facebook has on their side is that these companies, despite having a product worth using, have bills to pay. They must pay their personnel. They have to purchase or typically rent equipment to run the site. And they have to rent out an office which may be very expensive in depending what location they are in. When these expenses are factored together it makes young companies relatively easy to purchase if Facebook can get to them before they grow too big.

Facebook has purchased over thirty different startup companies to fight off having any real competition. While the Instagram purchase might make this strategy sound expensive, for the most part the purchases are far cheaper than that. While Instagram cost over $700 million, the entire expenditure of Facebook for all acquisitions only comes to $1.2 billion.[574] When we consider the position that Facebook holds in the market because of these acquisitions, it appears the money has been well spent.

What makes this situation easy for Facebook is that some companies may go into the business with the expectation that they will be bought up by a monopoly like Facebook. It is also not unusual for this to be an implicit agreement between the entrepreneur and the venture capitalist that an acquisition will happen. Zuckerberg himself sought to avoid his kind of situation when taking funding from venture capitalists during the startup stage.[575] A lot of venture capitalists don't care about changing the world; they just want to get the return on their investment.

It is this desire by venture capitalists for money and the desire of corporations to remain monopolies that keeps things the way they are in Silicon Valley. And if this system seems unreliable to maintain market dominance in the tech world, consider that Google and Microsoft each have purchased over 100 companies with an expense of $20 billion since they were founded. Those numbers do not even consider the products that these companies developed to destroy the market positions of those who tried to fight them.[576]

As long as the money keeps coming in, Facebook will be around just as long as the rest of the giants have been. Right now, Facebook is bringing in about $5 billion a year with advertising and fees.[577] They need the money to increase substantially if they are going to make it to where these industry giants are in terms of staying power. Do not make the mistake of thinking that Facebook cannot do this because they are still a relatively young company and we have not seen everything they must show.

Currently the revenue is not where it could be right now because of how much time and resources Facebook has spent on growth. Facebook is in a building phase still. But once that phase is over, there will be enough money coming in that Facebook will be able to pressure or buyout any competition that comes in its way. Rest assured that competition will include companies both foreign and domestic.

15. Facebook Global

While some networks in Facebook's envious position might spend some time reflecting on how they can keep their users safe from danger, Facebook instead has chosen to focus on unmitigated growth. Increasing their numbers is Facebook's stated mission as a company and they will not let concerns over privacy, safety, or even revenue stand in their way. Growth is all that matters to them because they know the strength it provides in the global marketplace. The more users they have, the more users they can get, the more powerful they are.

But to continue this quest for endless growth, Facebook must turn outside of the United States to find more users. The market in America has been saturated for some time now which is evidenced by Facebook's stable domestic growth in the past four years.[578] Foreign markets on the other hand offer Facebook the chance of capturing large numbers of people who have yet to join any social network. As some may have already discovered however, there are reasons why these areas lay unused.

Let Us In

Every time Facebook expands into a new country, the expansion brings with it the possibility of gaining tens of millions of users into Facebook's network. What is efficient about this strategy of expansion is that it requires no real innovation. Facebook can just be itself without having to develop any new bells and whistles to please people. Unlike existing users, the new foreign markets may not be accustomed to Facebook's platform, or any platform for that matter. This gives the company some time before the user starts getting bored with what Facebook must offer.[579]

The strategy for the most part is working and could be credited with helping Facebook reach the billion-member milestone in 2012. And while the United States has given Facebook the most users of any other country (166 million), foreign countries make up close to 85% of what Facebook is today.[580] This could mean that 10 million users come from one country while 50 million come from another, but when combined those numbers add up significantly. The potential for this strategy is very high when we consider that over 1.5 billion internet users exist in the combined areas of the Middle East, South America, Africa, and Asia. Of that number close over a billion are not yet Facebook members.[581]

While for the most part the effort to conqueror the world has gone smoothly, there are some obstacles that stand in Facebook's way. One barrier is that Facebook must face rival websites in those foreign regions. What these websites may lack in sheer size, the make up for in localization. Because the rivals are familiar with the languages and customs of the surrounding area so they can concentrate more heavily on the technical aspects of running an internet company.[582]

When Facebook wants to establish itself in a foreign country, it has to change its network to match the area it is targeting. This could require registering a national domain name like gr. or .ru. It may also involve improving the translation features to fit the local language dialect.[583] Facebook also has to worry about having enough server capacity to handle the increase in site traffic even if the site can be localized to the desired location. All of this stuff has to happen in a timely manner before some homegrown website establishes itself with the local population. Timing is important because once those users are on another social platform; it can be difficult to get them off.

This staying power could be the result of better localization by the home website or it could be that Facebook just doesn't have anything new to offer. The lack of originality is made even worse by the fact that many rival websites are fashioning themselves after Facebook. These rival social networks are often referred to as clones or copycats due to their similar layouts and business models. A good example of this is Russia's VKontakte, which not only looks startlingly like Facebook, but it also markets itself as the Facebook of Russia.[584] While Russia does allow Facebook in the country, the bulk of Russia's users go to VKontakte and other clone networks. With the low hanging fruit all but snatched out of their hands, Facebook may only be able to offer a brand name that while well-known is certainly not unbeatable.[585]

To avoid getting in these turf battles with other websites, Facebook is smart to penetrate developing countries that have the necessary infrastructure but lack the technical environment to generate substantial competition. These countries provide the perfect situation for Facebook because users have few options about which networks they can join. A good example of this kind of region is the Middle East which as of August 2013 has just over 90 million internet users, approximately 23 million of whom are on Facebook. Another case worth examining is Africa which has 167 million internet users with 51 million of them on Facebook.[586] These are numbers that Facebook cannot afford to turn away from.

We should remember that these two regions are not always the most hospitable places in the world to do business. Author Michael Parenti once said that "the problem with the third world is not that it is underdeveloped but that it is overexploited."[587] This kind of logic applies very well in the regions that Facebook is trying to expand into. The lack of competition in these countries comes from lack of freedom by order of the dictator or foreign government that controls the country. While Facebook would aid in giving freedom to individual involved in the Arab Spring, it would also bring consequences for Facebook reputation around the world for better or for worse.

The Arab Spring

First beginning in December of 2010, the Arab Spring involved 17 countries throughout the Middle East and North Africa. What characterized and may still characterize some of these countries is oppression. The people in some if not all of these countries had oppressive governments that prevented the freedom of expression necessary for a democratic society.[588] To meet this deficit, activists and journalists in the regions turned to social media to speak about their concerns. Of the numerous social media sites that were used by the protestors, Facebook was one of the most popular and instrumental networks in bringing about change in the region.

A major role that Facebook played in the Arab Spring was as a facilitator for political discussion. Facebook gave people a place to discuss political issues in a digital public square without having the fear of imprisonment, execution, or exile. This ability to speak freely was important in countries like Egypt were open dissent was a punishable offense. While Facebook was not entirely neglected by state security monitors in the Arab Spring, it provided enough anonymity and participation to make mass persecution for free speech unfeasible.[589]

This degree of digital freedom would also play a major role in the citizen journalism that would take place on Facebook. Users could bypass the state run media by putting up their own news stories on Facebook for concerned peers to read. This ability was especially important with the barrage of police brutality incidents that helped to galvanize more protestors to the cause of freedom. One specific instance of police brutality was the inspiration for the *Kullena Khaled Said* page for the Egypt revolution.

In his book *Revolution 2.0*, Wael Ghomin describes how after seeing the photo of a police brutality victim on Facebook he started a Facebook page to commemorate him. The man in the photo, Khaled Said, was beaten to death by two police officers in Cairo on June 6, 2011. Said's story pulled a lot of viewers to Ghomin's page and resulted in rounds of political discussion and citizen journalism to take place on Facebook regarding the Egyptian government. Ghomin even managed to organize thousands of protestors in Egypt through the Said Page all while he was changing location back and forth between America and the Middle East.[590]

Ghomin's ability to organize the first protests, known as the Silent Stands, was the result of Facebook's features for mass communication. For example by having people like the Kullena Khaled Said page, Ghomin could send them updates through the Newsfeed about protests that were taking place throughout Egypt. He was also able to moderate discussion and pay attention to the mood of the people who he was trying to reach. All of this was probably very simple for Ghomin seeing as he was a marketer for Google, but that is another matter of discussion.[591]

In addition to getting these protests started, Facebook provided a source of awareness for what was going on. Government as well as independent news sources could not just write off these revolutions like other civil unrests of the past. Social media had helped turn the rebellions into a statement of technological progress that the media was able to attach a story to. Because of that, more news coverage and more news viewers paid attention to the Arab Spring than the other foreign rebellions that normally go ignored.[592]

This attention that got paid to the Arab Spring helped generate a very important momentum factor. While the protestors may have disagreed about what they were fighting about, the knowledge that there were a large number of people standing with them was a major motivator. Facebook's event feature particularly played an excellent role in this regard by telling people when the rally would begin days in advance of the actual date.[593] The event lists particularly can be helpful in the beginning of a movement when numbers are small and people may be demoralized.

Understanding Facebook's role in the Arab Spring is important because now Facebook is tied to the success or failure of the movement. For the most part the media still views the Arab Spring as a positive occurrence regardless of any relapses that may have occurred. A part of this is that many westerners still seem to relate the American Revolution with the very different revolutions that have occurred in the Arab Spring. Because of this the media is giving the movement time to still play out in countries that may have fallen into disarray as of late.

Rejection

While this use of Facebook may have won praise from revolutionaries as well as journalists and media pundits, there are foreign governments who are not pleased to see Facebook have a role in revolution. Currently there are four countries, China, Cuba, Iran, and North Korea that ban Facebook.[594] There are also other countries such as Saudi Arabia, Syria, and Vietnam that have shown hostility towards Facebook while not totally banning it.[595] In addition to standing in the way of internet freedom, these countries are a major obstacle in preventing Facebook from connecting the entire world.

All of these countries have internet users that Facebook would want, but China has the most valuable market for Facebook. China currently holds over 500,000 million internet users who Facebook would like to have at least a part of.[596] These people also live in a country with a vibrant economy that could add billions of dollars to Facebook revenue stream. Unfortunately for Facebook the Chinese government is very hesitant to allow for the freedom of speech that the social network would permit.

American companies in general are also seen with a degree of distrust because they are believed to be connected to the American intelligence community. This is a suspicion that is held in China as well as in the Middle East. China takes significant efforts to maintain a closed society by creating their Golden Shield program that makes connecting to American websites very difficult.[597] They are not about to let another American company come in that can leak information on their citizens while bringing with it the possibility of starting a revolution.

This suspicion is not necessarily groundless. Because Facebook is such a massive and great depository of foreign intelligence it would be difficult for intelligence agencies to ignore it. As one intelligence official quoted in *Wired* put it, "We would be marked as incompetent if we didn't monitor it."[598] Monitoring Facebook for information on foreign countries would yield a wealth of intelligence. The photos that users upload would give agencies a ground level spy camera. Reports and posts made by users would tell analysts about potential targets such as restaurants and movie theaters. Examining posts and comments would also give analysts an ear into the attitude of the nations they are watching.

China's intelligence community paranoia is combined with a history of Western tech companies failing to follow orders after being given access to the Chinese market. A well-known example is Google who refused to censor their searches and turn over account information to the Chinese government after initially agreeing to do so.[599] Yahoo! is another company that originally agreed to the Faustian bargain and then reneged on the deal. Both of these failed business deals were the result of Congressional pressure being applied to the corporations to end their anti-democratic behavior.

And then there is the cause of protectionism. The Chinese government is protecting the position that their local monopolies have over social media by keeping companies like Facebook outside of their borders. One example is Tencent, which is a holding company run by Huanteng "Pony Ma" Ma that controls several communication platforms and gaming companies. Notable products and investments include: QQ, QZone, WeChat, Riot Games, and Epic Games. Altogether Tencent has 600 million active users for social media channels they control.[600]

There are also other major social media players in China such as Sina Weibo which is a Twitter clone and RenRen which is a clone of Facebook. Sina Weibo has over 500 million members and is the 4th most popular site in China while RenRen has over 160 million and is 27th most popular site in China as of July 2013.[601] As to be expected, all of these Chinese internet companies actively censor and monitor their site on the behest of the Chinese Communist Party. It also should be mentioned that this censorship was made possible with the help of Cisco Systems who sold China the equipment for their Golden Shield in 2002.[602]

What becomes clear after seeing how eager these western and Chinese companies are to participate in the subjugation in the Chinese people is that the Arab Spring is really incidental to Facebook's plans. They might use it as a PR tactic for domestic audiences, but democracy is by far not their greatest concern. Growth is all that matters. If growth means going to China and censoring every post that the communist parties wants, than that is what they will get.

If this seems like an extreme prediction, consider how much assistance that Facebook has provided to the American government. Facebook not only complies with the thousands of data requests that the U.S. government makes every year, but they provide online guides of how to obtain the data and make web pages to capture more of it.[603] While the Arab Spring may have prevented immediate access to China, if anything Facebook deserves to be let into China for the communist dictatorship standard for good behavior.

Fighting the inevitable

While this might seem like a permanent block against Facebook's plans for world domination, Facebook has a long term strategy that is designed to withstand the resistance of any hostile government such as China. By gathering all of the low hanging fruit that we talked about earlier, Facebook has received a position of dominance that no clone or rival has achieved. This dominance brings with it the capital necessary to expand beyond that current position. Other networks while able to expand cannot spread out the way that Facebook has.

The value of what Facebook has accomplished in the past few years is best illustrated in their proliferation around the world. Facebook is present in over 127 of 137 countries according a *Washington Post* article that cited Alexa.com.[604] In doing so Facebook has encircled any country that wishes to keep them out in the near future. This scenario is parallel to the position that Facebook was in during the 2003-2006 growth period. During this time, Facebook was getting requests from universities all over the country to become part of the Facebook network. Facebook had to restrict this growth because of their limited server capacity. If Facebook would have just let any school into the network, they would have been crippled by the large influx of traffic.   Until Facebook was able to take on a new school, a Facebook clone would form on the campus in anticipation for its arrival.[605]

This strategy prevented another original site from entering the university and converting potential members. According to author Kirkpatrick, if the clone was reluctant to give up its local hero status once the servers were ready, Facebook would use an encirclement strategy. This would involve admitting all the surrounding schools in the area to isolate the members of the holdout school. Eventually the holdout's members would flock to Facebook, leaving their clone managers standing in the dust.[606]

What is important to this plan is that no "revolutionary" types of social networking sites develop in countries that are not fully saturated by Facebook. Imagine a piece of hardware like Freedombox that provided an alternative to Facebook while still showing concern for privacy. Freedombox is an open source project to create a machine that can do social networking without having to use an outside service that stores information.[607] Needless to say Facebook and the rest of Silicon Valley does not want anything like that to happen.

Despite the small amount of competition they present, Facebook benefits from an environment with clones. The good thing about the clones is that they saturate local populations while getting them used to the platform.   When Facebook has managed to fully encircle a country like China or Russia the saturation will make the transition to Facebook easier.   No one will be wringing their hands saying what an intrusion this is. And no one will have developed an alternate form of social networking because people were too busy trying to be Facebook or too weak to become them.

While some of the clones do seem stronger than others, none of them have the capacity to become what Facebook can become. This is as true for VKontakte in Russia as it is for RenRen in China or Google+ in America. No other company has the combined characteristics of infrastructure, brand name, user base, funding, and corporate integration that Facebook has. The rivals and clones may have one of these qualities individually, but none have them all in one place.

Because none of these companies have any real offensive capability against Facebook, they will be forced to sit by while Facebook works its strategy. Obviously the strategy could be subject to unforeseeable events such as the rise of a new super website or a massive catastrophe.   Facebook even acknowledges in their annual earnings statement that regulations could be passed to infringe on their growth and revenue. These are all possible occurrences, but as for right now, Facebook is in a position of immense strength in the world of social networking.

16. The Internet of Things

What should be understood as we move forward is that the planned future of the internet does not depend on Facebook being the number one or only network in the world. Facebook could become the social network of the world but that is not a necessary outcome. Facebook is only a part of a much larger movement known as the Internet of Things. Facebook is one of many social networking sites that make up this movement, it just happens to be a very big one. To provide more elaboration, let us provide an explanation as to what this movement is in detail.

This Internet of Things is a paradigm shift in the way that mankind's technology collects and stores information about the world around us. The idea behind this movement is to turn every product into a receiver of data. Every car, t-shirt, refrigerator, and whatever else that can be bought in stores will be able to collect information on its environment. This storage will be facilitated through the implementation of Radio Frequency Identification (RFID) chips into every consumer product. These chips will go with the product wherever it goes and some can even track where the product goes.[608]

There are two types of chips that are being used for tracking. The first kind of chip is a passive RFID Tag. Passive RFID Tags have information placed on them such as the product's serial number, name, and distributor. For the product's distributor or owner to access that information they use a device called an E-Reader. The E-Reader sends out a radio signal that the chip receives through a miniaturized antenna. The chip then uses energy obtained from the signal to report the information it contains on the product. Once the process is over, the chip shuts off and waits to receive another signal.[609]

Active RFID tags however do not wait for a radio signal to be turned on. These kinds of tags have their own power source which allows them to stay on without using having to rely on another device. They also can be read at longer distances than passive tags because they have a bigger antenna and more power. While both passive and active tags receive and store information from their readers, active tags can store more data because of their larger size.[610]

Smart devices that have active RFID placed in them can communicate their tag's information through Near Field Communication or NFC. A smart phone uses NFC by activating a transmitter that generates an electromagnetic field along the back of device. This prevents a smart phone from reading and transmitting data to every RFID tag in the surrounding area. Generally, a device using NFC will only read tags that are a few inches away from its transmitter.[611][This is different from E-Readers that are developed to read hundreds of tags at once in larger settings such as warehouses and stores.[612]

What this is heading towards is for people to be read much like how objects are read. The proliferation of social media has resulted in billions of people creating digital identities that will eventually interact with the objects that are being tracked. This interaction leads to the creation of data which is attached to the individual's digital identity. While the identity is managed by the individual, it is owned by a social media company that has control over who can see the information.

Facebook represents an early stage of what the Internet of Things will eventually become. Right now, its role in this movement is to eliminate anonymous interaction in online as well as real world communication. That objective will be achieved by Facebook's spread around the world and the construction of infrastructure around the identity of the individual. It will not be until later that we see the full extent of what this movement can become. When a digital identity is necessary for an individual to function in their daily life, all of society will be completely visible to whoever controls the surveillance state at that time. There will be no more privacy for anyone, ever.

Current Usage

In many ways products that consumers use are already being thoroughly tracked by the manufacture, without even using RFID. UBC barcodes and QR codes are located on nearly every product that is sold in the world. The codes are used to identify the products and where they go. This identification helps sellers do inventory and pricing by scanning the barcode whenever someone buys it at the checkout line. When the code is scanned, the business knows which item was purchased and how much it was supposed to be sold for.[613] The code may be somewhat unsightly but it has improved the efficiency of the modern consumer goods store dramatically

What makes RFID chips different from a bar code is its ability to be discreet. RFID tags do not have to be placed on the external area of the product but can be hidden subtly inside of it. This could be done for products such as furniture or newspapers that traditionally do not come with bar codes because of the methods that they are sold. Bar codes also do not give the owner the ability to scan hundreds of items simultaneously with the click of a button. This is what makes warehouse inventory with RFID so fast, and it could also be used for police searches as well.

While bar codes might rule the day for now, the implementation of RFID technology into our daily lives has already begun to wear away at its dominance. Companies that specialize in the production of these devices have already arisen to meet the expected demand. Some of the more well-known ones include TagSys, TrueIQ, RealID, and Verichip. These companies along with several others will compete for dominance in this emerging market as it unfolds in the coming years.

One industry that this battle will take place in is resource distribution. Major retail corporations such as Wal-Mart and Target use RFID for logistics tracking. As early as 2003, Wal-Mart was using RFID chips to track their products to and from their shipping locations.[614] They also use it to save time while doing warehouse inventory.[615] Because this helps distributors make more money, they are encouraged their suppliers to embrace RFID as well.

Major retail suppliers such as Kimberly Clark, Proctor & Gamble, Johnson & Johnson, and Gillett were some of the first major commercial adopters of RFID. They were shipping billions of products a year with RFID as early as 2005. While the suppliers used RFID for the same efficiency reasons as Wal-Mart, Gillett was especially concerned about RFID to prevent shoplifting. Even today it is still difficult to keep people from stealing razor blades despite putting them behind glass.[616]

Another current example of RFID usage is in passports. As of 2008, all American passports have been outfitted with an RFID chip to prevent impersonation.[617] This allows the American government to track every person that leaves or enters the country through designated areas such as airports and train stations. The system does not however track illegal immigrants who come into the country through other avenues, but it does serve to document what legal American citizens do.

Along with international borders, RFID is also being used to help monitor crossing points within America. Car owners are now able to put an RFID tag in their car that will be scanned when they cross at a toll checkpoint. By having this tag, the individual can cross toll roads without stopping because it will report that they have already paid. This will document every time the car passes a toll point in the car that is registered.[618]

In addition to objects, RFID is also being used to track animals such as pets and livestock. Since 1989 animals were being equipped with RFID tags to help track where they went to prevent them from getting lost or running away. There are also tags that measure the health factors of the animal to allow for the necessary treatment and euthanization in a quicker amount of time. This will help to save money and time as well as prevent the animal from spreading any disease they may be carrying to others.[619]

Despite FDA approval of RFID chip implementation in humans, it is unlikely that chips will ever be surgically implanted at full scale like their bovine counterparts. There are numerous medical risks that go along with implementation under the skin such as chip migration, infections, and even cancerous tumors.[620] This is combined with the psychological discomfort that many people have over the idea of a computer chip being used to track everything they do. RFID for some people is associated with the Mark of the Beast as foretold in the Christian Bible's Book of Revelation.[621] It seems that for now RFID will have to stay in the machines.

Barriers to Full Scale Implementation

The wide range of uses that were expected for RFID, implementation of the technology were not enough however to bring it out of the state of stagnation it currently exists in. While distributors like Wal-Mart and groups like the State Department are still making use of RFID in relatively small instances, we are years away from a fully chipped society.[622] There are number of reasons for this, most of which were not acknowledged by RFID's advocates when groups were gearing up for the RFID revolution.

A major factor holding full implementation back is cost. It simply is not cost effective now to have RFID technology in every consumer product right now. Manufactures that use this technology have to pay for the chips, the meters, the software, and the personnel to set up the networks; this can be very expensive. As more companies make use of RFID and as time goes on the cost for the process is expected to go down. But until the cost of RFID is outweighed by the profits generated from it, RFID will only be seen as a novelty.[623]

Another major barrier to implementation is range. These chips need to be able to reach certain distances to be effective. Right now, active RFID tags can reach over 100 feet but passive chips at a short distance only a few meters at most.[624] The goal is to be able to communicate with the smart products from anywhere. But even for commercial purposes like inventory management the distance needs to be in hundreds of meters. When the range is marketable, the product will be marketable.

While range may be an issue for somewhat "dumber" products that only have a passive RFID chip, other smarter products must combat the battery life problem. The goal in this case will be to have the chip always on at all times. This means that the battery will have to be able to store energy from the sun or whatever energy source that is chosen when the product is not receiving energy. Solving this problem will help for implementation into things such as monitors and appliances. By having that product always turned on it will always be receiving information from its environment. That intake of information will allow the product to make judgments on its own about decisions that a human would normally have to make. A television knowing to turn to a certain channel when someone walks into the room could be an example.

Another problem that stands in the way of this technology being effective is virtualization.[625] By virtualization we mean whether the product will be connected into a cloud where people can have access to the information that the product receives. Virtualization will help identify if there is a problem with the product that needs to be addressed, but the real drive for virtualization is obtaining information.[626] Having these products connected to the cloud will make them become little cameras that detect everything in their environment.

What seems at the heart of these problems is that the money is not where it needs to be with RFID. Every technology has expected or hidden costs that must be carried by a company before mass acceptance drives the price down. What makes certain technologies worthwhile is their ability to absorb these costs by receiving the benefit of what the device does. Increasing efficiency in logistics and inventory may be great for a corporation like Wal-Mart, but if the rest of the business community is going to embrace RFID they are going to need a stronger incentive.

Smart Technology

The real commercial drive for RFID comes with the advent of smart technology. While definitions vary, we will refer to smart technology as electronic devices that can seamlessly communicate with other machines. Smart phones, smart grids, smart cards, smart boards, and smart televisions are the kind of things that fall in this category. While these devices have existed for some time now, their recent proliferation among the public has made them an essential technology for the 21st century.

What makes these devices important for RFID is that they allow the everyday person to interact with RFID chips that they may come in contact with. Now RFID is not just a way for organizations to track objects and animals, but also a way for people to get utility out of the system. That utility will lead to people using that system more and more as time goes on, a way to pay for it all will be created.

The most important of all the smart devices for the Internet of Things will be the smart phone however. This will be because of their popularity as well as the wide variety of communication features that smart phones have. For example, the original iPhone at its launch in 2007 gave the user the ability to use GPS, Wi-Fi, Bluetooth, and cellular connectivity.[627] In addition to their ability to communicate wirelessly with a wide variety of devices, today's smart phones have the long battery life and small size that are necessary for them to be easy to use.

What makes this device a wise purchase for low income individuals is its versatility and low price. Instead of buying say a laptop, an iPod, and a cell phone, a person can just buy an iPhone and get all those features in one. And if the person wants to get free internet connection too they can just go to an area that has Wi-Fi and connect to the internet that way. This wide range of benefits for low income individuals may help explain why 1.162 billion people in developing countries own smart phones compared to the 934 million people in developed countries that do as of December 2012.[628]

But while smart phones do allow for a wide variety of benefits to be given to the user they of course are very intrusive to privacy. And for the most part this fact is well known. Most brand name smart phones such as iPhone, Android, and Samsung contain GPS tracking devices that can monitor everywhere the user goes. A company known as Carrier IQ was even caught storing the locations of people who used Android and iOS operating systems on their smartphones.[629] This was only stopped after a researcher named Trevor Eckhart exposed how Carrier IQ was doing this in a YouTube video that went viral.[630]

Despite the risks that these devices pose to the public, they are still widely accepted as good technology. Current estimates say that there are approximately 2.1 billion smart phone users in the world today. That is an increase from 1.093 billion users in 2011.[631] This wide acceptance of technology despite its risks to privacy is important because it allows companies to get away with murder while the user thinks they are being provided an excellent service.

There are other smart devices which play a role in the Internet of Things as well. Most of these devices except for headsets and tablets are sedentary devices that the user does not take with them outside of the store, work place, or home. Examples could be smart electricity meters that interact with equipment inside the house to determine appropriate levels of electricity usage or surveillance cameras that send alerts to computer when they detect suspicious activity. Some of the companies that will market this kind of technology include: General Electric, Texas Instruments, Microsoft, and Cisco.[632] The goal of these technologies is to eliminate wiring through the use of radio transmission technology such as Bluetooth, Dash7, and Zigbee. As a result, the mobile device can communicate with the sedentary smart devices that surround it.

The web of communication that is created from smart phones and smart objects allow for RFID to have a place in a world that had previously discarded it. There are numerous theoretical uses for RFID but its role in commerce will be most important for the generation of revenue to support its existence. The automatic checkout is one example of a well-connected individual being able to use RFID in their daily life while making money for those who use it for logistics. An individual with a smart phone could go through a store a store and pick out the RFID tagged products that they wanted to purchase. By having a smart card or smart phone on them the individual could pay for their items by walking through a gateway that would scan their products and bill their checking account.[633]

This fantasy along with many others is so desirable for corporations because it makes purchases easier for the individual. There are mental barriers such as concern for cost and value of the product that keep people from buying things that they have an impulse to purchase when they see them. But when corporations eliminate external barriers like writing checks and talking to cashiers they shorten that amount of time the resistance must kick in. The results are higher profits for the business and less savings for the consumer.

Along with the profit incentive smart technology brings with it the much larger benefit of relieving exhaustion from technology. The corporations understand that people can only take in so much innovation at once. At a certain point users become overwhelmed with what they have to handle and they begin to reject new and perhaps beneficial technologies. Corporations are working to solve this problem by creating more infrastructures that allows consumers to use technology without having to think about it. This trend in technology is known as ubiquitous computing and it will shape the way that people receive new products in the coming years.[634]

Applications

One of the ways that this ubiquitous computing will be implemented is with applications. As you will remember applications allow the user to download features to an already existing product. But along with this ability, applications also make it easier for the user to keep up with all the data that new technologies generate. This allows the user to get the benefits of a wide array of devices that an Internet of Things would bring without exhausting the individual's utility from the technology.

There are many applications that have arisen in the recent years that build a nice foundation for what the Internet of Things will be like. One major area is in location based applications. Foursquare is an application that takes down the user's location and tells other people in their area that they are near.[635] Yelp! is an application that gives the user reviews of restaurants based on their current location.[636] Applications like these get users accustomed to sharing a previously guarded piece of information (their location) with an unaccountable third party.

Another very important set of applications for the Internet of Things will be digital wallet applications. These services allow users to pay for goods by swiping a credit or debit card through a swipe attached to their cell phone. Well known examples of these applications include Swipely, Square, and Google Wallet [637] Through their usage another piece of guarded information is shared and another barrier for making a purchase falls.

The third and perhaps most critical application that we are seeing widespread use of now are the social networking applications. It is in this area of applications that Facebook's role becomes important. With the infrastructure that these companies have made about RFID, Wi-Fi, and cell phones there are a lot of possibilities for information collection. But to get the greatest accuracy in creating a digital doppelganger, corporations will need applications that delve deeper into the personal life of the individual than the hardware can. It just happens that Facebook can dig the deepest.

Having a detailed look at the identity of the individual will allow advertisers to market themselves to individuals through RFID the same way they would through Facebook. One expected future is that organizations will be able to identify individuals through their social media profile when they walk into a designated area such as a store or community center. Having the identity of what would previously be an anonymous individual will allow the organization to supply information to them though their wireless device. It will also allow for the certification that the individual belongs in an area that would normally be restricted to the public.[638]

But for this seamless identification to happen there needs to be a mass acceptance of the centralized social networking we see in the market place today. As we have seen Facebook has done a marvelous job at getting people to accept a life with very little privacy in exchange for small social and economic benefits. That is what the Internet of Things will be only in a much larger real-world setting. The result will be a gamification of life just like there is a gamification of digital interaction on Facebook.

For this technological movement to gain success it is important that Facebook's brand of doing things spread, but it is not so much important that Facebook spread or even exist in the future. Facebook could be overtaken by a well-funded rival in the future. At the current time, it seems doubtful that this could happen but even if it did it would not affect the grand scheme of things. All that is necessary is for the usurper to embrace the mass collection policies that

Facebook has popularized. If we consider what we have seen in domestic as well as foreign markets it appears that mass collection is what the foreseeable future holds.

Guidance

There is significant reason to believe that Facebook's role in the Internet of Things has not only been expected but guided by members of its board of directors. A major reason why these people are on the board is for their knowledge of the industries and companies associated with Facebook. It could be assumed that if these people have extensive knowledge of what other companies know about the Internet of Things that they would apply that information to their roles at Facebook.

One significant connection worth examining is former Facebook board member Jim Breyer who was on the board of Wal-Mart during his time at Facebook. Wal-Mart as we have seen is a major force for the implementation of RFID and would benefit greatly from a future built around Facebook. It should be noted that Wal-Mart also does business with Facebook for marketing, but that is no reason to occupy a board seat on a social networking corporation like Facebook.[639] The Internet of Things is important to Wal-Mart which is why Facebook is important to Wal-Mart.

A second board member, Peter Thiel, also has a major connection to the Internet of Things. He earned his fame with helping to found the digital currency tool PayPal in 1999.[640] Digital currency through e-commerce sites like eBay was a significant stepping stone for the Internet of Things at the end of the 20th century. Worth noting is that in the Second Quarter of 2013, PayPal handled $5,445 worth of transactions every second. Every day they transact 7.7 million payments from their 100 million plus account holders.[641] It is safe to say that Peter Thiel may be harboring dreams of a cashless society that the Internet of Things would require.

Another board member, Reed Hastings, serves on the boards of Facebook, Wal-Mart, and Microsoft. For those who might not remember Microsoft gave Facebook $240 million in 2007. With the line of products that they are launching that involve embedded technology they are highly dependent on Facebook succeeding, as well as having a relationship with where Facebook goes as a company. Having a board member on a company that has a major role to play in the future is a wise move on their part.

A fourth connection to this agenda is Marc Andreessen who also serves on the board of Hewlett Packard which has significant interests in wireless technology. Andreessen is also a founding member investment firm Andreessen Horowitz which has invested in several digital currency companies such as Foursquare, Stripe, and Signifyd that all hope to profit from this Internet of Things.[642]

A recent addition to Facebook board of directors is Susan Desmond-Hellmann who is also on the boards of Bristol-Myers Squibb and Proctor & Gamble.[643] Bristol- Myers Squibb has interests in using RFID for medical purposes that could be helped by a widespread acceptance of Facebook. Her relationship to P&G is also significant because of their push for RFID in resource distribution.[644] What other knowledge she could add to a social networking company like Facebook seems hard to imagine.

In addition to these board members with ties to somewhat out of place organizations, there are numerous Facebook employees who have come from Google in recent years. Board member Sheryl Sandberg being the most notable; she spent several years working for the world's most popular search engine. Other notable former Google employees include Ben Ling, Eliot Schrage, Lars Rasmussen and Omar Hamoui.[645] While edging the competition is one reason for this Google focused recruitment, their experience dealing with a company heavily involved in the Internet of Things surely has had some effect.

These connections are not solely presented to suggest that there no legitimate reasons for these directors to exist on the board. Breyer and Thiel have significant Silicon Valley business experience. Andreessen helped to invent Netscape which was a major milestone in the history of the internet And Susan Desmond-Hellman worked at Genentech, where CFO David Ebersman also held a position several years ago.[646] The connections are pointed out to understand what effect the Internet of Things would have on Facebook, not suggest that these directors are there only for the implementation of RFID/Smart Technology.

But what can be said from these connections is that these people are making decisions at Facebook which may be based on their knowledge of what these other companies are planning for the Internet of Things. And that same logic can go the other way as well. Perhaps these individuals are using their knowledge of what Facebook plans to do to help guide their corporations like Wal-Mart and Proctor & Gamble down the right path. There is something going on with these companies, and the connections should prevent us from ever thinking otherwise.

Uses for the public

What should be troublesome about this shaping of technology for corporate gains is that wireless technology can have great uses for the use public. This is not an inherently evil system; it is only being shaped into something evil by opportunistic individuals. Radio frequency is a way for mankind's machines to communicate with one another. This should be a way to make life easier, not harder. And we should not forsake wireless technology, we should protect it.

One needed use for this technology is in energy conservation. Appliances and even buildings can be outfitted with monitoring technology that will communicate with other machines to determine appropriate energy usage. Think of a refrigerator that adjusts its temperature when it knows it's getting too hot or cold.[647] It is a way of applying a system of intelligence to something that before would only change when someone told it to. Applying this kind of strategy to the entire grid could serve to end a system of waste and environmental degradation that has characterized our energy usage for so long.

A second needed use for this technology could be in weather prediction. By taking in the necessary information about the environment weather forecasters could make more accurate forecasts in a faster amount of time. While things such as rainy and sunny days might seem trivial, predicting tsunamis and tornadoes would save the lives of people who receive emergency warnings earlier.[648] Extreme scenarios like this could become more common as global climate change continues its progression at the behest of our corporations.

A third use is in overall efficiency. Wireless technology can make life easier when it is made to do so. Whether that is in the operation of a business or in the management of a home, this technology has a place. It goes beyond energy conservation to the act of having tasks take care of themselves though automation. A robot that can clean my house is one example.

The final and perhaps the most pivotal use that wireless communication brings to mankind are in spreading the internet's use among the population. For many years, the internet was kept only for those who could afford internet access. That constriction is no longer what it is today because of Wi-Fi networks that allow low income individuals to access to the public work known as the internet that everyone should be able to enjoy. The internet is not free, but because of wireless technology it is not kept in the hands of the few either.

But these are not the benefits that are driving the Internet of Things. This technology is being crafted into a commercial technology. And that is what will shape the implementation and usage of the Internet of Things. Any benefit to infrastructure or the environment will be secondary and only used to lure people into the system. The primary goal of the corporations is to track what makes people buy what they buy. To accomplish that goal there needs to be information coming in as fast as possible.

It could also be assumed that without this negative corporate influence that is obsessed with profit, this technology could be used for some good. For that to happen this would have to be driven by a scientific community and a conscious public that is willing to look at the risks as well as the benefits of using wireless technology. We have already received the predictable result of surveillance and exploitation by letting corporations do what they want, perhaps if innovation were decided on a more democratic basis we would get a different result.

Insecurity of the System

What adds to the unacceptability of this system is that RFID chips can easily be hacked. This is mainly because most chips lack the necessary encryption standards to ward off an attack. And even encrypted chips that are present in smarter devices can be broken into with a moderate effort. Encryption standards for these devices are generally low because it would cost too much power for the device as well as money for the people who sell these things to spend money on the higher standards of encryption.[649]

Keeping costs down is one of the most important requirements to having RFID implemented on a full scale. This is especially true for passive or "dumb" RFID tags that are located on boxes and other non-electronic goods. These RFID tags are designed to be sold by the billions. A fluctuation in price by a few cents would have major consequences for the technology's adoption.[650] Until the technology improves to the point where it is almost free to encrypt these devices, RFID will remain an easy target for hackers.

An effective way to access the information contained on an RFID chip is for a hacker to build an E-reader. With the necessary materials and access to an internet connection, an individual can make their own E-Reader which will allow them to read any RFID tag they should come upon that is not encrypted. It should be remembered that these E-Readers are not that complicated to begin with. They consist of an antenna, a communication module, and a tag to bounce the signal off of. If an individual needs instructions there are numerous videos online that will take them through the construction process.[651]

The need for the construction of an E-Reader assumes that the hacker is not willing to risk the functionality of their smart phone which will be able to scan RFID chips for commercial purposes. These smart phones will be able to "read" but they will not be able to "write". Writing will be reserved to the manufacturer of the chips and the company that uses them. Writing requires impersonation of the chips designated signal, which would require augmentation of the phone to mimic the signal of the writer.[652]

Once the hacked reader or "cloner" as they are sometimes called is assembled, the hacker can then begin the process of impersonation. This impersonation will be possible because the cloner can elicit a signal that will allow reading the RFID tags of nearby objects. Once that signal has been read, the cloner can than record the signal for future usage. When the owner of the device wants to use that scanned signal, they can than mimic the signal to other products and e-readers.[653]

An example of how this could be useful is in the impersonation of people who are carrying RFID smart cards. All the hacker would have to do is get within the vicinity of the person with the smart card and then find it on their cloned E-Reader. Once they have captured the RFID signal, they can then repeat the signal of the person to get access to things like buildings and doors that use RFID security.[654] Cloned E-Readers can also be used for changing data that is stored on RFID chips. This has examples such as switching prices on products that have RFID or using it to obtain information contained by the chip when it scanned someone else's chip.[655]

This begs the question however of the liability by the RFID companies about security. A defense could be that the companies do not know how unsafe this technology is. This counterargument might be credible were it not for a clear example of the corporations behind RFID acknowledging the failure of this technology. In 2011, the Discovery Channel show *Myth Busters* tried to do an entire episode exposing how simple it is to hack into RFID chips. When the interests involved in RFID technology heard about this, they ordered discovery channel to pull the episode. These interests included various credit card companies and resource distributors who stand to lose money if RFID's insecurity is known. To this day *Myth Busters* host Adam Savage is not allowed to discuss just how unreliable RFID chips really are and the public is once again denied access to important information.[656]

The *Myth Busters* incident shows that RFID technology is recognized as unsafe by the industry. They may not acknowledge how insecure their product is, but they know. They know just like Facebook knows how insecure their service is. But the corporations can get away with this insecurity because most people will not be able to create an RFID signal impersonator. Just like how Facebook accounts are relatively easy to hack into but most people do not know how to do it either.

While RFID should not be trusted, we should also show hesitation with putting our trust in smart phones that also have vulnerabilities because of their connection to the internet. Along with having the same range of attacks such as social engineering and malware, mobile devices can be even less secure than desktops because of their wide spread usage of unsecure Wi-Fi networks. The threats of online attacks also assume that the user has not lost their phone or had it stolen. According to the 2012 Norton Cybercrime Report 1/3 people have either lost or had their cell phone stolen before.[657]

No Control

After looking at these insecurities we should try to keep our eyes on the bigger picture that exists with surveillance. This argument over security in the Internet of Things misses the crucial point of ownership. The data that these smart devices take in is not really theirs to take.   Corporations or governments do not deserve to have this information any more than criminals do. If these RFID security problems are ever solved, it will only give the individuals who they track a false sense of security. The goal of the public should be the elimination of this form of surveillance instead of its perceived pacification.

It could be assumed that actors who would have control and access to the information created by this system would be unaccountable for the most part. As we have seen with the information that Facebook has collected so far, there has been few obstacles between this information and those who want it. The government is getting increasingly good at collecting the information without even a warrant and corporations only have to pay the necessary price. A moderately skilled hacker could break into Facebook, the smart devices, and the RFID products that will soon go along with it. The security of this technological government is an illusion.

A danger from this perversion of what could be a very useful technology, the Internet of Things will probably either become a surveillance tool or it will not be implemented at all out of fear. Conserving energy, making buildings and appliances more efficient, helping predict changes in weather, these are beneficial uses for a technology. The problem is that these benefits are going to be tied with surveillance and commercialization for the sake of profit. Human good will not be the goal of this technology, profit will be.

By most accounts the RFID devices that will make up this surveillance network will be so numerous that resisting them once the infrastructure is in place will be futile. In Katherine Albrecht and Liz McIntyre's seminal work *SpyChips (2006)*, they detail how companies wish to subtly place RFID in every product and piece of identification that they can while the public stays unaware. This strategy is what authors Albrecht and McIntyre refer to as "delay the debate until it is too late."[658] By the time any real resistance is mounted against this surveillance it will be considered impossible for the infrastructure to be removed.

That type of strategy is what makes technology so much more powerful in advancing a national security state than any legal or political maneuvers ever could. This is largely because technology often seems inevitable in how it turns out. People seem to think for example that social networks have to be geared around data collection and that any other method is infeasible. Cars that run on gasoline as compared to electricity are another example that has been proven false. All technology is guided to go in a certain direction. This is something that venture capitalists understand very well which is why they spend so much money trying to influence technology to suit their interests. It is the job of the public to make sure that they exert their influence on technology or else it will be used for their exploitation. Because most of the technology that the public has been given in recent years (cars, the internet, television, and phones) have been used for their exploitation, it is safe to say they need to start looking at how the technology they use will benefit them instead of just passively accepting what they are given.

17. Central Intelligence

After looking at where Facebook has come from and where it is headed, it seems that there are still unanswered questions as to how Facebook has developed into what it has become. While we have examined numerous aspects of society such as venture capital, the computing industry, and even Facebook's creator Mark Zuckerberg, we still have not addressed the role that the government has played in all of this. It would seem strange if there was not some input by government when we consider how beneficial Facebook has been in giving them information about the world.

And if there was some degree of cooperation between the government and Facebook, it would not be out of keeping with what has happened in the past. Previous intelligence gathering operations have used private companies and illegal monitoring to carry out their agendas. Other consumer technologies in the past have had government influence that was widely acknowledged by the public at the time. Oddly enough, some of the people who worked for those governments funded technologies are employed at Facebook today. When examine this relationship between the United States government, and Facebook, the relationship is quite substantial.

Convenience

The driving reason for why we are looking for a link between the government and Facebook is how good Facebook is for advancing the government's objectives. Previous chapters have covered the amount of information that is collected and the ways that it can be used, but there is more to Facebook than just a lot of data. Any intelligence gathering program for better or for worse can collect information; however it is the way that a program collects information that determines its worth to the agency that uses it.

Facebook for instance goes beyond what the average intelligence gathering program can do by being mostly independent of government. On paper Facebook does not have a government budget. It does not employ government personnel. It does not occupy space in a federal building. But at the same time, the government has access to whatever information that they believe they need from Facebook. It is almost like a gift from the tech community to the intelligence community.

A reason why the government goes to Facebook for information so often is that Facebook can go where the government simply cannot go. Theoretically the intelligence community could develop a program that would collect all the information that Facebook did. But if that program did exist it would be very difficult to keep a secret and if it became public it would be subject to regulation. That regulation while not very strict would still be more burdensome than what Facebook lives under. Facebook can solicit billions of photos and comments out of people every day and from a legal standpoint no one is able to do much about it.

Having a privatized intelligence program also allows for the recruitment of highly skilled workers that would normally be out of reach for government payroll budgets. The marketplace brings with it the ability to pay the best people what they believe they should be paid. Because of that financial elasticity, the talent pool available for the program increases and in turn creates a culture of innovation that encourages people to work hard at what they do.

What has also happened is that Facebook allows for a more relaxed atmosphere than what someone might experience at an intelligence agency or even a contracting firm. The people at a contractor like SAIC for example are probably ex-NSA or ex-CIA types that deal in very serious issues every day that are depressing and at time boring. The people at Facebook or Google on the other hand probably play video games in their spare time and are still young enough to believe that what they are doing is okay. There are tradeoffs for both scenarios of course, but there is a benefit to having the hip, fun experience that a worker gets at a Silicon Valley internet company.

Patterns

What also should draw our suspicion to Facebook is that domestic spying has never been out of bounds for the U.S. government. There have been numerous government programs which were specifically designed for that purpose throughout the history of the United States. While these projects have come and gone, their legacy remains as a testament to what the government will do when it perceives danger. With the years of Cold War intrigue that filled the public's consciousness over the past century, what follows should not come as a surprise.

A pointed example of this is Operation Shamrock that started at the end of World War II. Shamrock was a surveillance program that was run by the NSA's forerunner the Foreign Surveillance Agency. It functioned through cooperation between the FSA and telecommunications companies such as RCA Global and ITT World Communications. These companies among others turned over millions of telegrams to the FSA no questions asked. It was also alleged that the FSA and later NSA had rooms in these communications companies that were specifically designed for the warrantless copying of domestic and international communication.[659] After thirty years the program was officially closed for being considered unconstitutional by a senate judiciary committee popularly known as the Church Committee, headed by Senator Frank Church in 1975.[660]

Following the findings of the Church Committee and the passage of the Foreign Intelligence Surveillance Act in 1978, domestic monitoring still continued from what the record shows. The strongest example came from the massive Echelon program run by the NSA. Echelon was a global satellite network that monitored nearly all electronic communication on earth. This network included participation from the United Kingdom, Canada, Australia, and New Zealand to expand the NSA's reach around the globe. While Echelon has been rendered somewhat obsolete with the mass acceptance of hard to tap fiber optic cable, by all accounts it is still functioning on some level to capture communication signals that leave the atmosphere.[661]

A program of far smaller size that was perhaps equally controversial to Echelon was DCS1000 or "Carnivore" that was run by the FBI. Carnivore was a packet sniffing program that allowed FBI agents to read emails of domestic targets. To use the program on a suspect, an agent had to go through several lines of authorization. If the requirements were met, the FBI would contact the service provider and have them set up a bug on the suspect's network. This would allow the agents to monitor the traffic on that network until the system known as carnivore came across the packets they were looking for.[662] After years of use the project was disbanded and replaced with less invasive software.[663]

As computing technology became more powerful, government data mining continued to get more and more sophisticated and aggressive. The first real testament to this pattern came with Able Danger, an intelligence gathering operation that utilized data mining techniques and link theory on open source intelligence. The program founded in 1999 was co-managed by the U.S. Special Operations Command in conjunction with the Defense Intelligence Agency. The way it operated is still largely classified, but a large amount of information was made available to the public in 2006 following a Senate investigation into the mishandling of information regarding the September 11 terrorist attacks. Following the termination of Able Danger out of civil liberties concerns, plans were then made for a follow up program known as Able Providence that would achieve similar goals with less abuse.[664]

In addition to the data mining programs of the DIA, the NSA came up with a program around the time of 9/11 known as Thinthread. Thinthread worked essentially by pooling large amounts of data and analyzing it immediately for relevancy. Certain information such as telephone numbers would be encrypted until authorization was gained from a judge. This prevented extraneous information that may have included data on innocent citizens from reaching prying eyes. If someone decided to decrypt without authorization, the system would show that the corrupt activity had taken place.[665]

In this respect, Thinthread aided privacy and also reduced the strain on the NSA's already overburdened data collection system. The program was also considered a fast and effective form of data collection when compared to its contemporaries. On the other hand, Thinthread picked up lot information on American citizens that is wasn't allowed to do by law. This reason as well as Thinthread's small size and cost led to it being overcome by a much large program, more expensive program known as Trailblazer.[666]

Trailblazer was another project started by the National Security Agency to track electronic communication. It worked in the same manner as Thinthread did except it didn't have the encryption privacy feature. This would allow irrelevant information to be seen without gaining a court order. Along with intruding constitutionally protected privacy, the program would cost hundreds of millions of dollars more than Thinthread. The heavy price tag along with its approval led some to suggest it wasn't result of the agency's collusion with government contractors. It predictably failed to produce good intelligence and was discontinued in 2006.[667]

Another failed as well as incredibly costly intelligence program was the Multistate Antiterrorism Information Exchange or MATRIX as it was aptly named. MATRIX was an information sharing system conceived in 2003 by Seisint Inc. The purpose of MATRIX was to help combine databases for state law enforcement departments much like a fusion center would.[668] The defenders of MATRIX point out that the system only organized information that would be available to law enforcement anyway. This argument failed to prove MATRIX'S legitimacy for domestic intelligence gathering, and was discontinued in 2003. The major reason for its cancellation was the inability to reconcile privacy concerns.[669]

The third of the big modern domestic spying programs was Total Information Awareness or (TIA) that was started by John Poindexter of the CIA. Poindexter as you may remember was a former defendant in the Iran-Contra Scandal and member of the Regan administration. The purpose of his program was to assemble a major database that took in as much information as possible on as many people as it could. With the database, it was hoped the government could identify existing and potential terrorists by using complex algorithms based off a profile. After congressional funding for the project was withdrawn over feared abuses, the project was closed in 2003.[670]

The current manifestation of government surveillance that Americans are under now comes from the Terrorist Interdiction Program. In 2002, President George W. Bush issued an executive order allowing the National Security Agency to monitor communications within the United States and without obtaining a court issued warrant. This went beyond current laws such as FISA that made illegal the wiretapping of American citizens without obtaining a warrant. The program covers various forms of electronic communication such as phone calls, emails, internet activity, and text messages.[671]

While originally promising to end this surveillance during his election campaign, President of the United States Barack Obama has expanded government surveillance. He has signed bills for its reauthorization through laws such as FISA and the Patriot Act. He has also publicly supported this type of surveillance during the leak by NSA whistleblower Edward

Snowden.[672] Should the President try to end this monitoring, the Congress that we discussed in earlier chapters would probably not support him. Obama is not the solution to this problem.

These intelligence programs show that domestic monitoring has been going on for a long time. It could be assumed that if these actors were able to conduct a program like Shamrock or TIA that they would assume they could do it again. It is not a matter of if they would get caught so much as what they can get done before they get caught and have to start over again. Because of this lack of accountability, the government would probably assume that if a technology like Facebook were to arise that they would have relatively unrestricted access to it. If that were the case, then it would also not be out of order for them to try and shape that technology as it developed.

Creations

If the government had such power to watch whoever they wanted through electronic communication, there may also be a desire to create devices that would benefit their ability to gather and analyze intelligence as well. This would be done with the expectation that the intelligence community would have access to it eventually anyway if it developed outside of their grasp. Speeding up the discovery process along with shaping technology to suit their interest could be justified under the name of national security and preventing major crimes. This is not just an assumption about what would be nice strategy for future technologies because this is something that the government already does on a regular basis.

The government has several ways of developing technologies that they think they will need in the future. The first is through providing funding for research projects. In military research for instance, the Defense Advanced Research Project Agency or DARPA would fund a technology that they wish to see develop. This would be done knowing that the research cannot receive investment somewhere else. An example could be the invention of the Internet which only became a commercial venture decades after it started and was turned over to the public. Other relevant examples include GPS and video conferencing that also started off as military research projects. [673] Unlike the public, the military does not just sit idly by hoping their wishes will be granted by the corporations.

For more civilian focused technology, the National Science Foundation can be looked to for funding. The NSF typically gives money to universities and colleges to develop needed technologies that are far from commercial viability. An example that is related to the Internet is the Internet backbone or NSFNET that was started in 1987. The backbone created a necessary public highway for internet traffic to travel on that allowed the internet to expand to its current state. It continued to be funded by the NSF until it was commercially able to run on its own in 1995.[674]

Another example of this kind of development was Mosaic, a web browser developed at National Center for Supercomputing Applications at the University of Illinois Urbana Champaign. Someone who was critical in the development of Mosaic was Marc Andreessen, current board member of Facebook. Following his ground-breaking accomplishment with Mosaic, Andreessen would later turn Mosaic into commercial venture called Netscape.[675]

Along with web browsers, the government has also had a hand in the development of search engines. The world's most famous search engine, Google, was developed at Stanford University by founders Larry Page and Sergey Brin in 1996. They developed this search engine with the aid of a government grant and the use of a tax payer funded laboratory at Stanford. The grant was through a project known as the Digital Library Project which was funded with money from the NSF, DARPA and NASA.[676] After Google got up in running it received funding from the venture capital community until it went public.[677] Google now has open ties with the NSA for the purposes of cyber warfare and data mining.[678] There are also numerous former employees from Google that now work at Facebook.[679]

The intelligence community may also use investment to further technologies that have a more immediate place in the private market. This is done through the CIA venture capital arm In-Q-Tel that purchases equity in companies that they think will be helpful to them in the future.[680] An example of this could be Recorded Future that has a product which the market likes, but that also received In-Q-Tel investment in 2010 to survive as an intelligence analysis product. As a result of the support, the company is continuing their work and the intelligence community gets a product that they may not be able to get through government research.[681]

Another example of a company that received money from In-Q-Tel was Palantir, Peter Thiel's company. In-Q-Tel invested $2 million into Palantir in 2005.[682] A company that we discussed earlier, Visible Technologies, also received money from In-Q-Tel. They received $2 million in June 2009.[683] And to draw even more suspicion, Attensity also reportedly received an investment from In-Q-Tel in 2001.[684] This is why we covered these companies earlier. To not just show what these contractors are doing but to demonstrate their connection to government.

And then there are companies that do have an intelligence gathering component to them like Facebook or Twitter, but they do not need any direct government funding to make it through to the IPO. They have a good enough product that the public will want to use as much as the government does. But what may be happening with these companies is that they are being steered in the direction that the government wants them to head in. Government influence may also be needed to make sure the company becomes a success that can stand on its own. While there are plenty of good ideas; there are a lot fewer successful companies.

The question that needs to be answered now is how that influence would come from government. After all they are not directly giving funding to or supplying the facilities for Facebook to the best of our knowledge. But there may be another way that they are influencing this network. This could be done using connections the government has in Facebook. This type of influence would be done discreetly, but not entirely in the dark.

Connections

What cannot be ignored are the number of connections that exist between Facebook and the intelligence community. Some of these figures have played major roles in the development of Facebook while others are merely associates of the company. All of them however are significant and drive the suspicion that the government may have had an influence on the network.

To illustrate this government link, we should start with Peter Thiel. As the largest of the initial angel investors, Peter Thiel's money helped to kick start Facebook on its path to achieving a billion members. Along with helping start Facebook however, he also helped start Palantir Technologies and Quid which both helped to produce intelligence analysis tools.[685] To help steer Palantir, Thiel even put one of friends, Dr. Alexander Karp to help head the project.[686]

In addition to Karp, there are also several other former employees of Thiel that have worked at his intelligence contracting companies. CEO of Quid Kevin Freedman worked for PayPal and after that he also served as the CFO of Slide Inc.[687] Slide is also one of the first companies that the Founder's Fund invested in. Co-founder of Palantir Technologies Joe Lonsdale worked for PayPal as well as Clarium Capital.[688] All three are companies that were run by Peter Thiel. Executive Vice President of Palantir Stephen Cohen also previously worked for Clarium Capital after graduating from Stanford University.[689]

In addition to his own personal connection to the elite employees of Palantir and Quid, several of Thiel's former associates at PayPal have also invested in these companies. Former PayPal employee and Slide founder Max Levichin has put money into Quid. And former PayPal employee and LinkedIn, Square investor Keith Rabois has put money into Palantir.[690] In helping advance the will of the surveillance state, it appears that Thiel and his former employees stand to make a lot of money from their investments.

These individual investors are in addition to Thiel's venture capital firm the Founder's Fund which has invested in Palantir, Quid, and Facebook. Partners at the Founder's Fund include PayPal co-founder Ken Howery, PayPal employee Luke Nosek, former Google employee Brian Singerman, and former Facebook president Sean Parker.[691] Also interesting to note is the Founder's Fund support of a company known as RoboteX.[692] They literally make robots for law enforcement and military operations.[693] While the robots are still at what one might consider a prototype stage, they are still symbolic of a security state agenda.

A second major influence on Facebook's path has been Jim Breyer the CEO of Accel Partners. Breyer became a board member of Facebook in 2005 following Accel's $27.5 million investment in Facebook.[694] One of Breyer's most famous feats as a business man came with his sale of BBN Technologies to Raytheon in 2009 on the same day of his sale of Marvel Entertainment to Disney.[695] BBN Technologies is a social media monitoring company that fits very nicely into the government's monitoring of Facebook. Breyer was also the former Chairman of the National Venture Capitalists Association as well as the former chairman of the Harvard Business School.[696]

What makes Breyer's time at BBN also significant is that he served at the same time as former In-Q-Tel board member and DARPA overseer Dr. Anita K. Hill. Also connected to Breyer was In-Q-Tel's former CEO Gilman Louie. He served on the board of the National Venture Capitalist Association the same time as Breyer did.[697] Both of these actors could have possibly told Breyer information about what the government wanted. This could have then led him to shape Facebook accordingly to create an environment on the internet which urged domestic monitoring. At the very least Thiel managed to capitalize off of what his former board member may have been doing.

After Accel Partners made their investment with Facebook in 2005, Greylock Partners purchased equity in Facebook in 2006. This is significant because a member of Greylock's board of directors is Howard Cox, a former board member at In-Q-Tel. Prior to working for In-Q-Tel, Cox served in the United State military during Vietnam and later attended Harvard Business School. He would then go on to work under Secretary of Defense and World Bank President Robert McNamara in the Johnson Administration. Along with being a partner at Greylock, Cox was the head of the NVCA.[698] He now serves on the board of Greylock with Reid Hoffman who has served on the board since 2009.[699]

The fourth person to demonstrate a clear connection between Facebook and the government is Sheryl Sandberg. Following her employment for the World Bank, Sandberg worked as Chief of Staff of the Treasury for the Clinton Administration under then Treasury Secretary Larry Summers. After leaving government Sandberg than went to Google which also has suspicious ties to the intelligence community. Sandberg worked at Google until being recruited to work for Facebook in 2008.[700] Since her arrival Facebook's growth has exploded enormously and the features have become more intrusive than ever.

Another Facebook board member who also served under the Clinton Administration was Erskine Bowles in who joined the board in 2011. Bowles served as Chief of Staff for the Clinton Administration during Clinton's first term. While Chief of Staff he helped direct the federal government's response to the Oklahoma City Bombing. While Bowles is mainly responsible at Facebook for taking care of the financial books, this is still a service that is valuable to the company and no less demerits his connection to government.[701]

Also significant are the members of management who hold connections to the intelligence community. Former head of Platform development Ben Ling invested in Palantir in 2010.[702] Also interesting is that Ling originally worked at Google, but left to join Facebook. After going from Google to Facebook he eventually went back to Google in 2008.[703] Ling represents another Facebook connection that may be profiting off an opportunity that Facebook presents for intelligence contracting profits.

And finally, former Head of Counsel at Facebook Ted Ullyot served in the Bush Administration as Chief of Staff at the Justice Department and later as deputy assistant to the president. Before his time in the Bush Administration he clerked for Supreme Court Justice Antonin Scalia. Ullyot resigned his position at Facebook in 2013.[704] We cannot say for certain whether his resignation was tied to the NSA whistleblower leak that occurred around the same time. Either way, the Justice Department is still represented in the management levels of Facebook by Joe Sullivan who is the head of Facebook's security.[705]

If we consider the positions that these actors have held in Facebook it seems that they would certainly have the power to pressure Facebook to suit a certain purpose. This is especially true when we consider the tremendous amount of influence that Peter Thiel, Sean Parker and Jim Breyer would have had over Zuckerberg in the early years of his career. Other people such as Sandberg and Ling would be able to carry that influence into the product their management positions. And what influence Bowles may have had on Facebook is uncertain really, other than him perhaps being a fourth vote for whatever these other three may have wanted to implement. Greylock Partners employees Cox and Hoffman could have certainly played a similar role as that of Thiel or Breyer, just to a lesser degree.

To explain these connections there are two theories that may or may not totally explain what we are seeing. The first explanation could be that the government through institutions such as DARPA and In-Q-Tel may have used Gilman Louie, Anita K. Hill, and Howard Cox along with others to influence Facebook investors and board members. The government also could have used contacts such as Sandberg, Bowles, and Ullyot to make sure that Facebook ran smoothly. Meanwhile other less important players such as Levichin, Rabois, and Ling may have just profited from what Facebook had created in the intelligence analysis marketplace.

The second explanation could be that the connections between government and Facebook are simply opportunistic actors who are taking advantage of their role in Facebook. Thiel, Breyer, Hoffman, Levichin, Rabois, and Ling are just capitalizing off inside information about what the intelligence community wants. Bowles, Ullyot, and Sandberg are perhaps just there out of a professional coincidence of some sort. They take jobs that require an amoral attitude about life and then earn money and credentials from just going along with the way things are.

Perhaps the truth is somewhere in between these two theories. A combination of influence combined with opportunity may have led to Facebook becoming a perfect intelligence gathering machine. And as to what effect these connections have had on Facebook we can only speculate. It is possible that that these connections are at this company out of the increasing proximity of government to industry. That is not a wild assumption to make either, but it does require ignoring a lot of other information such as past intelligence programs and current usage of Facebook by government that really call any assertion of coincidence into question.

Coming Soon

If Facebook was shaped by some or all of these actors with the expectation of later government intrusion, there would be also later events that we could expect to take place. Much like the telephone networks and internet service providers, Facebook could be pressured into granting the government forced inclusion on the network. While the CALEA and FISA laws allow for the forced supplying of backdoors to government agencies, Facebook could also be pressured to legally allow law enforcement in with laws like CISPA. The leaks by whistleblowers in the recent years would suggest this is already happening, but with the passage of a law it could be used to imprison or kill people using evidence obtained from Facebook.

What we are also currently seeing is the legitimization of such behavior in the media. Instead of there being a public outcry over this issue, there is instead a debate that is brushed aside by many as unserious. The motto of national security and the length of time that domestic spying has gone on have made this behavior controversial, but not unacceptable. While it could be assumed the public would be in opposition to government involvement in the creation of Facebook, the monitoring of it does not cause much of a surprise.

With the acceptability of domestic spying and perhaps one day the manipulation of publicly available technology, we may see government abuse of the medium of communication. Not only would they be monitoring the communication, but they would be using it as a weapon against targets. The COINTELPRO scandal once again is an excellent example of a situation that society could be placed in with Facebook. But we could also look at more current examples like the censorship of Google searches as well as the use of Facebook and Twitter to promote a State Department agenda during the Arab Spring.[706] With the necessary power the government can either turn weapons of democracy against the people or they can create their own to serve whatever purpose they should desire.

18. Special People

The story unfortunately does not end with the United States government. It also appears that Facebook has connections to several elite international organizations that play a major role in determining world affairs. These organizations include members of the world's most powerful from all sectors of society. Numerous conspiracy theories surround these groups because of their secrecy and their influence on global politics. The examination of these organizations is not done to indulge in any paranoid fantasies, but only to help provide understanding for the role that they play in Facebook.

For our purposes, we will look at four specific organizations that hold connections to Facebook's leadership. They are: the Bilderberg Group, the Council on Foreign Relations, the Trilateral Commission, and the World Economic Forum. While there are probably more organizations who hold connections to Facebook that could be examined, these groups have the strongest links worth examining. The point of this section is not to chase every connection that exists out there, but to provide explanation for why Facebook developed into its current state.

The Bilderberg Group

The most controversial group of any elite association in the world is the Bilderberg Group. For the uninitiated, the Bilderberg Group is a forum of 120 individuals who meet to discuss matters that include economics, diplomacy, technology, business, and politics. The topics of the discussions as well the members list is available on a website known as Bilderberg Meetings that is run in cooperation with the organization. Attendees of Bilderberg meetings are told not to discuss what is spoken at the gatherings to ensure that members will speak freely.[707] Because of this members of the Bilderberg Group are sometimes treated with suspicion as though they are members of some sort of secret cabal.

The group meets annually at various locations around the world but they originally met in the Bilderberg Hotel in Oosterbeek, Holland 1954, which is where they get their name.[708] Famous American attendees of the Bilderberg Conference have included: Bill Clinton, Tom Daschle, Bill Gates[709], Gerald Ford, John Kerry, Henry Kissinger, Condoleezza Rice, Richard Pearle, and Colin Powell.[710] These individuals not only have prestigious names but they have also played key roles in the history of the United State of America. And these are just a few of the many big names that can be seen on the membership and attendee list of Bilderberg. One can only speculate at where they all might lead.

Among these less notable names are several figures associated with Facebook. They include: Reid Hoffman, Donald E. Graham, Alexander Karp, Peter Thiel, Chris Hughes, Sean Parker, Peter D. Sutherland, Craig Mundie, and Larry Summers. Some of these people have already been discussed, but for others there is some elaboration needed. Chris Hughes was one of the original founding members of Facebook. Peter D. Sutherland is the CEO of Goldman Sachs International. Craig Mundie is the Chief of Officer of Strategy and Research at Microsoft. And Larry Summers is the former president of Harvard University and Sheryl Sandberg's former mentor.[711]

These names do not just provide a connection between Bilderberg and Facebook, but they also shed light on causes for those connections. Chris Hughes for instance served as the vice-President of Public relations for Facebook from 2004 to 2008. Hughes is also credited with spearheading the internet campaign of Barack Obama. This is significant because of the major role that social media played in the 2008 election. Hughes masterfully utilized this tool that virtually went ignored by the McCain campaign.[712] The results of that election seem to speak for themselves.

Keep in mind that Hughes is not an official Bilderberg member but he was invited to attend the conference in 2011. We could assume that the Group wanted to know his role in Obama's campaign but there may have been more to his visit than that. They could have asked him to run another campaign or perhaps teach other people what he knows about Facebook. Because Hughes has never been invited back to Bilderberg it may also be that he didn't want to cooperate with their agenda.

Another notable attendee worth looking at is Donald Graham, CEO of the Washington Post and board member of Facebook.[713] He held such a major influence on Mark Zuckerberg that Zuckerberg named Graham to the board in 2005. When Zuckerberg had to choose between accepting an investment from the Washington Post Company and Accel Partners, Graham told Zuckerberg to accept the investment from Accel instead. According to author Kirkpatrick this recommendation gained Zuckerberg's trust from that moment forward.[714] Ever since then it has been said that Graham is some sort of mentor.

Craig Mundie of Microsoft represents just one more connection between Microsoft and the global power structure. They have invested in Facebook, the Internet of Things, the surveillance state, and they have a seat the one of the most powerful tables in the land. It would be more of a surprise if someone from Microsoft was not there than if they were. We could also note how Zuckerberg attended a lecture by Bilderberg attendee and Microsoft founder Bill Gates at Harvard his sophomore year.[715] This probably doesn't mean anything but it is a strange coincidence.

However, another associate of Harvard, Larry Summers, is quite important when we examine the indirect connections he has to Facebook. Perhaps coincidentally or perhaps not, Larry Summers rejected the Winklevosses ethics complaints about Zuckerberg when he was president of Harvard in 2004.[716] This prevented Zuckerberg from getting kicked out of Harvard which would have looked far worse than him dropping out. It is difficult to see how Summers and Thiel could have been in conspiracy this early in Facebook's development, but it is still something that should be remembered.

Summers role as Sheryl Sandberg mentor is also something that warrants investigation. After graduating summa cum laude from Harvard in 1991 Sandberg studied under Summers for her graduate thesis. She followed Summers to the various positions he would take at the World Bank and later as Treasury Secretary in the Clinton Administration. Her relationship with Summers along with her position as COO could certainly have shaped how Facebook has developed and where it may be headed.[717]

The rest of these characters may be just as important but their connections are easier to point out so they require less explanation. Reid Hoffman was an angel investor in Facebook as well as numerous other social networks like Twitter and his own company LinkedIn.[718] Alexander Karp is a friend of Peter Thiel and the CEO of Palantir Technologies which is widely used by the U.S. government for intelligence analysis.[719] Sean Parker helped found Facebook and is also force for developing Web. 2.0 And Web 3.0 with his venture capital firms the Founder's Fund.[720] Sutherland is CEO of the international division of Goldman Sachs that gave Facebook a billion dollars in investment. These people are key players in Facebook, and they are all attendees of the Bilderberg Conference.

Two people not related heavily to Facebook but also attendees of the Bilderberg Conference according to author Daniel Estulin are former Presidential candidate and Senator Walter Mondale along with former Senator Frank Church.[721] Both of these people played important roles in the Church committee that regulated the intelligence community during the 1970s. While Mondale's attendance could be attributed to his chances of being president, Church's attendance is most likely connected to famous committee that bared his name.

When we recognize that members of the current intelligence apparatus in America have also been Bilderberg attendees it certainly raises some suspicion as to how they are influencing the issue. Current director Keith Alexander was an attendee of the meeting at the same time as Facebook angel investor Peter Thiel in 2012.[722] This represents another connection between the intelligence community and Facebook. These officials meeting with one of the most powerful groups in the world may also reveal why intelligence gathering abuses continue to be exposed and ignored at the same time

Council on Foreign Relations

Another organization with ties to Facebook is the Council on Foreign Relations or CFR. The CFR was first founded 1921 and is perhaps most well-known for publishing the magazine

Foreign Affairs. The Council has over 4,700 members who are exclusively U.S. citizens. The members of the group are picked from the elite members of American society by invitation only.[723]

The allegations against the CFR are similar to those made against the Bilderberg Group. But the CFR is more focused on the manipulation of the U.S. as a geopolitical actor than on other countries. Controlling the United States is obviously important because they have the strongest military force and have a massive role to play in economic affairs. This manipulation of the U.S is done through their large membership. The CFR has members of not only key government and corporate positions, but also key media opinion makers who influence the thoughts of the public. By controlling not only what America's leaders think, but also what its people think, the CFR is able to push whatever agenda it should desire.[724]

This paranoia over the CFR is increased, not mitigated, by seeing who is on the members list that they release. Well-known members of the CFR include: Madeleine Albright, Zbigniew Brzezinski, Tom Brokaw, Richard Cheney, Bill Clinton, Chelsea Clinton, George Clooney, Thomas Friedman, Grover Norquist, Colin L. Powell, Condoleezza Rice, David Rockefeller, Angelina Jolie, George Soros, Paul Wolfowitz, and Fareed Zakaria.[725]

People connected to the Council through Facebook include: Sheryl Sandberg, Erskine Bowles, Peter Thiel, Anita K. Jones, David Kirkpatrick, and Eliot Schrage.[726] These are the usual suspects except for Schrage, and Kirkpatrick. Eliot Schrage formerly worked at Google and is now the VP Communications and Public Policy at Facebook.[727] David Kirkpatrick is the author of *The Facebook Effect (*2010) and is an editor for *Forbes* magazine. *The Facebook Effect* is marketed as the "official story" about how Facebook came to be and serves to contradict *the Accidental Billionaires* and *The Social Network*. Kirkpatrick's membership to the CFR may explain why his book so heavily favors Zuckerberg's opinion of himself and his version of how he created Facebook.

Along with being influence by the CFR, it could also be that Kirkpatrick is a journalist who is hungry for access to a good news story like Zuckerberg and he is worried about angering him. The same question can be raised for Kirkpatrick's article about Sean Parker which appeared in Vanity Fair.[728] The piece, as you may have guessed, was very boastful of how great Sean Parker is.

What makes this CFR even more powerful is that it is funded through corporations who wish to influence policy making. Notable associates that are pertinent to Facebook include:

Goldman Sachs Group, Booz Allen Hamilton, Google, Raytheon, Palantir Technologies, Microsoft Corporation, T. Rowe Price Group, Sullivan & Cromwell, Wal-Mart, and General Atlantic.[729] Both T.Rowe Price and General Atlantic have invested millions of dollars into Facebook in 2011.[730] Booz Allen Hamilton and Raytheon are both major surveillance contractors for the NSA. And Sullivan Cromwell is the law firm that Peter Thiel used to work for after he left Stanford.[731]

As we can see there are a lot of connections between the CFR and Facebook. What makes this situation ironic however is that the conspiracy with the CFR is that the media that has led to social media being a news source.[732] With Facebook also being heavily influenced by the CFR and its members, they are playing on both sides of the court. The Council controls mainstream media, and now it controls social media. They cannot lose.

Trilateral Commission

A third major elite international organization with ties to Facebook is the Trilateral Commission. Founded in 1973 by David Rockefeller, the Trilateral Commission is designed to promote discussion between North America, Europe, and Asia with the objective of building cooperation among their nations.[733] Like the Bilderberg Group and the Council on Foreign Relations, politicians are not allowed to be members of the Trilateral Commission until they leave public office. Susan Rice for instance is a former member of the Commission but she is expected to return when her public service is over.[734]

The Trilateral Commission is also similar to the Bilderberg group and CFR in that members are permitted entry only by invitation. Invitations are given on a national basis with a cap of how many individuals can come from one nation. How the invitees are selected is not public information at this time.[735] Notable members of the Trilateral Commission include: Madeleine K. Albright, David Brooks, Austan Goolsbee; Richard Haass; Henry Kissinger, John Negroponte, Condoleezza Rice, and David Rockefeller.[736]

Also among the members of the Trilateral Commission who are connected to Facebook are Managing Director of Goldman Sachs Gerald Corrigan; former U.S. Director of National Intelligence Admiral Dennis Blair, former President of Harvard University Larry Summers, CEO of Goldman Sachs International Gerald Corrigan, and Washington Post CEO Donald Graham.[737] Blair is rather significant because he represents another member of the American intelligence community that is attending a secret elite meeting with several people who have played a hand in Facebook. While Blair is no longer the DNI of the United States, he still has valuable knowledge about how the system works that would prove very beneficial to the Commission.

What is said at these meetings will probably never be revealed. But what we do know is that the Trilateral Commission is designed to make the world more interdependent upon each other. They are big supporters of globalization. It seems that while the CFR's goal is to control the role that the United States plays, the Trilateral Commission's goal is around promoting interdependence through globalization.[738] This agenda is very important as we will see later.

World Economic Forum

The last major elite organization that Facebook has ties to is the World Economic Forum or WEF. The WEF was first founded in January 1971 under the name of the European Commission until it officially changed its name to the World Economic Forum in 1987.[739] The Forum boasts of memberships from 1,000 different companies, it does not accept members by country. The average company that is a member to the WEF has more than five billion dollars in turnover globally.[740] Every year since its founding the WEF meets annually in Davos, Switzerland, which is why people often refer to the meeting as "Davos."[741]

The idea behind the three-day conference is to discuss matters dealing with globalization, much like that of the Trilateral Commission. The subject matter for the discussions is the reason why the highly affluent and or wealthy are invited to speak at the forum. After all, the people who shape the world economy are the ones that the Forum wants to hear from, not experts or policy analyst who have no real role to play.

Among the Facebook associated attendees of the WEF are Sheryl Sandberg, Peter Thiel, Sean Parker, Jim Breyer, Mark Zuckerberg, and David Kirkpatrick.[742] A lot of the concerns that one might have about the previous three elite organizations are not the same as the WEF. The membership is a lot larger so it means that there are more ideas being discussed and more viewpoints being heard. The WEF is also held in an open setting where cameras are allowed. The videos featuring discussions with Zuckerberg or Sandberg are available to watch online.

The criticisms that are made against the WEF and groups like them that promote globalization is that they only give voice to the rich and powerful. The WEF seeks to address issues like poverty and authoritarianism by asking for solutions from people who promote it.

Although the public can send in their questions as well, the conflict of interest remains. That irony is even pointed out during the talks by the hosts of the forum from time to time.[743]

The Forum rebuts this criticism by claiming that economic development improves the conditions of everyone, not just the rich. By listening to what the corporations or developers have to say, the Forum claims they can get a better look at what needs to be done in the developing nations of the world. This way of thinking ignores the idea that economic development can be a zero-sum game where people do lose at the success of others. If anyone understands this point it is developing nations, and if anyone misses this point it is corporations.

Why they Love Facebook

There are numerous reasons why the individual actors associated with Facebook have relationships with the elitist organizations. Involvement in these groups brings with it powerful connections that can make or break careers. Becoming a part of an organization like the Council on Foreign Relations is also seen by many as a major achievement and something that gives respectability to the member. Aside from career aspirations, what is important to understand is why these organizations have taken an interest in Facebook. This can be done by looking at the goals of these organizations and by examining how Facebook can achieve those goals. Because Facebook is a very powerful machine, there is a lot to say about what Facebook can do.

Each one of these organizations is a heavy supporter of corporate dominate globalism. They support this idea of globalization because they believe it is the cure for a number of social problems such as poverty, war, and the like. At the same time, it also makes yields incredible corporate profits that may be blurring the judgment of those involved. But implementing this "solution" requires the destruction of barriers that exist between people such as geography, language, or even borders. By erasing these obstacles to interaction, it is hoped the problems society faces will go away as a result of increased trade and communication.

Facebook helps promote these benefits of globalization in a number of ways. Facebook's ability to bring people together who are separated by vast distances is one way they aid globalization. Facebook's large and diverse user base helps create a smaller world than what existed before. Every year more and more countries make Facebook their number one social networking site. And every year more and more people get devices such as smart phones that allow them to connect to the internet and consequently Facebook.[744] Distance is no longer the barrier that it used to be.

Tied to the bridging of geographic barriers is Facebook's ability to erase cultural barriers. The translation feature for instance allows individuals separated by language to communicate with each other to exchange views and ideas.[745] Translation also allows for users to look at what people in other countries think about certain places and topics that are present on Facebook. This ability to almost erase the effect of language has resulted in a new type of social network that is far more international than American.

While ending these barriers is important, there are also economic barriers that must be eliminated for globalization to gain full acceptance. Facebook as we have seen is a force for a digital currency system. This is being done right now through their Gifts feature and will be boosted later as the Internet of Things progresses.[746] Digitalized currency would allow for an easier transition from the present currencies based on a national level to future currencies based on a regional or even a global level. In the end, there will be fewer currencies, which will mean that the people who control those currencies will have more power.

Features of globalization bolstered by Facebook such as digital currency help expose that there is another more obvious reason than any humanitarian goal the elite organizations might claim. By pushing their system of doing things, the elite make more money by having fewer obstacles to trade. The members of groups like the Bilderberg, Trilateral, CFR, and WEF have a substantial amount to gain by seeing globalization take effect in every way possible. Social goals such as developing the third world are only minor side effects needed to further the true concerns of their efforts.

Along with the centralization of economic control, there are also negative externalities that globalization causes for the public. Globalization, as Naomi Klein author of *The Shock Doctrine* would tell us, can stimulate the problems it seeks to fix such as "inequality, corruption, and environmental degradation."[747] This stimulation can lead to social upheavals which may over throw existing institutions that promote the system. If the elite members of society intend to reap the rewards of that system, they must be able to protect their wealth and well-being from the masses.

Facebook is certainly an excellent tool to keep people in their place. It strengthens the intelligence gathering capabilities of local and national police forces that regulate citizens on a day to day basis. Police forces will be needed to control riots and demonstrations against globalization just like they do today. Having a system of total information awareness through Facebook will allow not only for the prosecution of those who resist the system, but it will prevent people from even considering it.

Having a Facebook life that is tied to the Internet of Things will prevent individuals both radical and passive from straying away from the pack. Not cooperating with existing economic power structures could mean that the individual will be punished or just rejected from society all together. This will force the individual to choose between their cause and being a functioning member of society. Sadly, this is the situation that most Facebook resistors are put into today.

What we see now after painting this picture of these organizations and the uses that Facebook can have for them is that it leads to the creation of a trap. Technological developments such as Facebook help guide people towards a globalized way of living that disregards previous societal barriers that stood in the way of that lifestyle. Once people are used to this way of living, governments with access to Facebook can use it to punish those who reject the system for the negative effects that it causes. These people will be easy to identify and at the very least easy to marginalize should they ever become a significant threat to the current state of affairs.

Arrangement

Now that we have identified the important actors, the groups they belong to, and the agendas of those groups, it is now time to determine what role they may have played in Facebook. What seems likely given the information available is that Zuckerberg created Facebook, either by stealing it or coming up with it on his own, and then he went to Silicon Valley. While there he was introduced to Peter Thiel and Reid Hoffman through his relationship with Sean Parker.[748]

During the time that Zuckerberg spent with Sean Parker at his house in Palo Alto, the dark influence on Facebook could have begun. This influence would have refined an already well-suited intelligence gathering project that Zuckerberg did a good job of making. Parker would have served to aid the product in its development until it got to Peter Thiel. After that Parker would become Thiel would both become board members.[749]

Following the ousting of Eduardo Saverin through stock dilution, Parker would also be pushed out of the company for criminal behavior. He was arrested in North Carolina for doing drugs with underage girls at a party in 2005. He would later go on to deny this.[750] It has also been reported that Peter Thiel and Breyer wanted Parker to leave the company following the arrest.[751] With both Saverin and Parker gone, Thiel and Breyer would have the largest amount of control over Zuckerberg and the company. And after funding PayPal, Facebook and Palantir, along with numerous other ventures, Thiel began attending the Bilderberg Conference in 2007.[752]

Something interesting to note is that one year after both Thiel and also Larry Summers started attending the Bilderberg Conference in 2007;[753] Sheryl Sandberg was recruited to be the Chief Operations Officer of Facebook in 2008.[754] This was a departure from her previous job at Google which she took following the close of the Clinton Administration in 2001. Sandberg also arrived at Google the same year that Google CEO and Bilderberg, CFR, WEF member Eric Schmidt did.[755] It seems that Google needed some "direction" to make sure the founders cared about the wishes of the venture capitalists.[756]

Schmidt, who began attending the Bilderberg Conference in 2010, is responsible for pushing the privacy envelope with Google.[757] What makes Google somewhat odd is that unlike a majority of venture capital deals, the investors actually kept the original founders of Google, Larry Paige and Sergey Brin, as heads of the company. They weren't kicked out like founders of Apple, Cisco, YouTube, and countless other companies were.[758] Instead Google let the founders stay while giving them a chaperon in the form of Schmidt to make sure the business end of things got carried out.

This scenario sort of describes what has happened at Facebook. Mark Zuckerberg, despite being originally seen as a naïve and careless, but capable CEO, could remain the head of his company as long as he listened to the two parent venture capitalists on his board Thiel and Breyer. These people may or may not have influenced him to serve their outside interests in the areas of technology, intelligence analysis, and globalization. But it would very surprising if they didn't have something to say about it.

In addition to the advisors that allowed Zuckerberg to stay, there was also a secret advisor that gave him instructions on how to be a good CEO. According to *The Facebook Effect* author David Kirkpatrick, workers at Facebook took to calling the secret advisor Wormtongue after the character in Lord of the Rings. In LOR, Wormtongue is an aide to a king that has lost his mind. As a result of Wormtongue's influence the king destroys his dominion. So it is safe to say that the executives didn't approve of what Zuckerberg's Wormtongue did. Several of them resigned as the result of Zuckerberg's decisions under this mysterious mentor. Why these people resigned and who this man named Wormtongue remains a mystery.[759]

Later Zuckerberg would receive a much closer advisor with Sheryl Sandberg as his COO. This may have been a needed addition because Thiel and Breyer could have wanted to concentrate on other projects that needed more help at the time. Seeing as Sandberg is a member of the Council on Foreign Relations, the Bilderberg Group, the World Economic Forum, a former Chief of Staff for the Secretary of the Treasury, and a former employee of Google, she probably had similar ideas as that of Thiel and Breyer.[760] This would have worked well with Zuckerberg's obsession with company growth that drives every action he takes. Sandberg would later become a board member in 2011, cementing the role she would play in the Facebook.[761]

Before Sandberg reached the board room, Marc Andreessen would be the fourth board member added in June of 2008.[762] Andreessen has no reported ties to the influential organizations. But he does have a history with a successful government sponsored project known as Mosaic that he later turned into a Netscape.[763] Andreessen's knowledge of a browser is also significant because Facebook itself is becoming a browser with its search options, social plugins, recommendations, and algorithms. You could almost say that Facebook has the best person to make a master browser of the internet.

In March of 2009, Bilderberg and Trilateral commission member Donald Graham joined the board.[764] Even before he acquired the seat, Graham and Zuckerberg were close in the aftermath of Accel Partners investment. Had Accel not offered Facebook a better deal, the Washington Post would have invested in Facebook in 2005. Graham let Zuckerberg out of the verbal agreement he made to sell equity to the Washington Post. The young CEO would often look to him for advice in matters dealing with Facebook.[765]

Graham, much like Sean Parker, also has a very suspicious story about how he came into his relationship with Zuckerberg. In an interview given for radio host Kojo Nnamdi, Graham said that Olivia Ma, daughter of late Washington Post vice president Chris Ma, was a former class mate of Zuckerberg's at Harvard. She had heard Zuckerberg was coming to Washington D.C. and arranged a meeting between Zuckerberg, her father, and Graham. This would have been the first venture style investment that the Post ever made, which Graham says was part of

Zuckerberg's reason for originally saying yes. After getting the offer from Accel, Zuckerberg tearfully called Graham and asked to be let out of his "moral dilemma."[766]

The next board member to join Facebook would be Reed Hastings in June of 2011. Hastings also serves on the board of Microsoft in addition to being the CEO of Netflix and a board member to Facebook.[767] His seat is a result of the investment made by Microsoft for $240 million.[768] Microsoft has a large interest in the Internet of Things and Facebook is crucial to that future. In 2012, Facebook would also begin sharing information with Netflix to boost advertising revenue.[769]

Following Hastings, CFR and Bilderberg group attendee Erskine Bowles would be appointed to Facebook in September of 2011. Bowles primary role on the board is as the head of the auditing committee.[770] While influence on product development seems unlikely, he could be serving more of a monitoring capacity given his government connections. And he certainly wouldn't be a friend to anyone hoping to steer the company in a more public friendly direction.

Throughout this period of increasing influence on Facebook by these actors, the site changed dramatically. At an almost suicidal pace, Facebook embarked on a campaign of rapid expansion and evolution that would result in the network having information on over a billion internet users by December 2012.[771] This campaign would see features developed such as the Newsfeed, the Timeline, the Platform, the Search Bar and Home.[772] These features are all incredibly intrusive on privacy and show the true intentions of the people who run Facebook. Their membership to the elite organizations is only icing on a candle lit cake.

19. Privacy

As we head towards this Internet of Things with Facebook and the global elite at the front of the charge, we must confront the world that this will create. A world without privacy is not livable by today/s standards. It is not even comfortable by what most people are accustomed to. But aside from preferences, we also cannot expect the existing power structures to respect the total information awareness that will be accessible to them. These are problems that must be answered or at least discussed; because once this Facebook world is constructed there will be little chance to take it apart.

For some people living in Facebookland might seem like a good idea. These people don't need privacy to function in society. They may even see privacy as an outdated idea that should be reconsidered when the costs and benefits are taken into account. While that might be a good option for them, there are also people who cannot afford to sacrifice their privacy. And not only can these people not function in a world built on identity, but they should at least choice in whether they are going to sacrifice their privacy or not.

Right to Privacy

Privacy is a valuable thing that many people take for granted. The simple reason for its value is that privacy allows for us not to worry about every action that we take. It allows customers to bargain from a position of strength against companies they buy from. It gives journalists the freedom to say what they want without fear of retribution against them. Privacy is more than just a nice thing. It is the foundation on which other freedoms are built upon.

In the U.S. Supreme Court case of Griswold v. Connecticut, the majority opinion found that while privacy is not enumerated in the Constitution, it is a right that several of the Amendments to the Constitution depend upon. The Justice speaking for the court in that case, Stephen Douglas, lays out in the opinion what he refers to as penumbras of the constitution. The term penumbra refers to the partial shadow that the earth casts on the moon when it goes in front of the sun. The majority held that such penumbras also existed within certain amendments in the Bill of Rights.[773]

Examples of penumbras that Douglas gives for privacy are things such as the freedom of speech and freedom of association found in the 1st Amendment. Without some degree of privacy members of certain groups may experience discrimination because of their membership to those groups. If they cannot associate in private and say what they wish in private, they do not have freedom of speech or association.[774]

The Court does not stop with the 1st amendment however. Also cited are the 3rd Amendment's right against quartering soldiers that was built on the value of privacy in one's home. The 4th amendment's right to no unlawful search and seizure that was considered dependent on the same reasoning. The 5th Amendment right against self-incrimination was based on the idea that you must have some level of privacy to maintain a level of presumed innocence. The 9th amendment was considered an effort to prevent against any legislature from making laws that invaded one's privacy that had been protected by the states. And this was further bolstered by the incorporation of these rights to the states with the passage of the 14th amendment.[775]

While we are on the subject of penumbras, we could also throw in the 2nd amendment's right to bear arms. The value of having a gun might be significantly diminished without some element of surprise. The 6th amendment's right to an impartial jury requires some degree of privacy for a defendant. The 8th amendment's ban cruel and unusual punishment might consider a lifetime of surveillance a form of torture. We could also talk about slavery with regard to a zero-privacy life and the constitution, but hopefully you get the point by now.

However, this right to privacy is not considered absolute by the Supreme Court either. There are strong examples given by later Courts such as terrorism and sexual predation that gives cause to violate a suspect's right to privacy. But that right is to be suspended by an elected or appointed magistrate that is presented with lawful documentation. And even in the cases were documentation isn't obtained such as in intelligence gathering, there is still congressional oversight with that activity which puts some degree of control in the hands of the people.

It should be understood by now that this right to privacy is to be taken seriously. But to some of those among us it is an old custom to be dismissed with a smirk and a wave of the hand. Facebook CEO and Founder Mark Zuckerberg would recommend that users throw away their right to privacy. He encourages them to forfeit their privacy with his words, with his company, and with his product. In interviews and conferences, he openly says that privacy will and should be a thing of the past.[776] In Washington Facebook actively lobbies against legislation that would promote more privacy on the internet.[777] And the very machine of Facebook itself intrudes on privacy and exploits the information that its users so generously give. The framers of the Constitution and Facebook have some significant differences between each other.

Risks of losing Privacy

Despite what Facebook's CEO might tell us, there are reasons why we hold on to privacy hundreds of years after the signing of the Constitution. While the vast majority of people may believe they have no secrets to hide, there are people in this society that do have reasons to keep things about themselves private. These are the individuals that the majority rejects out of fear or misunderstandings about who or what they are. For these people having privacy does not revolve around concealing a crime, it revolves around protecting personal dignity or even personal liberty.

An example could be an investigative journalist who writes stories about government corruption. Another person could be an activist who marches in protests for causes that are deemed "radical" by the majority. Whistleblowers that report abuses about powerful corporations or government agencies need to protect themselves through anonymity and secrecy. Lawyers who represent assumed guilty clients need to protect their client's "presumption of innocence".

People with illnesses such AIDS or Schizophrenia deserve to have their condition kept to themselves if they do not pose harm to anyone else. LGBT individuals who are not ready to publicize their sexuality deserve to have privacy. Illegal immigrants who are forced to work for slave wages under the threat of expulsion or discrimination deserve privacy. Victims of violence need privacy to avoid being harmed again. And members of minority groups that are mistreated by society such as Muslims or African Americans deserve to have their privacy as well.

Along with these people who have broken no law in keeping their secrets, there is the general public that needs to maintain a degree of privacy. Their right to privacy prevents abuses from corporations in the form of predatory business practices. And it prevents governments from controlling what people do through endless regulation and suspicionless surveillance. There are real concerns when you create a society without privacy; these are not just rightwing or leftwing boogeymen.

Before with social security numbers and license plates there was a system to track what humans did in. But with a Facebook style collection system, every action the person takes will be matched with that identity. The result is that a person would have to become accountable to the powers that be (family, government, business) for every action that they would take. What this would leave society with is an unbreakable system of slavery.

Because most behavior and activity would be attached to one's identity, it would be easy for a computer to tell when someone did something unacceptable to the current establishment. If the action was deemed criminal, law enforcement could easily find where the person was, and they could penalize however they felt necessary. This would mean that if the identity was blamed for something the person did not do, the person would never be able to obtain innocence. It is easy to argue with eye witnesses, it is difficult to argue with computers.

This efficient system of tracking and punishment would ensure that the vast majority of people did exactly as they were told at all-times. Work, consume, sleep, repeat would be the motto of this world. While crime is a problem that must be controlled, it is a necessary evil that allows people to maintain a degree of liberty in their lives. With the eradication of crime there would come the eradication of personal freedom.

Embracing a world without privacy like that of what Facebook intends would risk the end of free thought. Without privacy, individuals will suffer costs for having thoughts or behaviors about taboo or controversial subjects that society condemns. This condemnation would be a system of conditioning that dictates a person's entire life.

The inspiration for this model of conditioning is known as the panopticon. First envisioned by Jeremy Bentham in the 19th century and later elaborated on by philosopher Michel Foucault, the Panopticon is a prison that gives its occupants the idea that they are always being watched. Because they hold this assumption, they refrain from behaviors that their prison guards would punish them for. Because they do not know when they are not being watched, they embrace this conditioning at all times. Eventually, there is no longer a need for a prison at all because the person has changed their way of thinking to suit that of the system's criteria.[778]

This idea of thought controlling actions is also something the Supreme Court spoke on with the case of Cantwell v. Connecticut (1940), which held that government can only regulate religion when it the regulation is based out of a secular policy. The majority rooted their position on the assumption that in order to worship, one must also act on the beliefs of their religion. In other words, the distance between thinking and doing is not as far as some people might believe. Because of the assumption the court makes, they determined that actions enjoy protection in some instances as much thoughts do.[779]

Zeitgeist

There is an old German word known as "Zeitgeist" that translates in English to "sprit of the times." This word was also the title of a documentary film series that looked at the current state of world affairs and what their causes were. In that work, the director exposed the dangers that the corporate state presented to the world and also ways to mitigate those dangers. The current Zeitgeist has gotten even worse since that documentary was made, and it should be faced if we intend to understand what world without privacy would specifically mean. The truth hurts, but it helps.

There is a reason why internet users are being asked to sacrifice their privacy in exchange for convenience. This is not just some coincidence as we have seen with the CIA and its connections to Facebook. And despite what people like Zuckerberg might say, they know privacy is important. If they didn't know they wouldn't be so busy trying to take it away from the average person all of the time.

Also think back to that corporate oligarchy we talked about earlier and the secret meetings that they have every year. This oligarchy rules over the United States along with many, many, many other countries. The evidence for this dictatorship is in the crimes that the elite commit which go unpunished. We see it in finance with the Too Big to Fail and Libor scandals. We see it in foreign policy with countries such as Iraq, Chile, Iran, Egypt, Guatemala, Panama, and numerous others that become dictatorships at the behest of corporations. We see it in the economy with the richest 1% controlling half of the world's wealth. We see it in the environment with global warming and other destruction caused by using fossil fuels going unaddressed. The list is long and the crimes are many of what this corporate dictatorship has done.

These crimes speak not just to the power corporations have in our society, but they also point to the major causes of anger for the average citizen. Imagine the frustration a person would feel after losing their house to foreclosure while they watch broadcasts about how Wall Street is getting bailed and avoiding going to prison. Or imagine being a parent that knows their child has no future because of the greed of a few major energy companies that are destroying the global biosphere. These are just a few sources of anger for the average citizen because corporations have been allowed to get away with these crimes. To not expect a public response is naïve at best.

And there have been a variety of responses to the actions taken by this corporate state. The 9/11 terrorist attacks could largely be attributed to the foreign policy and economic actions taken against Muslims countries on behalf of corporations. This rage is best represented in that the targets of those attacks were the World Trade Center and the Pentagon. These are two major symbols of globalization that are a product of the corporate state created by elite international organizations. They should not be treated as incidental by any means.

Along with this act of terrorism among others, there have also been major protest movements that are a result of globalization. The Seattle WTO protests in 1999 gave a major boost to anti-globalization efforts throughout the world. Occupy Wall Street is another protest that speaks to these issues that America is experiencing as a result of globalization right now. And perhaps the most substantial of all recent protests movements was the Arab Spring that overthrew many corporate, American favored leaders in the Arab countries. When we look at these actions by the public they represent a public that is waking up and that needs to be controlled.

To defend the oligarchy from the social upheaval caused by their actions, a security state is being developed with the support of corporations. Warrantless wiretapping, unreasonable searches and seizures, and the suspension of habeas corpus are all features of this society. Intelligence agencies are allowed to roam unrestricted over the world's communications. Police agencies have become more high tech to aid in watching citizens at all times. Tools such as drones and RFID are expected to become common weapons for the military and law enforcement in the next ten years.[780] American citizens are increasingly being searched for no reason. Along with electronic surveillance, Stop and frisk programs go unchecked in New York City despite being unconstitutional and in violation of the ruling in Terry v. Ohio.[781] The response to public anger is very real and substantial.

What makes this system even more powerful is that law is being used to not end it but to defend it. Legislation such as the Patriot Act, the Protecting Americans from Terrorism Act and the FISA Amendment of 2007 all serve to protect an unconstitutional system of surveillance. The law was designed as a tool to protect American citizens from their government but now it is a tool for the government to not just rule but oppress their citizens. This is combined with the Congress being bribed away from making privacy an issue for the internet by internet companies and surveillance contractors with deep pockets.

All of this occurs while the intelligence agencies operate secret prisons in foreign countries. These prisons may detain their occupants without any trial or hearing to determine their innocence. The prisons also conduct prohibited forms of punishment such as torture and indefinite detention. With the creation of these prisons there is the creation of the tortures who man them. At close of their duty those torturers will be released onto the open market for the world to enjoy.[782]

People who try to expose these abuses are persecuted as traitors by the American government. James Risen of the New York Times was doggedly pursued for his sources in writing his book *State of War*.[783] The book helped to expose the torture and warrantless wiretapping programs that took place during the Bush administration. NSA whistleblower William Binney was held at gun point in his shower by FBI agents that broke into his home in 2007 after he tried to reveal the corruption and bribery going on within the agency.[784] He was an NSA program director for 40 years prior to the incident. And CIA agent Jon Kiriakou was sentenced to 30 months in prison for going public over the illegal torture program.[785] As of this writing, the Obama administration has filed cases against more whistleblowers than all past Presidential administrations combined.[786]

To avoid the stain that these activities put on government, we are seeing the increased use of mercenary forces such as BlackWater to handle military operations.[787] Not only are combat operations being lifted from service member's hands, but intelligence analysis is as well. Most intelligence analysis is done not by government agencies but by intelligence contractors.[788] These actions are all taken to avoid the backlash that results from having a standing army do anything. Because public relations and secrecy no longer works they are now trying outsourcing.

For domestic control, civilian police departments are increasingly being militarized against their own populations. This is being done to avoid the restrictions of the Posse Comitatus Act which prevents the use of the Army to enforce laws passed by Congress or enumerated in the Constitution. Instead of using soldiers to work as policemen they are turning policemen into soldiers.[789] Ironically this works because of the threat that comes from terrorism.

This current Zeitgeist will be joined by an Internet of Things that will track every move that individuals make. Its proponents do not even acknowledge the current flaws in the human experience that would make such a world unsustainable. Instead they create advertisements that speak of a utopia from the surrender of privacy and the embracement of corporate idealism. The real world is simply not suited for this fantasy. To pretend that it will not make the problems that corporate globalization causes worse is insane.

In Naomi Wolf's work *The End of America,* she compares the current state of affairs in the United States to former totalitarian regimes in history. She noticed that all the totalitarian regimes had many similar characteristics as that of the United States. They included: the creation of a surveillance system, the formation of a paramilitary force, the use of external threats to justify losses in civil liberties, the use of secret prisons, subversion of the rule of law, monitoring of innocent civilians, arrest and detain individuals for no reason, the targeting of key individuals, and the infiltration of citizens groups.[790] This government has looked at Wolf's work and decided to give it the old college try.

What exactly will follow from the end of privacy is uncertain. That could lead to a number of utterly terrible results that are simply not foreseeable now. The decisions made now regarding privacy may not show life and death consequences until years have passed. That dilemma applies on both a societal and individual level. Whether it's a database filled with names or an employer looking over a user's Facebook account, the level of privacy one needs is determined in the future. The only way to address the problem is to show restraint in the past. It comes down to forward thinking, either you exercise it or you don't.

Lessons from the past

This type of corporate collusion with oppression is not new by any means. Corporations are frequently the enemies of democracy outside of their television advertisements and press releases. The animosity that corporations have is not because they are totally evil.   The problem they have with democracies is that they tend to have trade unions and laws which protect workers' rights. They also have regulations which prevent against monopolies, pollution, and the like. These are not things that national or multinational corporations want to deal with. So they support policies and politicians that cause the country to turn into a dictatorship.

To provide some examples we could look at Nazi Germany during the 1930s. Adolf Hitler was only able to make his rise to power because of help from some of the wealthy industrialists who lived in Germany at the time. In William Shirer's *The Rise and Fall of the Third Reich,* he discusses how funding from the coal and steel industrialists were essential for Hitler to rise through the 1930-1933 period.[791] Shirer also notes the less substantial but still important support that came from the rubber, chemical, potash, insurance, publishing, banking, and railroad interests in Germany at the time.

Aside from the domestic business community, Hitler also had help from outside business interests as well.   Chase Bank helped the Nazi Party raise funds on the stock exchange. Coca Cola supplied Germany with soft drinks through their subsidiary Fanta. Ford Motor Company, General Motors, and Chrysler have all been accused of selling vehicles to be used by the Germans in battle. The list could go and on of American corporations that were more than willing to lend their support to the Nazi regime.[792]

But Germany and its collaborators are not the only examples that history provides us with of corporations fueling fascism. The capitalists of 1920's Italy also helped fuel Mussolini's rise to power.[793] Corporations such as ITT used connections with the CIA to get rid of democratically elected president Salvatore Allende in Chile and give rise to General Augusto Pinochet.[794] Mosaddegh's regime in Iran also suffered a similar result due to his defiance of

American-British petroleum interests. Julio Arbenz in Guatemala was overthrown largely because of his opposition to the United Fruit Corporation. The corporate state is old, powerful, and very hostile to true democracy.[795]

We should also not forget another company who has been kind to non-democratic regimes: Facebook. They were willing to bend over backwards to get into China despite its human rights abuses. Facebook would have even helped out with those abuses just like the other social networks in China do. "Censorship, surveillance, propaganda, whatever it takes just let us in", is essentially what Facebook tells the world with their efforts to get into China. Unfortunately for Facebook; Google, Yahoo and Cisco botched that deal for American companies, so Facebook will have to try some other way.

And while Facebook itself might sound like an original story, it too has a historical parallel that is worth examining. In Edwin Black's powerful book *IBM and the Holocaust,* he investigates the connection that existed by the International Business Machine corporation and the Third Reich. The volume reveals how IBM and their CEO Thomas J. Watson aided the Germans in all six stages of the Jewish Holocaust in Europe. This was done through the use of a punch card machine system that identified and tracked all of the Jews in Germany. Not only did IBM assist the Germans in this macabre census taking, but they did so with amazing efficiency. IBM worked wonders as they assembled massive amounts of information on Jews that ranged from profession, country of origin, native tongue, marital relationship, and numerous other aspects that before would have been impossible to count all at once.[796]

Despite participating in one of mankind's worst atrocities, today IBM is still seen as good company. They are listed on the New York Stock Exchange. They bring in billions of dollars every year with their business solution products. They have clever commercials that can be seen on TV. In 2011, they even created a super computer named Watson to compete on Jeopardy.[797]

What makes this so demoralizing is that Black's book came out ten years ago. No apology has ever been issued by IBM for their role in the Holocaust. No boycott has successfully destroyed their business. They never even responded to the charges that Black has leveled against them. IBM has nothing to fear 80 years after their very profitable relationship began with the Nazi's in 1933.[798]

The example of IBM was also lauded against Apple Computer when their machines started making their way into everyone's home during the 1980s. In Walter Isaacson's biography on Steve Jobs, he notes how people compared Apple to a punch card system for identification.[799] It is likely that if this connection between IBM and Facebook is used in the public discourse, it will be dismissed much like IBM and Apple similarities were. That suspicion of personal computers may have been unfounded during the birth of the PC, but it is troubling how well iPhones and iPads are used to track what people do now. And I hate to beleaguer this point, but Isaacson also happens to be an attendee of the Bilderberg Conference.[800] You have to keep your eyes and mind open at all times.

A Grain of Salt

When corporations tell their customers or their users that they do not need their privacy, those customers and consumers should take that advice with a grain of salt. The past as well as the present shows us that privacy is very necessary for one's own safety. It is not some abstract concept or a metaphor with a hidden meaning, privacy is a right that must be protected.

History has also shown us that the corporate source of any advice, whether it is IBM, Facebook, Yahoo, Chase Bank, should be treated with suspicion. Corporations have a separate agenda than that of those they serve. Occasionally that agenda will match that of the public, but it may also match that of authoritarian leaders. History does not forgive such amnesia. Facebook users should be very careful with the trust they place in this company.

20. Deletion

"Lose me, Hate me, Smash me, Erase me, Kill me."

"Eraser" - Nine Inch Nails

There are several options that users could take regarding Facebook. They could protest the site through petitions and marches that would generate awareness for the issue. They could write their congressmen and pressure them to look into this issue of warrantless surveillance and intrusive social networking. Users could even adopt new social networks that provide reasonable alternatives for privacy conscious users.

But there is only one true solution to the problem of Facebook and that is deletion. Facebook must be destroyed to prevent it from getting any stronger than it already is. That means as many people as possible need to leave this network as soon as possible. Deletion will require people to leave a social network that may have been addicted to for a number of years and that they get a lot of enjoyment out of using. This will increase the difficulty of getting those users to leave, but deletion must be done. The other solutions cannot work, and there are many reasons why.

Change will never come

What needs to be made clear in the conversation about Facebook is that it cannot be fixed. Facebook is doing what it was designed to do and it will continue to do that until people leave. Currently there is no real pressure for Facebook to change. There are no mass desertions of Facebook that are happening right now. On the contrary Facebook is constantly expanding around the world. With their domestic users thoroughly addicted and their foreign markets eager to sign on, Facebook has no plans on deviating from its current business model.

Even the institutions designed to regulate companies like Facebook have failed to pressure for the necessary changes. Congress, the regulatory agencies, and the court system will never come to the rescue of users. They are too slow, uninformed, complicit, and unaccountable to make any real changes with this site. This is not to mention that the government has never been effective at policing the internet or the products related to the internet. Examples include: Microsoft, Apple, IBM, CISCO, Yahoo, and Google to name just a few. They seem to like just having a few monopolies to deal with when they go to get information on the American people.

For some it will seem obvious that the government has failed them. They might even say that government has no business interfering in the affairs of the market. But what is also a problem is that the current market will allow Facebook to continue existing with little challenge. Most of the social networking sites that are launched today are basing themselves off Facebook. They understand that this is the way to make money. As a result, most of the alternatives are the same as Facebook. Because of these clones, there is no real reason to leave Facebook for something else. It is becoming all the same.

Another place that people look to when government fails is the media. It would be expected that a real media would intervene in a situation like this because of the opportunity for sensationalism regarding a tech company and the intelligence community. Instead, the media embraces Facebook as a place for outsourced reporting and typically sings its praises for citizen journalism. While mainstream media does occasionally provide criticisms on privacy, those stories are never in depth. They also don't say much when the news organization that reports the story typically has a Facebook page.

If there was enough external pressure on this site to change, there is a second major reason why things will not change. Facebook's board of directors is there to see Facebook collect massive amounts of information. They have a professional interest in seeing Facebook progress into what it is planned to become. It is also difficult to pressure these people because most of them with the exception of Zuckerberg and Sandberg are not well known. Jim Breyer for instance is hardly well known outside of the business world and he has already left the company.[801] His relatively discreet presence and exit from Facebook may prevent him from being a focus for any future scandal that should be unearthed later.

But even if we were to assume that these people could be persuaded to change their company, they would face an impossible task of tampering with the design of the network. It is inherent in Facebook's design to collect lots of information. This design is the result of an evolution of internet companies over a decade that has shaped Facebook's very DNA as a website. The problem is bigger than centralized social networking or even a set of intrusive features that could be rescinded. These executives couldn't change things if they wanted to, which is why their decision to keep expanding Facebook data collection is so easy.

Here to Stay

The myth that is often told by the media is that people will get bored of Facebook eventually. Facebook is one of many companies that people get tired of after the thrill wears off. The problem with that way of thinking is that it assumes that Facebook is just a product or a service that can be forsaken. The sad truth is that Facebook is an addiction; it is not just a website. It is a part of a routine that some people go through every day. When they wake up they login to Facebook. When they sit down in front of the computer they login to Facebook. It is just something that people are used to doing, and that makes it hard to get away from.

Like most bad habits, Facebook lacks the immediate reasons why it should be broken. For Facebook, the dangers of identity theft or wrongful arrest are also seen as too remote for most people to show concern. And for the most part that is true. Most users will not have their identity stolen or be arrested because of the information they put on Facebook. Because of that, the user can rationalize that the risk of using is not as great as the reward. Cigarettes are a good analogy to this. Everyone knows that cigarettes cause diseases and preventable deaths, but millions of people still smoke. They continue to do so because the threat of cancer or a heart attack caused by smoking is too remote in their minds for them to break from the routine.

Gambling addiction also provides us with some parallels worth examining. Using Facebook itself is a gamble because every user runs the risk of sharing too much information that could cause problems for themselves or someone else. The unsuccessful gambler is the person who falls into the trap of sharing lots of information with Facebook to get their enjoyment from it. The successful gambler is the person who can share very little information while getting a lot of utility from it. Negative effects might happen to the user that over shares just like they would a gambler who spends too much of their money. Nevertheless, because there are plenty of both unsuccessful and successful gamblers on Facebook, the problem is seen in the individual and not in the design.

The difficulty with this addiction is that if Facebook does naturally disappear without user rejection, it will most likely be usurped by a corporate rival who offers users the same thing in a different way. That network could actually be even worse than Facebook because it would lend to the myth that its existence is also temporary. Internet users have been spoiled in recent years with the rise in fall of companies who gathered too much information on their users. Because of this people do not take the excessive sharing on social networking very seriously.

Fear

If there is anything that demonstrates to us how real this addiction is it is the consequences that users may suffer from deleting their Facebook account. This is akin to the withdrawals that people will experience when they go through detoxification. The knowledge of what lies beyond the gate is what helps keep the user from ever truly leaving their addiction.

And the effects that users predict are not necessarily all in the users head. Deletion of Facebook could mean cutting off connections with a large number of people. Just about everyone has a friends list with people they only hear from while on Facebook. There could be more than one hundred people that the user will become disconnected from after leaving. They may even go years without hearing or seeing a large portion of those people. That is a big change in a person's social life which can also be scary if the user has a few real social connections in the real world.

However, leaving Facebook is not just a social fear but a business one too. Professionals and entertainers may see Facebook as essential to building a reputation. Without it they may slip into obscurity and never be heard from again. That doesn't have to necessarily happen, but in the mind of someone who uses Facebook for their career it could seem very real. A career can be greatly aided by embracing Facebook, and with the same token it is also possible that it could be broken by abandoning it.

A more mental but equally powerful tool to keep users loyal is the fear of boredom that many people address by getting on Facebook. Like any cell phone game, Facebook is something that can keep a user busy when they have downtime throughout the day. For some people, the idea of having any boredom is bad and there are a number of reasons why that could be, but that is a separate matter. In this circumstance Facebook, itself is not so much important as it is filling a space that exists in the users mind for a brief period of time. Idle hands are the devil's playground so the old saying goes.

There are things that can be done to mitigate the concerns of leaving Facebook. The user could start spending time with the people in their life. They could always use other forms of communication such as telephone, text messaging, or email to reach people they want to communicate with. Or if the user wants to try something more engaging they could find a social hobby that brings them around people who they wouldn't normally get to see.

But for most people this will not do at all. They want to be able to use a social networking platform to communicate with large numbers of people all at once. What a user should look for if they want the same type of behavior to occur again is to go to Twitter, Google+, Tumblr, Pinterest, or Instagram. They should go to these collection-based websites, register for an account, and begin sharing all the same information they shared before.

But if the user wants to have different results, they should go to a social network that gives them control over their information. Some alternatives worth exploring are Diaspora, GNUNet, FreedomBox, and Friendica. These networks will be lesser known in comparison to the likes of Facebook or Twitter, and therefore they will have fewer members that the user is likely to know. They will also have fewer features due to their concern for increased privacy as well as their inability to generate funding. Most are still in development which means that they have bugs which occur from time to time as well. As a result of these flaws it is nearly certain that no alternative can ever truly replace what Facebook gives to its users.

And perhaps what Facebook has should not be done ever again. The user and the developer should forgo the perks that came with centralized, mass collection of their information. Embracing alternative forms of online communication means embracing less sharing which means receiving fewer benefits for better privacy and security.

Part of that answer is not new social networks, but no social networks. The best way for a user to break the spell that Facebook has on them is to break from social networking for a while. This will help to destroy the addicted, excessive sharing mentality that all social networks promote in some way. Just going from one social networking site to another would put users at the mercy of whoever develops the network. It is an addiction that does not have an easy fix that gives people what they want without the cost. That is just how it is.

Clock

Aside from the policy of aggressive expansion that Facebook has embarked on, there are also forces that are pushing for involuntary social network membership. The first source is job recruitment. Having a social network profile may eventually be required to get professional occupations. This would eliminate the need for a resume and would make the recruitment process go faster. While this requirement only applies for certain professional occupations at the current moment, it could eventually include even menial service jobs may require this form of identification because of the Internet of Things.

The next source of involuntary membership is internet application development. Developers and websites are increasingly creating and linking their content to social platforms to spread their applications. This is significant when we consider that over a million websites have Facebook social plugin code embedded in their web page.[802] As Facebook's user base grows this platform gains more and more gravity to outsider who have yet to use it. This is not to mention that the platform is easier to code on most of the other platforms on the internet. In the end, every website on the internet could wind up looking like Facebook.

As more and more websites take a shine to Facebook's information gathering model, they will require the user to be connected through social networking. This requirement will be justified for the sake of using the applications that developers only choose to build on Facebook.

Already there are websites who ask for users to login to Facebook so they can use their webpage. As time goes on, websites without a mandatory log in will lose out on advertising revenue compared to websites that choose to connect with Facebook. Eventually, advertisers may only choose to publish on sites with a Facebook connection. This would starve the holdouts of the advertising revenue that every website needs to survive.

As the Internet of Things becomes more and more integrated into society, Facebook will become necessary for an individual to function in daily life. It is difficult to tell exactly how much of a role that the Facebook identity will play, but it will play a role in this future. They will need an accurate way to track what people do. The best way to do that is through a social network profile. Every year the internet becomes larger but it also becomes more personalized to what the user wants. Social plugins are an example of this. Facebook and its clones are helping to turn the internet into a place for corporations to watch what people do. Whether the internet user is okay with that will not matter in a short period of time. The infrastructure will simply exist and the user will have to deal with it.

As a result of these involuntary forces along with natural attractions to the site, Facebook will continue to get stronger and stronger. By having a gargantuan membership base Facebook will have a greater capability to attract even more people than ever before. It is hard to say if there is a certain point where Facebook is bound to have ever user on the internet, but that number could very well exist. There are close to 2.4 billion internet users in the world right now. Facebook already has 1.1 billion.[803] Having the whole internet on one social networking site only sounds impossible until it happens.

While world domination is not so much a certainty, increased revenue from an increased membership base will happen. Currently Facebook only brings in a few billion dollars every year as of right now. This is relatively small when we compare it to other technology companies such as Apple, Google, and Microsoft.[804] As Facebook grows and it advertisers begin to master social media advertising, Facebook's profits will rise. It has a lot of potential when we consider the amount of information it contains on users. The only obstacle in its way is time and users' becoming aware of what is going on.

The money that they earn will give Facebook the financial power it needs to protect its monopoly from challengers. We are already seeing this with their donations to House and Senate campaigns to prevent regulation. Those donations will be able to grow and be distributed more equally as Facebook makes more money. More money will also allow for more acquisitions, more employees, data centers, and the like. Once Facebook gets the money they need they will be untouchable like the other Silicon Valley giants are.

Removing the batteries

The same thing that makes Facebook powerful is the same thing that makes it destructible. Facebook is a business that requires money to survive. Even if every employee were to work for free, the website would still fail because of the upkeep it requires financially. The shareholders will not hold their stock if the company does not make money. The servers and the external contractors that Facebook needs will not function without money.

Facebook is worth nothing if it does not have users to look at advertisements or to collect information from. The stock price of Facebook is also heavily dependent on the number of people that use the network. If enough users are removed from the machine the machine will die. It will not take every user to delete their account but enough will have to leave if Facebook is to be defeated. To better achieve that goal an exact number such as 500,000,000 should not be focused on. Instead the destroyers of Facebook should try to get as many people out of the machine as possible. There is no such thing as having too many Facebook deletions.

The destruction of Facebook could have a range of effects around the world. One message it would send is that Silicon Valley can no longer do what it likes with computers. No more collecting personal information for advertisements. No more monopolizing internet communication and search capability. These are simple ideas that could be taught to hundreds of internet companies in a single day of Facebook deletions.

The massive deletions could also cause major harm to the corporate version of the Internet of Things. This technological movement relies on an online identity to catalogue information to.[805] It can be assumed that other forms of identification such as license number of even some form of registration would take Facebook's place, but that would dramatic improvement from Facebook. Facebook already knows too much as it is, it is time that users pull the plug.

While the cyber criminals won't go away entirely, they will be set back. Facebook and the rest of its social media spawns let hackers grow lazy off easy information. Once Facebook is gone they may actual have to learn how to code if they want to break into someone's computer.

The same idea goes for those corporate spies who just hack the Facebook account to find out private conversations.

Local and state law enforcement will be unable to utilize profile information on their suspects. The police will have to return to their old methods of talking to witnesses which will make them care about the department's reputation. No number of cameras will ever be able to get the information that Facebook did. As a result, crimes will be harder to solve but citizens will also be freer to do what they want.

Other issues such as warrantless wiretapping and the influence of the elite organizations will take other strategies. They will be addressed somewhat by the elimination of Facebook but that will not make them go away. Those issues require separate forms of resistance that are more demanding than just deleting a Facebook account. They require attention by the media and political participation by the citizens. In the end, these are political problems that demand political solutions. Protesting is not enough. It will require democratic action by those who care. If Facebook has shown us anything, it is that it takes more than the click of a button to make for political change.

And aside from the much larger effects that elimination of Facebook will have on the world, there are also more immediate benefits that come on an individual level. One direct effect will be that the user will have more privacy in their daily lives. Users will not have to worry about their parents or their employers seeing a tag of an embarrassing photo. They can avoid the confusing post that lead their friends to wonder if the person has lost their mind. The barrier between the user and the people who they have in their life can go back up. This is the barrier that allows us to still feel close, but not intruded on. Everyone needs their space.

Another basic benefit for the user will be more free time. Studies show that Facebook usage cuts into the productivity of those that use it.[806] It stands to reason that if the user is not wasting their time on Facebook there is a chance they may accomplish more meaningful with their day.

There is also reason to believe that the average person would use their computers and mobile devices less if they didn't use Facebook. If people were to substitute the time they spent on Facebook with doing an activity that didn't require an electrical device, they could save a lot of energy. But avoiding Facebook to begin with would help save energy by decreasing the number of servers they need. This is assuming that everyone doesn't abandon Facebook resulting in the total shut down of all server locations. Either way, the server centers cause a lot of pollution and waste of energy; it would do some good to cut down on their usage.[807]

Altogether there are a lot of benefits for the world and the individual that come with the end of Facebook. They demonstrate how much weight that users are carrying by being a member of this network. Self-surveillance is a taxing experience for anyone, but because users are given rewards for that surveillance they put up with it. And the more users that put up with it, the more ordinary the costs will seem.

Don't be a Hipster

If the user chooses to delete their Facebook account, they may find themselves marginalized by the remaining Facebook users who hold prejudices against those who choose to leave. People who delete their Facebook account are sometimes labeled under a group known as Hipsters. These people are thought of as pretentious and self-aggrandizing for their concern with trendy brands and activity. Hipster behavior includes but is not limited to: wearing vintage clothes, playing Frisbee, eating organic foods, sporting thick, black frame glasses, wearing fedoras or cabbie hats, and they are typically a Mac user. The list is far longer than just a few, annoying behaviors, but that will have to do to describe the Hipster to the uninformed.

The problem with this group is that they typically delete their Facebook account and then proclaim it to the world like a badge of honor. Their reasons tend to vary. Some delete their account because they see Facebook as old news in the social media world. They will then choose a lesser known site like Tumblr or Google+ to appear like a trend setter. And when everyone is on that site they will then complain on how they were there before everyone else.

Another reason that Hipsters leave may be social alienation. These users will say that Facebook is ruining the relationships they have in the real world. After deleting their account, they will vow never to use Facebook again and resort to hanging out with people in real life. Following this proclamation, the Hipster may return to Facebook in shame. Or they will discover they don't have any real relationships and live life in isolation.

And then there are those who do care about their privacy. Those individuals may be the most vocal of all the Hipsters because they see Facebook as a tool of oppression. They ruin the reputations of those who leave by treating those who are still members as lacking in intelligence.

"Facebook is for sheep", is something they might say. While that may very well be true, that kind of attitude only pushes the remaining Facebook users further away from the exit sign.

The problem with these hipsters is that they muddle understanding of the true problems with Facebook. They make things like privacy and corporate control seem like trendy issues. It is almost as though this is their chance to be ahead of the rest of us. This isn't about being hip; it is about being free from surveillance on the internet. That is all anyone needs to know.

Deletion

If you are a Facebook user, this is how to delete your account. Go to the log in page. Look in the bottom right hand corner and click the small lettering that says HELP. Then click on Facebook Basics. After you have reached the basic information page, click on the account settings and the deletion button. The first option to select is "how to delete my account". Click on the option. It will then tell you to click on a link that will send a request to Facebook for deletion. The request will take 14 days to complete. Do not return to your account during those 14 days or else your request will be cancelled. I will leave you with this: Don't look back.

Acknowledgments

At a time of extreme hopelessness during this book I cursed those who had motivated me to be a writer when I was younger. I had wished they had never complimented my ability or made me feel like I could do anything writing. Well now that I have come to my senses, it is time to thank those teachers and professors in my life who have helped me get to where I am today. I would just like to say thank you to:

Mrs. Carinci-Bell; Ms. Julia Bond; Mr. Dwight McUmar; Ms. Cindy Jividen; Mr. Edward Samoraj; Mr. John Collabreze; Mr. Phil Carey; Mrs. Elizabeth Ann Cain; Ms. Jaime Kegg; Mr. Andy Pintus; Dr. Beverly Hinton-Lintz; Dr. Alana Querze; Dr. David Hoinski; Dr. Kim Jones-West; Dr. Gregg Noone; Dr. Susan Hunter; Mr. Jim Ebel; Mr. Daniel Brewster; Dr. Phil Michelbach; Dr. Erin Cassese; and Dr. Richard A. Brisbin.

This book was also written with the help of strangers who guided my research along the way. I owe these people a debt of gratitude for teaching me what my professors and instructors were unable to do. They include:

Peter Joseph, Jacob Appelbaum, Sut Jhally, Moxie Marlinspike, Christopher Soghoian, Dmitry Kleiner, Richard Stallman, Rop Gonggrijp, Frank Rieger, Ira Winkler, James Bamford, William Binney, Ben Mezrich, David Kirkpatrick, Michael Parenti, Noam Chomsky, Katherine Albrecht, Alex Jones, Aaron Russo, Julia Angwin, Richard Clarke, Naomi Wolf, Chris Hedges, James Risen, George Orwell, Philip K. Dick, and Aldous Huxley.

I would also like to thank Mr. Adam Howell; Mr. Ray Pernell; Mr. Jeff Lewis; WTF with Marc Maron; The Joe Rogan Experience; The Monday Morning Podcast with Bill Burr; Trent Reznor, Marilyn Manson, and Henry Rollins.

253

Special thanks go to my family for the love and support they gave during this work. They will have to remain anonymous for the present time.

Index

End Notes

Introduction

[1] First Quarter Earnings Statement, Investor Relation, Facebook, http://files.shareholder.com/downloads/AMDA-NJ5DZ/2544109454x0x660034/7eb4acb8-d90a-42c3-96b1-eb49f6c990c4/Transcript_FB_May-01-2013.pdf (accessed: August 5, 2013).

[2] Ibid.

[3] "Social Media Use in Law Enforcement Investigations," *LexisNexis,* 2012. http://www.lexisnexis.com/government/investigations/ (accessed: July 25, 2013).

[4] "Information for Law Enforcement Authorities," Facebook, http://www.facebook.com/safety/groups/law/guidelines/ (accessed: July 25, 2013).

[1] "Facebook.com Site Info," *Alexa,* http://www.alexa.com/siteinfo/facebook.com (accessed: April 22, 2013).

Mandy Zibart, "IDC-Facebook Always Connected," *IDC,* Aug 2, 2013, https://fb-public.app.box.com/s/3iq5x6uwnqtq7ki4q8wk as cited in Chris Taylor "Smartphone users check Facebook 14 times a day,", Mashable, March 28, 2013 www.cnn.com/2013/03/28/tech/mobile/survey-phones-facebook

[2] "Messaging," Help Center, Facebook, http://www.facebook.com/help/?ref=pf#!/help/326534794098501/ (accessed: August 1, 2012).

[3] "About Apps," Help Center, Facebook, http://www.facebook.com/help/?ref=pf#!/help/493707223977442/ (accessed: August 1, 2012).

[4] Max Chafkin, "How to Kill a Great Idea!" *Inc. Magazine,* Jun 1, 2007, http://www.inc.com/magazine/20070601/features-how-to-kill-a-great-idea_pagen_2.html (accessed: August 1, 2012).

[5] "I am Getting Too Many Notifications. Can I adjust what notifications I hear about?" Help Center, Facebook, http://www.facebook.com/help/254180001276638#!/help/390022341057202?q=notifications%20&sid=0CLPnNweGg7K52Owi (accessed: August 1, 2012).

[6] "Connect with People You May Know," Help Center, Facebook, http://www.facebook.com/help/?ref=pf#!/help/501283333222485/ (accessed: August 1, 2012).

[7] World Map of Social Networks, *VincosBlog,* June 2013, http://vincos.it/world-map-of-social-networks/ (accessed: August 1, 2012).

[8] "About CNN iReport," *CNN,* http://ireport.cnn.com/?hpt=sitenav (accessed: August 1, 2012).

[9] "How Newsfeed Works," Help Center, Facebook, http://www.facebook.com/help/?ref=pf#!/help/327131014036297/ (accessed: August 1, 2012).

[10] "Links," Help Center, Facebook, http://www.facebook.com/help/?ref=pf#!/help/335697046510763/ (accessed: August 1, 2012).

[11] Chad Little, Facebook in Translation, *The Facebook Blog,* June 23, 2008, https://blog.facebook.com/blog.php?post=20734392130 (accessed: August 1, 2012).

[12] "Platform," Newsroom, Facebook, http://newsroom.fb.com/Platform (accessed: August 4, 2012).

[13] "Ad & Sponsored Stories Copy, Image, Targeting & Destination," Help Center, Facebook, http://www.facebook.com/help/adpolicy#!/help/199766486817238/ (accessed: August 4, 2012).

[14] Clara Shih, *The Facebook Era: Tapping Online Social Networks to Market, Sell, and Innovate,* Prentice Hall, 2009.

[15] Dennis Wilcox, Glen T. Cameron, Bryan H. Reber, and Jae-Hwa Shin, *Think Public Relations,* (Pearson 2013).

[16] Clara Shih, *The Facebook Era, 123-141.*

[17] John Koetsier, "Facebook: 15 million businesses, companies, and organizations now have a Facebook page," *VentureBeat,* March 5, 2013. www.venturebeat.com/ 2013/ 03/ 05/ facebook-15-million-businesses-companies-and-organizations-now-have-a -facebook-page/ (accessed: August 18, 2013).

[18] "Three out of four workers (75 percent) access social media on the job from their mobile devices at least once a day, and 60 percent access it multiple times," *Business News Daily,* http://www.businessnewsdaily.com/3220-employee-social-media.html (accessed: August 4, 2012).

Sharon Gaudin, "Study: Facebook use cuts productivity at work Survey finds 77% of Facebookers use the social networking site while on the job", *ComputerWorld,* July 22, 2009, http://www.computerworld.com/s/article/9135795/Study_Facebook_use_cuts_productivity_at_work (accessed: August 4, 2012).

[23] "Introducing Hash tags on Facebook," Facebook Studio, June 12, 2013, http://www.facebook-studio.com/news/item/introducing-hashtags-on-facebook

[24] Derrick Harris, "How Facebook keeps 100 petabytes of Hadoop data online," *Gigaom,* June 13, 2012, http://gigaom.com/2012/06/13/how-facebook-keeps-100-petabytes-of-hadoop-data-online/

[25] Nicholas Carlson, "In 2004, Mark Zuckerberg Broke Into A Facebook User's Private Email Account," *Business Insider,* Mar. 5, 2010, http://www.businessinsider.com/how-mark-zuckerberg-hacked-into-the-harvard-crimson-2010-3#ixzz2N7kV8LsJ

[26] "Confirm Your Email," Help Center, Facebook, http://www.facebook.com/help/460711197281324/#!/help/376335499080938/ (accessed: July 30, 2013).

[27] "Notifications," Help Center, Facebook, http://www.facebook.com/help/460711197281324/#!/help/327994277286267/ (accessed: July 30, 2013).

[28] "Information We Receive about You," Data Use Policy, Facebook, http://www.facebook.com/about/privacy/your-info (accessed: July 30, 2013).

[29] Ibid.

[30] Ibid.

[31] Ibid.

[32] Ibid.

[33] "Cookies," Facebook, http://www.facebook.com/help/cookies (accessed: July 30, 2013).

[34] Ibid.

[35] Eva Galperin. "How to Turn on Do Not Track on Your Browser," Electronic Frontier Foundation, June 14, 2012, https://www.eff.org/deeplinks/2012/06/how-turn-do-not-track-your-browser (accessed: July 30, 2013).

[36] "Uploading Profiles and Profile Photos," Help Center, Facebook, http://www.facebook.com/help/cookies#!/help/118731871603814/ (accessed: July 30, 2013).

[37] Form 10-K Annual Report. Facebook, Inc., February 1, 2013, http://investor.fb.com/secfiling.cfm?filingID=1326801-13-3&CIK=1326801 (accessed: August 3, 2013).

[38] "People You May Know," Help Center, Facebook, http://www.facebook.com/help/cookies#!/help/501283333222485/ (accessed: August 10, 2013).

[39] "Update Your Basic Info," Help Center, Facebook, http://www.facebook.com/help/cookies#!/help/334656726616576/ (accessed: August 10, 2013).

[40] Ibid.

[41] "Get Started," Help Center, Facebook, http://www.facebook.com/help/cookies#!/help/467610326601639/ (accessed: August 10, 2013).

[42] Get Started. Introducing Timeline, Facebook, http://www.facebook.com/help/www/437430672945092?rdrhc#!/help/www/467610326601639/

[43] "Reports," Help Center, Facebook, http://www.facebook.com/help/cookies#!/help/132408693504322/?q=reports&sid=0kdU08yU0bX4HXh4C (accessed: August 10, 2013).

[44] Explore Your Activity Log, Facebook, http://www.facebook.com/help/www/437430672945092?rdrhc (accessed: August 8, 2013).

[45] "Adding Friends and Friends Request," Help Center, Facebook, http://www.facebook.com/help/cookies#!/help/360212094049906/ (accessed: August 10, 2013).

[46] Ibid.

[47] "How Do I change my relationship status from my timeline?" Help Center, Facebook, http://www.facebook.com/help/cookies#!/help/251060974929772/?q=family&sid=0w66801oVWtQQGV66 (accessed: August 10, 2013).

[48] "How the News Feed Works?" Help Center, Facebook, http://www.facebook.com/help/cookies#!/help/327131014036297/ (accessed: August 10, 2013).

[49] Ibid.

[50] "Page Basic," Help Center, Facebook, http://www.facebook.com/help/?ref=pf#!/help/281592001947683/ (accessed: August 10, 2013).

[51] "Commenting," Help Center, Facebook, http://www.facebook.com/help/search/?query=delete#!/help/499181503442334/ (accessed: August 5, 2013).

[52] "Tagging," Help Center, Facebook. http://www.facebook.com/help/search/?query=delete#!/help/366702950069221/ (accessed: August 5, 2013).

[53] "Messages," Help Center, Facebook, http://www.facebook.com/help/search/?query=delete#!/help/326534794098501/ (accessed: August 5, 2013).

[54] "How Do I start a video call with a friend," Help Center, Facebook, http://www.facebook.com/help/240197935990595/ (accessed: August 5, 2013).

[55] "Pokes," Help Center, Facebook, http://www.facebook.com/help/?ref=pf#!/help/451424538215150/ (accessed: August 5, 2013).

[56] Social Plugins, Facebook for Websites, Facebook Developers, http://developers.facebook.com/docs/guides/web/ (accessed:

August 5, 2013).

[57] Ibid.

[58] "Open Graph Overview," Documentation, Facebook Developers, http://developers.facebook.com/docs/opengraph/overview/ (accessed: August 5, 2013).

[59] "About Apps," Help Center, Facebook, http://www.facebook.com/help/?ref=pf#!/help/493707223977442/ (accessed: August 5, 2013).

[60] "Learn How Apps Interact with Your Info," Facebook, http://www.facebook.com/help/?ref=pf#!/help/262314300536014/ (accessed: August 5, 2013).

[61] David Kirkpatrick, *The Facebook Effect: The Inside Story of the Company That is Connecting the World,* (New York: Simon & Schuster, 2010), 215.

[62] App Center, Facebook, http://www.facebook.com/appcenter/?ref=pf (accessed: August 5, 2013).

[63] Ibid.
[64] Ibid.

[65] **3. Addiction**
App Center, Facebook, http://www.facebook.com/appcenter/?ref=pf (accessed: August 5, 2013).

Gabe Zichermann and Christopher Cunningham, *Gamification by Design: Implementing Game Mechanics in Web and Mobile Apps,* O'Reilly Media, 2011., xv.

[66] Form 10-K Annual Report, Facebook Inc. Investor Relations, Facebook, Feb 1, 2013, http://investor.fb.com/secfiling.cfm?filingID=1326801-13-3&CIK=1326801 (accessed: August 1, 2013).

[67] Fourth Quarter 2012 Earnings Call Facebook Inc., Investor Relations, Facebook, Jan 30, 2013, http://files.shareholder.com/downloads/AMDA-NJ5DZ/2449166033x0x631892/cc895d21-303f-4afe-a564-dd2641a04ab9/Facebook_Q412EarningsTranscript.pdf (accessed: August 1, 2013).

[68] "Second Quarter 2013," Investor Relations, Facebook, July 24, 2013, http://files.shareholder.com/downloads/AMDA-NJ5DZ/2605021042x0x679671/78c697f6-a66a-43fb-9d17-a5cdae0041a7/Transcript_FB_July%2024_2013.pdf (accessed: August 2, 2013).

[69] "Other information we receive about you," Data Use Policy, Facebook, December 11, 2012, http://www.facebook.com/full_data_use_policy (accessed: August 2, 2013).

[70] "Logging in to another site using Facebook," Data Use Policy, Facebook, December11, 2012, http://www.facebook.com/full_data_use_policy#ip (accessed: August 2, 2013).

[71] "About instant personalization, Logging in to another site using Facebook," Data Use Policy, Facebook, December 11, 2012, http://www.facebook.com/full_data_use_policy#ip (accessed: August 2, 2013).

[72] Form 10-K Annual Report. Facebook, Inc. Investor Relations, Facebook, February 1, 2013, http://investor.fb.com/secfiling.cfm?filingID=1326801-13-3&CIK=1326801 (accessed: August 1, 2013).

[73] "People You May Know," Help Center, Facebook, http://www.facebook.com/help#!/help/501283333222485/ (accessed: August 2, 2013)

[74] Startups - Jonathan Abrams-TWiST #303, ThisWeekIn, November 6, 2012, http://www.youtube.com/watch?v=GDs2nJf6lro (accessed: July 24, 2013).

[75] "Blocking People," Help Center, Facebook, http://www.facebook.com/help/104941232944896/#!/help/290450221052800/

[76] Roger Scruton, "Hiding Behind the Screen," *New Atlantis: A Journal of Technology & Society*, (2010), Vol. 28, p48-60, (accessed: July 24, 2013).

[77] "How to Report Things," Help Center, Facebook, http://www.facebook.com/help/124970597582337/#!/help/181495968648557/ (accessed: August 2, 2013).

[78] "Facebook.com Site Info," Alexa, http://www.alexa.com/siteinfo/facebook.com (accessed: April 22, 2013).

[79] "Cookies," Facebook, http://www.facebook.com/help/cookies

[80] Keith Hampton, Lauren Sessions, Cameron Marlow and Lee Rainie, "Why most Facebook users get more than they give," *Pew Internet Research*, February 3, 2012, http://www.pewinternet.org/Reports/2012/Facebook-users/Summary/Power-Users.aspx

[81] Roger Scruton, "Hiding Behind the Screen," *New Atlantis: A Journal of Technology & Society*, (2010), Vol. 28, p48-60.

[82] Browser Media, Socialnomics, MacWorld Research, as cited in "Social Networking Statistics," Statistics Brain, December 11, 2012, http://www.statisticbrain.com/social-networking-statistics/ (accessed: August 2, 2013).

[83] Second Quarter 2012 Earnings Call, Facebook Inc., Investor Relations, Facebook July 26, 2012, http://files.shareholder.com/downloads/AMDA-NJ5DZ/2449170695x0x586612/755f05ca-750e-4e49-827c-e9acd9560cc8/FacebookQ212EarningsCallTranscript.pdf (accessed: August 2, 2013).

[84] Form 10-K Annual Report. Facebook, Inc., February 1, 2013, http://investor.fb.com/secfiling.cfm?filingID=1326801-13-3&CIK=1326801 (accessed: August 3, 2013).

[85] "Facebook facelift! Social network to launch new version of the News Feed amid concerns over user fatigue," *Associated Press*, March 7, 2013, http://www.pewinternet.org/Media-Mentions/2013/Social-network-to-launch-new-version-of-the-News-Feed-amid-concerns-over-user-fatigue.aspx (accessed: August 3, 2013).

[86] "Deleting and Deactivating Your Account," Data Use Policy, Facebook, December 11, 2012, http://www.facebook.com/full_data_use_policy#ip (accessed: August 3, 2013).

[87] Form 10-K Annual Report, Facebook, Inc. Investor Relations, Facebook February 1, 2013, http://investor.fb.com/secfiling.cfm?filingID=1326801-13-3&CIK=1326801 (accessed: August 1, 2013).

[88] Form 10-Q. Facebook, Inc. United States Securities and Exchange Commission. Investor Relations, July 31, 2012, http://investor.fb.com/secfiling.cfm?filingID=1193125-12-325997&CIK=1326801

[89] Lee Rainie, Aaron Smith, and Maeve Duggan, "Coming and Going on Facebook", February 5, 2013, *Pew Internet Research*, http://www.pewinternet.org/Reports/2013/Coming-and-going-on-facebook.aspx (accessed: August 2, 2013).

[90] Form 10-K Annual Report, Facebook, Inc., Investor Relations, Facebook, February 1, 2013, http://investor.fb.com/secfiling.cfm?filingID=1326801-13-3&CIK=1326801 (accessed: August 1, 2013).

[91] "What's a recognized device?" Help Center, Facebook, http://www.facebook.com/help/339635806085622 (accessed: August 7, 2013).

[92] "How do I use my security question to get into my account?" Help Center, Facebook, http://www.facebook.com/help/221138037913489 (accessed: August 18, 2013).

[93] "Extra Security Features," Help Center, Facebook, http://www.facebook.com/help/?ref=pf#!/help/413023562082171/ (accessed: July 31, 2013).

[94] Active Sessions, Extra Security Features," Help Center, Facebook, http://www.facebook.com/help/?ref=pf#!/help/413023562082171/ (accessed: July 31, 2013).

[95] Ibid.

[96] "What's the difference between deleting a story and hiding a story from my timeline?" Help Center, Facebook, http://www.facebook.com/help/?ref=pf#!/help/229406343794650/?q=hiding&sid=0vxvp6I7TztfMbWg9 (accessed: July 31, 2013).

[97] What's the difference between deactivating and deleting my account?" Help Center, Facebook, http://www.facebook.com/help/125338004213029/ (accessed: July 31, 2013).

[98] "Active Sessions," Extra Security Features, Help Center, Facebook, https://www.facebook.com/help/?ref=pf#!/help/413023562082171/ (accessed: July 31, 2013).

[99] "State of Security," *MacAfee and Evalueserve*, 2012, http://www.mcafee.com/us/resources/white-papers/wp-state-of-security.pdf (accessed: August 2, 2013).

[100] "Facebook & your privacy: Who sees the data you share on the biggest social network?" *Consumer Reports Magazine*. June 2012. http://www.consumerreports.org/cro/magazine/2012/06/facebook-your-privacy/index.htm (accessed: August 2, 2013).

[101] Data Use Policy, Facebook, http://www.facebook.com/about/privacy (accessed: July 31, 2013).

[102] "Downloading Your Info," Facebook, https://www.facebook.com/help/?ref=pf#!/help/131112897028467/ (Date of Access: July 31, 2013).

[103] Help Center, Facebook, https://www.facebook.com/help/?ref=pf#!/help/ (accessed: July 31, 2013).

[104] "How Do I report a violation," Help Center, Facebook, http://www.facebook.com/help/?ref=pf#!/help/263149623790594/ (accessed: July 31, 2013).

[105] "What's secure browsing (https)? How do I turn it on?" Help Center, Facebook, https://www.facebook.com/help/156236274442491#!/help/156201551113407?q=encryption&sid=0jSBcuoK813LmpYVW (accessed: July 31, 2013).

Peter Eckersley, "How secure is HTTPS today? How often is it attacked?" *Electronic Frontier Foundation*, October 25, 2011, https://www.eff.org/deeplinks/2011/10/how-secure-https-today (accessed: August 3, 2013).

[106] Christopher Soghoian, "Your ISP and the Government: Best Friends Forever," *DEFCON 18*, YouTube, October 26, 2010, .http://www.youtube.com/watch?v=t0aQojDGSD4 (accessed: July 31, 2013).

[107] Ibid.

[108] Ibid.
[109] Alex Rice, "A Continued Commitment to Security," *The Facebook Blog*, January 26, 2011,

https://www.facebook.com/blog/blog.php?post=486790652130 (accessed: July 31, 2013)

[110] Andrew Cunningham, "Keep it secret, keep it safe: A beginner's guide to Web safety understanding encryption is key to protecting yourself on the Web", *ArsTechnica*, Jan 30, 2013, http://arstechnica.com/security/2013/01/keep-it-secret-keep-it-safe-a-beginners-guide-to-web-safety/ (accessed: July 31, 2013).

[111] James Bamford," Confronting the Surveillance Society" at ACLU Washington, http://www.youtube.com/watch?NR=1&v=V0jZOaJ6gpk&feature=endscreen (accessed: July 31, 2013).

[112] Moxie Marlinspike, "New Tricks For Defeating SSL," Blackhat 2009 http://www.blackhat.com/presentations/bh-dc-09/Marlinspike/BlackHat-DC-09-Marlinspike-Defeating-SSL.pdf (accessed: August 7, 2013).

[113] Kashmir Hill, "Facebook's Top Cop: Joe Sullivan," Forbes February 22, 2012, http://www.forbes.com/sites/kashmirhill/2012/02/22/facebooks-top-cop-joe-sullivan/ (accessed: September 20, 2013).

[114] "Protecting People On Facebook," Facebook, February 15, 2013
https://www.facebook.com/notes/facebook-security/protecting-people-on-facebook/10151249208250766 (accessed: September 7, 2013).

Max Kelly, Facebook Security: Fighting the Good Fight," Facebook, August 7, 2008
https://blog.facebook.com/blog.php?post=25844207130

[115] Steven Musil, "Facebook awarded $711 million in spam lawsuit," CNet. October 29, 2009, http://news.cnet.com/8301-1023_3-10387021-93/facebook-awarded-$711-million-in-spam-lawsuit/ (accessed: September 6, 2013).

Elinor Mills, "At Facebook, defense is offense," CNET, January 31, 2011, http://news.cnet.com/8301-27080_3-20029954-245.html (accessed: September 6, 2013).

[116] Elinor Mills, "At Facebook, defense is offense."

[117] Facebook Bug Bounty, https://www.facebook.com/BugBounty (accessed: September 7, 2013
[118] Important Message from Facebook's White Hat Program, Facebook, June 21, 2013,
https://www.facebook.com/notes/facebook-security/important-message-from-facebooks-white-hat-program/10151437074840766 (accessed: September 5, 2013).

[119] Facebook Security, https://www.facebook.com/security (accessed: September 5, 2013)
[120] AV Marketplace, Facebook, https://www.facebook.com/security/app_360406100715618 (accessed: September 5, 2013).

[121] Julie Bort, "Facebook Has A Full-Time Team Of 30 Fighting Spam And Hackers," *Business Insider*, Jan. 14, 2012,
http://www.businessinsider.com/facebook-is-spending-millions-to-thwart-spammers-and-hackers-2012-1#ixzz2e8vKbneZ (accessed: September 6, 2013).

[122] Facebook's Continued Fight Against Koobface," Facebook Security, January 17, 2012,
https://www.facebook.com/notes/facebook-security/facebooks-continued-fight-against-koobface/10150474399670766 (accessed: September 5, 2013).

[123] "Facebook for Business," Facebook, http://www.facebook.com/business/overview (accessed: July 31, 2013).

[124] "Connect with people," Facebook, http://www.facebook.com/business/connect (accessed: August 2, 2013)

[125] "Targeting Options," Help Center, Facebook, http://www.facebook.com/help/337584869654348/#!/help/131834970288134/ (accessed: August 3, 2013)

[126] "Campaign Cost & Budgeting," Help Center, Facebook,
http://www.facebook.com/help/337584869654348/#!/help/318171828273417/ (accessed: August 3, 2013)

[127] "Account Spending Cap," Help Center, Facebook, http://www.facebook.com/help/?ref=pf#!/help/317877674969069/ (accessed: August 2, 2013).

[128] Where will my ad show on Facebook?" The Basics, Ads & Sponsored Stories, Facebook,
http://www.facebook.com/help/337584869654348/#!/help/326113794144384//

[129] Ads Reporting, Facebook, https://www.facebook.com/help/www/336893449723054?rdrhc#!/help/www/251850888259489/ (accessed: August 20, 2013).

[130] Social %, Facebook,
https://www.facebook.com/help/www/336893449723054?rdrhc#!/help/www/133004883442468?q=social%20%25&sid=01aNWleQFDmBPR5IV (accessed: August 19, 2013).

[131] "Facebook Advertising Guidelines," Facebook, July 26, 2013, http://www.facebook.com/ad_guidelines.php (accessed: August 2, 2013).

[132] "Adware," Help Center, Facebook, http://www.facebook.com/help/399392800124391/#!/help/380632641992051/ (accessed:

August 2, 2013).

[133] "Privacy For Apps and for Website," Help Center, Facebook, http://www.facebook.com/help/?ref=pf#!/help/403786193017893/ (accessed: August 3, 2013)

[134] Yonggui Wang, Hui Feng, "Customer relationship management capabilities: Measurement, antecedents and consequences", *Management Decision*, Vol. 50 Iss: 1, 2002, pp.115 – 129.

[135] Clara Shih, *The Facebook Era: Tapping Online Social Networks to Market, Sell, and Innovate,* (Boston: Prentice Hall, 2009), 85-90.
[136] Ibid.

[137] Steven Greenhouse, "Even if It Enrages Your Boss, Social Net Speech is Protected," *The New York Times*, January 21, 2013, http://www.nytimes.com/2013/01/22/technology/employers-social-media-policies-come-under-regulatory-scrutiny.html?pagewanted=all&_r=0 (accessed: August 3, 2013).

[138] Clara Shih, *The Facebook Era, 43-57.*
[139] Lauren Drell, "4 Ways Behavioral Targeting Is Changing the Web," *Mashable*. April 26, 2011, http://mashable.com/2011/04/26/behavioral-targeting/ (accessed: August 3, 2013).

[140] Federal Trade Commission, *Self-Regulatory Principles for Online Behavioral Advertising,* N.p.: n.p., 2009, ii, http://www.ftc.gov/os/2009/02/P085400behavadreport.pdf (accessed: July 9, 2012).

[141] Sut Jhally, "Advertising and the Perfect Storm: Global Warming, Peak Oil, and Consumer Debt," at Green Field Community College, October 14, 2010, http://www.youtube.com/watch?v=WNy9s5qR4i0 (accessed: August, 11, 2013).

[142] Ibid.

[143] 2012 Annual Norton Cybercrime Report, Symantec, http://now-static.norton.com/now/en/pu/images/Promotions/2012/cybercrimeReport/2012_Norton_Cybercrime_Report_Master_FINAL_050912.pdf (accessed: August 18, 2013).

[144] "Facebook & Your Privacy: Who sees the data you share on the biggest social network?" *Consumer Reports Magazine*, June 2012, http://www.consumerreports.org/cro/magazine/2012/06/facebook-your-privacy/index.htm (accessed: August 3, 2013).

Second Quarter 2012 Earnings Call, Facebook, Inc., Investor Relations, Facebook, July 26, 2012, http://files.shareholder.com/downloads/AMDA-NJ5DZ/2449170695x0x586612/755f05ca-750e-4e49-827c-e9acd9560cc8/FacebookQ212EarningsCallTranscript.pdf

[145] Michael B. Sauter, Adam Poltrack, and Ashley C. Allen, "Nine Major Ways Criminals Use Facebook," *Yahoo!*, May 16, 2012, http://finance.yahoo.com/news/nine-major-ways-criminals-use-facebook.html?page=1 (accessed: August 18, 2013).

"Facebook Fraud: Identity Theft through Social Networking," *Experian,* 2010, http://www.protectmyid.com/images/education_center/pdf/050TypesofFraud/7_types%20of%20fraud_social%20networking.pdf (accessed: August 18, 2013).

[146] Ira Winkler, "How to Recruit Spies on the Internet," *RCA Conference*, 2011, http://www.youtube.com/watch?v=bUpFXEa-B24 (accessed: August 2, 2013).

[147] Ibid.
[148] Federal Bureau of Investigation, "Internet Social Networking Risks," *Counterintelligence*, Aug 11, 2012, http://www.fbi.gov/about-us/investigate/counterintelligence/internet-social-networking-risks (accessed: August 3, 2013).

[149] 2012 Annual Norton Cybercrime Report, Symantec.

[150] Privacy Rights Clearinghouse, "Fraud on Social Networks," *Fact Sheet 35: Social Networking Privacy: How to be Safe, Secure and Social*, 2013, https://www.privacyrights.org/social-networking-privacy#malware (accessed: August 18, 2013).

[151] Michael B. Sauter, Adam Poltrack and Ashley C. Allen, "Nine Major Ways Criminals Use Facebook."

[152] Federal Bureau of Investigation, "Internet Social Networking Risks," *Counterintelligence*, Aug 11, 2012, http://www.fbi.gov/about-us/investigate/counterintelligence/internet-social-networking-risks (accessed: August 3, 2013).

Mathew J. Schwartz, "Facebook Revamps Pages Administrator Security Controls". *Information Week*, May 31, 2012, http://www.informationweek.com/security/management/facebook-revamps-pages-administrator-sec/240001282 (accessed: April 5, 2013).

[153] 2012 Annual Norton Cybercrime Report, Symantec.

[154] "Report a Violation," Help Center, Facebook, http://www.facebook.com/help#!/help/263149623790594/ (accessed: August 6, 2013).

[155] Jim Edwards, "How Facebook Is Hunting Down And Deleting Fake Accounts", *Business Insider*, December 29, 2012, http://www.businessinsider.com/facebook-fake-likes-and-accounts-2012-12

Joseph Menn, "Social networks scan for sexual predators, with uneven results," *Reuters*, July 12, 2012, http://www.reuters.com/article/2012/07/12/us-usa-internet-predators-idUSBRE86B05G20120712 (accessed: August 6, 2013).

[156] Research, Cyber Bullying Research Center, http://cyberbullying.us/research/ (accessed: August 18, 2013).

"Cyber/Bullying Statistics," Bureau of Justice Statistics, US Department of Health and Human Services, Cyberbullying Research Center, *Statistics Brain*, May, 7, 2013, http://www.statisticbrain.com/cyber-bullying-statistics/

Cyber Bullying: Statistics and Tips, iSafe, http://www.isafe.org/outreach/media/media_cyber_bullying (accessed: August 18, 2013).

Corey Murray, "25 Eye-Opening Statistics About Cyberbullying [Infographic]," *EDTech Magazine*, Jhttp://www.edtechmagazine.com/k12/article/2012/07/cyberbully-takedown-infographic (accessed: August 18, 2013).

[157] Jordan Crook, "Facebook Still Reigns Supreme With Teens, But Social Media Interest Dwindling," TechCrunch, April 10, 2013, http://techcrunch.com/2013/04/10/facebook-still-reigns-supreme-with-teens-but-social-media-interest-dwindling/ (accessed: August 18, 2013).

[158] "What is Bullying? What Happens when I block someone?" Facebook, http://www.facebook.com/help/search/?query=blocking#!/help/131930530214371/?q=blocking&sid=0zGgpZtNFDdoUIAtD (accessed: August 18, 2013).

[159] "How to Report Violations," Facebook, https://www.facebook.com/help/263149623790594 (accessed: August 12, 2013).

Justin W. Patchin, "Help With Fake Facebook Profile Page", *Cyberbullying Research Center*, July 25, 2012, http://cyberbullying.us/help-with-fake-facebook-profile-pages/

[160] "Cyberbulling," *KidsHealth*, http://kidshealth.org/parent/positive/talk/cyberbullying.html (accessed: August 12, 2013).

[161] Amanda Lenhart, Mary Madden, Aaron Smith, Kristen Purcell, Kathryn Zickuhr, and Lee Rainie, "Teens, kindness and cruelty on social network sites," *Pew Internet Research*, November 9, 2011, http://pewinternet.org/Reports/2011/Teens-and-social-media/Part-1/Facebook.aspx (accessed: August 3, 2013).

[162] Kimberly J. Mitchell, Ph.D.*, David Finkelhor, Ph.D., Lisa M. Jones, Ph.D., and Janis Wolak, J.D. "Use of Social Networking Sites in Online Sex Crimes Against Minors: An Examination of National Incidence and Means of Utilization," *Journal of Adolescent Health* (2010) 1–8 http://www.unh.edu/ccrc/pdf/CV174.pdf Enough is Enough. 2013.

[163] Mary Madden, Amanda Lenhart, Sandra Cortesi, Urs Gasser, Maeve Duggan, Aaron Smith, Meredith Beaton, "Teens, Social Media, and Privacy," *Pew Internet Research* May 21, 2013, http://www.pewinternet.org/Reports/2013/Teens-Social-Media-And-Privacy/Summary-of-Findings.aspx (accessed: August 6, 2013).

[164] "Facebook & your privacy: Who sees the data you share on the biggest social network?" *Consumer Reports Magazine*, June 2012, http://www.consumerreports.org/cro/magazine/2012/06/facebook-your-privacy/index.htm

[165] Donna L Stewart, "Victim Grooming: Protect Your Child from Sexual Predators", *Parenting.org*, http://www.parenting.org/article/victim-grooming-protect-your-child-sexual-predators

267

166 Kimberly J. Mitchell, Ph.D.*, David Finkelhor, Ph.D., Lisa M. Jones, Ph.D., and Janis Wolak, J.D. "Use of Social Networking Sites in Online Sex Crimes Against Minors: An Examination of National Incidence and Means of Utilization," *Journal of Adolescent Health* (2010) 1–8 http://www.unh.edu/ccrc/pdf/CV174.pdf Enough is Enough. 2013

167 Chelsea Shilling, "Kids Raped, Sodomized on Facebook Pages Bombshell! America's favorite social network is child-predator playground," World News Daily, May 6, 2012, http://www.wnd.com/2012/05/kids-raped-sodomized-on-facebook-pages/ (accessed: August 18, 2013).
168 Ibid.
169 Joseph Spector, "Investigation Claims Facebook the target of child predators," *USA Today*, September 24, 2007, http://usatoday30.usatoday.com/tech/news/2007-09-24-facebook_N.htm (accessed: August 18, 2013).

170 Form 10-Q. Facebook, Inc. United States Securities and Exchange Commission. Investor Relations, July 31, 2012, http://investor.fb.com/secfiling.cfm?filingID=1193125-12-325997&CIK=1326801 (accessed: August 18, 2013).

Heather Kelly. "83 million Facebook accounts are fakes and dupes", *CNN*, August 2, 2012, http://www.cnn.com/2012/08/02/tech/social-media/facebook-fake-accounts

171 Title 18 U.S.C., Section 1831.

172 "Definition of Industrial Espionage," Investopedia, http://www.investopedia.com/terms/i/industrial-espionage.asp (accessed: August 18, 2013).

173 C. Frank Figliuzzi Assistant Director, Counterintelligence Division Federal Bureau of Investigation Statement Before the House Committee on Homeland Security, Subcommittee on Counterterrorism and Intelligence, Washington, D.C., June 28, 2012, http://www.fbi.gov/news/testimony/economic-espionage-a-foreign-intelligence-threat-to-americans-jobs-and-homeland-security (accessed August 2, 2013).

174 Emil Protalinski, "NSA: Cybercrime is 'the greatest transfer of wealth in history," *ZDNet*, July 10, 2012, http://www.zdnet.com/nsa-cybercrime-is-the-greatest-transfer-of-wealth-in-history-7000000598/ (accessed August 3, 2013).

175 Ira Winkler, "How to Recruit Spies on the Internet," *RCA Conference*, 2011, http://www.youtube.com/watch?v=bUpFXEa-B24 (accessed: August 2, 2013).

176 Ned Smith, "Three out of four workers (75 percent) access social media on the job from their mobile devices at least once a day, and 60 percent access it multiple times", *Business News Daily*, October 4, 2012, http://www.businessnewsdaily.com/3220-employee-social-media.html (accessed August 3, 2013).

Sharon Gaudin, "Study: Facebook use cuts productivity at work Survey finds 77% of Facebookers use the social networking site while on the job."

177 Ira Winkler, "How to Recruit Spies on the Internet," *RCA Conference*, 2011, http://www.youtube.com/watch?v=bUpFXEa-B24 (accessed: August 2, 2013).

178 Gabriel Weiman, "How Modern Terrorism Uses the Internet", *The Journal of Internet Affairs,* Number 8, 2005, http://www.securityaffairs.org/issues/2005/08/weimann.php (accessed July 29, 2013).

179 Catherine A. Theohary, "Terrorist Use of the Internet: Information Operations in Cyberspace", *Congressional Research Service*, March 8, 2011, http://www.fas.org/sgp/crs/terror/R41674.pdf (accessed August 3, 2013).

180 Joseph Kunkle, "Social Media and the Homegrown Terrorist Threat", *Police Chief Magazine*, July 2013, http://www.policechiefmagazine.org/magazine/index.cfm?fuseaction=display&article_id=2692&issue_id=62012

181 Theohary, "Terrorist Use of the Internet: Information Operations in Cyberspace."

182 Damien Gayle, "FBI arrest Facebook 'cybercrime ring' after they 'infected 11m computers with viruses and stole £525million," *The Daily Mail*, December 12, 2012, http://www.dailymail.co.uk/sciencetech/article-2246857/Facebook-helps-FBI-bust-cybercriminal-ring-infected-11m-

computers-viruses-stole-525million.html

[183] Riva Richmond, "Web Gang Operating in the Open," *The New York Times*, January 16, 2012, http://www.nytimes.com/2012/01/17/technology/koobface-gang-that-used-facebook-to-spread-worm-operates-in-the-open.html?pagewanted=all&_r=0

[184] "Facebook and the FBI Partner to Take Botnet Offline," Facebook, December 12, 2012, https://www.facebook.com/notes/facebook-security/facebook-and-the-fbi-partner-to-take-botnet-offline/10151134554125766

[185] Gabriel Weiman, "How Modern Terrorism Uses the Internet", *The Journal of Internet Affairs,* Number 8, 2005, http://www.securityaffairs.org/issues/2005/08/weimann.php (accessed July 29, 2013).

[186] Christopher Soghoian, DEF CON 18 Hacking Conference Presentation: Your ISP and the Government BFF . ISPs, April 27, 2013, http://www.youtube.com/watch?v=U9nWgZ0yGpI (August 6, 2013).

[187] Facebook's Continued Fight Against Koobface," Facebook Security

[188] Orin Kerr, "Digital Evidence and the New Criminal Procedure," in *Cybercrime: Digital Cops in a Networked Environment,* ed. Katz Eddan, James Grimmelmann, Nimrod Kozlovski, Shlomit Wagman, Tal Zarsky (New York University Press. 2007), 221-246.

[189] "Social Media Use in Law Enforcement Investigations," *LexisNexis,* 2012. http://www.lexisnexis.com/government/investigations/ (accessed: July 25, 2013).

[190] Nick Summers, "Walking the Cyberbeat," *The Daily Beast*, April 30, 2009, http://www.thedailybeast.com/newsweek/2009/04/30/walking-the-cyberbeat.html

[191] "Information for Law Enforcement Authorities," Safety Center, Facebook, http://www.facebook.com/safety/groups/law/guidelines/ (accessed: August 12, 2013).

[192] Information for Law Enforcement Authorities," Facebook.

[193] National Security Letters, Electronic Frontier Foundation, https://www.eff.org/issues/national-security-letters (accessed: August 12, 2013).

[194] Information for Law Enforcement Authorities, Facebook.

[195] "Federal Judge Finds National Security Letters Unconstitutional," *Wired*, March 15, 2013, www.wired.com/threatlevel/2013/03/nsl-found-unconstitutional/ (accessed: August 18, 2013).

[196] Information for Law Enforcement Authorities, Facebook.

[197] Julie Masis, "Is this lawman your Facebook friend? Increasingly, investigators use social networking websites for police work", *Globe Correspondent*, January 11, 2009, as posted on Boston.com, http://www.boston.com/news/local/articles/2009/01/11/is_this_lawman_your_facebook_friend/?page=full (accessed: August 18, 2013).

[198] "Evolution of the Redwood City Police Department's Social Media Program presented by Lt Rhonda Leipeit, Officer Chris Rasmussen of Redwood City Police & Geneva Bosquez of Freemont Police, SMILE, http://smileconference.com/live/

[199] Julie Masis, "Is this lawman your Facebook friend? Increasingly, investigators use social networking websites for police work".

[200] International Center for Social Media, "Building Your Presence with Facebook Pages, a Guide for Police Departments," Facebook, http://www.iacpsocialmedia.org/Portals/1/documents/FacebookPagesGuide.pdf (accessed: August 3, 2013).

[201] Ibid.

[202] Thomas Fingar, Chapter 1: Analysis in the Intelligence Community: Purpose, Masters, and Methods, in *Intelligence*

Analysis: Behavioral and Social Scientific Foundations, National Research Council, Washington, DC: The National Academies Press, 2011, 9-13.

203 James Bamford. *The Shadow Factory: The NSA from 9/11 to the Eavesdropping on America*, 2008,   Anchor Books, Random House.

204 National Reconnaissance Office, Members of the IC, Director of National Intelligence, http://www.dni.gov/index.php/intelligence-community/members-of-the-ic#nga (accessed: August 18, 2013).

205 National Geospatial-Intelligence Agency, Members of the IC, Director of National Intelligence, http://www.dni.gov/index.php/intelligence-community/members-of-the-ic#nga (accessed: August 18, 2013).

206 James Bamford, *Body of Secrets: The Anatomy of the Ultra Secret National Security Agency from the Cold War to the dawn of a new century,* (New York: Anchor Books, 2001), 358, 399.

207 "Mark Klein," *C-SPAN Video*, November 8, 2007, http://www.c-spanvideo.org/program/201508-6 (accessed: August 3, 2013).

"Exclusive: National Security Agency Whistleblower William Binney on Growing State Surveillance," *Democracy Now!* April 20, 2012, http://www.democracynow.org/2012/4/20/exclusive_national_security_agency_whistleblower_william

Dan Farber, "U.S. v. Whistleblower Tom Drake," *CBS News*, October 18, 2012, http://www.cbsnews.com/8301-503544_162-20122207-503544/thomas-drake-the-dark-side-of-data-and-the-nsa/

"Exclusive: Did U.S. Spy On Journalists?" *Countdown with Keith Olbermann*, MSNBC, January 21, 2009, http://www.youtube.com/watch?v=vqigfE0nBs0 *(accessed: August 4, 2013).*

208 Glenn Greenwald and Ewin MacAskill, "NSA Prism program taps in to user data of Apple, Google and others," *The Guardian*, June 6, 2013, http://www.theguardian.com/world/2013/jun/06/us-tech-giants-nsa-data?guni=Article:in%20body%20link&guni=Article:in%20body%20link (accessed: August 12, 2013).

209 Mark Zuckerberg, Newsroom, Facebook, June 7, 2013, https://www.facebook.com/zuck/posts/10100828955847631 (accessed: June 7, 2013).

210 Max Kelly, "Memories of Friends Departed Endure on Facebook," *The Facebook Blog*, October 26, 2009, https://www.facebook.com/blog/blog.php?post=163091042130

211 James Risen and Nick Wingfield, "Web's Reach Binds N.S.A. and Silicon Valley Leaders," *The New York Times*, June 19, 2013, http://www.nytimes.com/2013/06/20/technology/silicon-valley-and-spy-agency-bound-by-strengthening-web.html?pagewanted=all&_r=0 (accessed: August 4, 2013).

212 [216]James Bamford, "NSA Chief Denies Domestic Spying But Whistleblowers Say Otherwise," *Wired*, May 21, 2012, http://www.wired.com/threatlevel/?p=39308 (accessed: August 12, 2013).

213 Kimberly Dozier, "AP Exclusive: CIA following Twitter, Facebook," Associated Press, November 4, 2011, http://news.yahoo.com/ap-exclusive-cia-following-twitter-facebook-081055316.html

Catherine Herridge, FBI seeks developers for app to track suspicious social media posts, sparking privacy concerns, Fox News, February 16, 2012 http://www.foxnews.com/politics/2012/02/16/fbi-seeks-developers-for-app-to-track-suspicious-social-media-posts-sparking/#ixzz2f9ockPjV

214 Kimberly Dozier, "AP Exclusive: CIA following Twitter, Facebook,"

215 Tim Shorrock, *Spies for Hire: The Secret World of Intelligence Outsourcing 1ˢᵗ Edition, (*Simon & Schuster; 2008), 13-17, 23, 97, 151.

216 Ibid, 17-18.

[217] Rao Leena, "Palantir Technologies Raises $70 Million At $2.5 Billion Valuation," *Tech Crunch*, October 6, 2011, http://techcrunch.com/2011/10/06/palantir-technologies-raises-70-million-at-2-5-billion-valuation/ (accessed: August 4, 2013).

[218] "About", Palantir, http://www.palantir.com/about/ (assessed: July 25, 2013).

[219] Alexander Karp, Interview by Charlie Rose, *The Charlie Rose Show*, PBS, August 11, 2009.

[220] Robin Wauters, "Social Media Monitoring Company Visible Technologies Lands $6 Million," *Tech Crunch*, March 31, 2011, http://techcrunch.com/2011/03/31/social-media-monitoring-company-visible-technologies-lands-6-million/ (accessed: August 4, 2013).

[221] "About Visible Technologies," Visible Technologies, http://www.visibletechnologies.com/about/ (accessed: August 4, 2013).

[222] Recorded Future, https://www.recordedfuture.com/

[223] "How Recorded Future Works," Recorded Future, https://www.recordedfuture.com/this-is-recorded-future/how-recorded-future-works/ (accessed: August 4, 2013).

[224] Social Media Command Center, InTTENSITY, http://www.inttensity.com/products/social-media-command-center/ (accessed: August 4, 2013).

[225] Quid, http://quid.com/

[226] BBN Web Monitoring System Version 2, *BBN Technologies,* http://bbn.com/products_and_services/web_monitoring_system/

[227] Defense Electronics, *Open Secrets.org*, 2012, http://www.opensecrets.org/pacs/industry.php?txt=D02&cycle=2012

[228] The 9/11 Commission Report: Final Report of the National Commission on Terrorist Attacks Upon the United States," (Authorized Edition), *National Commission on Terrorist Attacks*, (New York: W.W. Norton Company, 2004).

[229] James Igoe Walsh, The International Politics of Intelligence Sharing, Columbia University Press, 2010, http://cup.columbia.edu/book/978-0-231-15410-9/the-international-politics-of-intelligence-sharing/excerpt

[230] James Bamford. *The Shadow Factory, 17, 20*

[231] Department of Homeland Security, "Fusion Centers and Joint Terrorism Task Force Centers," http://www.dhs.gov/fusion-centers-and-joint-terrorism-task-forces (accessed: August 4, 2013).

[232] United States Senate, "Federal Support for and Involvement in State and Local Fusion Centers," *Permanent Subcommittee on Investigations*, October 3, 2012, http://www.hsgac.senate.gov/subcommittees/investigations/media/investigative-report-criticizes-counterterrorism-reporting-waste-at-state-and-local-intelligence-fusion-centers (accessed: August 4, 2013).

[233] "Homeland Security watches Twitter, social media," *Reuters*, January 11, 2012, http://www.reuters.com/article/2012/01/11/us-usa-homelandsecurity-websites-idUSTRE80A1RC20120111 (accessed: August 4, 2013).

[234]

[235] United States Senate, "Federal Support for and Involvement in State and Local Fusion Centers," *Permanent Subcommittee on Investigations*, October 3, 2012, http://www.hsgac.senate.gov/subcommittees/investigations/media/investigative-report-criticizes-counterterrorism-reporting-waste-at-state-and-local-intelligence-fusion-centers (accessed: August 4, 2013).

[236] [241] Federal Bureau of Investigation, 2011 Annual United States Crime Report, http://www.fbi.gov/news/stories/2012/october/annual-crime-in-the-u.s.-report-released (accessed: August 20, 2013).

[237] Christopher Westphal, *Data Mining for Intelligence, Fraud, & Criminal Detection: Advanced Analytics Information Sharing Technologies,* (Boca Raton, FL: CRC Press, 2009), xii.

[238] [243] Sir David Omand, Jamie Bartlett, and Carl Miller, *Introducing Social Media Intelligence (SOCMINT), Intelligence and National Security,* (Routledge, Taylor and Francis Group 2012), 1–23.

[239] "Facebook & your privacy: Who sees the data you share on the biggest social network?" *Consumer Reports Magazine,* June 2012, http://www.consumerreports.org/cro/magazine/2012/06/facebook-your-privacy/index.htm (accessed: August 2, 2013).

[240] Robert M. Clark, Intelligence Analysis: A Target Centered Approach 3rd Edition, CQ Press, 75
[241] Ibid., 253.
[242] Ibid, 253.

[243] 3. Robert A. Hanneman and Mark Riddle, *Introduction to social network methods,* Using graphs to represent social relation, Riverside, CA: University of California, Riverside, 2005) (accessed: August 12, 2013).

Robert A. Hanneman and Mark Riddle, *Introduction to social network methods,* 5. Using matrices to represent social relations, (Riverside, CA: University of California, Riverside, 2005), http://faculty.ucr.edu/~hanneman/nettext/C5_%20Matrices.html (accessed: August 3, 2013).

[244] Robert A. Hanneman and Mark Riddle, *Introduction to social network methods* , 11. Cliques and sub-groups (Riverside, CA: University of California, Riverside, 2005), http://faculty.ucr.edu/~hanneman/nettext/C11_Cliques.html#subgraph (accessed: August 3, 2013).

[245] Getting Started: The Graph API, Facebook Developers, http://developers.facebook.com/docs/getting-started/graphapi/ (accessed: August 4, 2013).

[246] Clark, Intelligence Analysis, 19.

[247] Ibid, 81-82.

[248] Clarke, Intelligence Analysis, 207

[249] Heather Kelly, "83 million Facebook accounts are fakes and dupes", *CNN*, August 2, 2012. http://www.cnn.com/2012/08/02/tech/social-media/facebook-fake-accounts (accessed: August 3, 2013).

[250] Christopher Westphal, *Data Mining for Intelligence, Fraud, & Criminal Detection*, 24, 53.

[251] Daniel S. Gressang IV, "The Shortest Distance Between Two Points Lies in Rethinking the Question: Intelligence and the Information Age Technology Challenge", Edited by Johnson, Loch K. Strategic Intelligence: Information from Overseas to the Highest Councils of Government. Roxbury Publishing, 2007, 129.

[252] Ibid., 129.

[253] Data Integration, Technopedia, http://www.techopedia.com/definition/28290/data-integration (accessed: August 20, 2013).

[254] "Updates to Custom Audiences Targeting Tool Downloads," Newsroom, Facebook, February 27, 2013, http://newsroom.fb.com/News/576/Updates-to-Custom-Audiences-Targeting-Tool (accessed: August 4, 2013).

[255] Arvind Narayanan and Vitaly Shmatikov, "Robust De-anonymization of Large Sparse Datasets," The University of Texas at Austin, 2008, https://www.cs.utexas.edu/~shmat/shmat_oak08netflix.pdf (accessed: August 4, 2013).

Gilbert Wondracek, Thorsten Holz, Engin Kirda, Sophia Antipolis, Christopher Kruegel, "Practical Attack to De-Anonymize Social Network Users," IEEE Symposium on Security and Privacy, IEEE Computer Society Press, May 2010, http://www.iseclab.org/papers/sonda-tr.pdf (accessed: August 20, 2013).

[256] Ibid.
[257] Technologies, Palantir, http://www.palantir.com/technologies/ (accessed: August 14, 2013).

Kapow, InTTENSITY, http://www.inttensity.com/products/kapow/ (accessed: August 14, 2013).

[258] Chris Morris. "The Sexiest Job of the 21st Century: Data Analyst," *CNBC*, June 5, 2013, http://www.cnbc.com/id/100792215

(accessed: August 5, 2013).

259 "Information for Law Enforcement Authorities," Facebook.

260 Developing a Policy on the Use of Social Media in Intelligence and Investigative Activities: Guidance and Recommendations, IACP Center for Social Media, http://www.iacpsocialmedia.org/Portals/1/documents/SMInvestigativeGuidance.pdf

261 Ibid.

262 James Bamford. *The Shadow Factory*, 32.
263 United States Senate, "Overview of the Senate Select Committee on Intelligence Responsibilities and Activities," Senate Select Intelligence Committee, http://www.intelligence.senate.gov/about.html (accessed: August 2, 2013).

264 Bamford, *The Shadow Factory*, 32, 230.

265 Church Committee Report on U.S. Spy Agencies," *C-SPAN Video*, September 21, 2006, http://www.c-spanvideo.org/program/194406-1 (accessed: August 2, 2013).

266 U.S. Congressman Mac Thornberry, Committees, http://thornberry.house.gov/biography/committees.htm

United States Senate, "Overview of the Senate Select Committee on Intelligence Responsibilities and Activities", Senate Select Intelligence Committee, http://www.intelligence.senate.gov/about.html (accessed: August 2, 2013).

267 Cyber Information Sharing Protection Act, (H. R. 624).

268 Ben Kersey, "Worse than SOPA, CISPA Bill Passes," *Slashgear*, April 27, 2012, http://www.slashgear.com/worse-than-sopa-cispa-bill-passes-27225004/ (accessed: August 5, 2013).

269 Samantha Murphy, "Cyber-attacks of 2012", *Mashable*, October 8, 2012, http://mashable.com/2012/10/18/cyber-attacks-201/ (accessed: August 4, 2013).

270 Andrew Couts, "CISPA supporters list: 800+ companies that could help Uncle Sam snag your data," *Digital Trends*, April 12, 2012, http://www.digitaltrends.com/web/cispa-supporters-list-800-companies-that-could-help-uncle-sam-snag-your-data/ (accessed: August 4, 2013).

Chris Burns, "Facebook defends CISPA with talk of protection," Apr 13, 2012, *Slashgear*, http://www.slashgear.com/facebook-defends-cispa-13222897/ (accessed: August 5, 2013

271The Cybersecurity Act of 2012 (S. 2105).

272Andrew Couts, "Senate Kills Cybersecurity Act of 2012," *Digital Trends*, August 2, 2012, http://www.digitaltrends.com/web/senate-votes-against-cybersecurity-act-of-2012/#ixzz2btT8Z5t2

273 Doak Jantzen, "House panel approves ISP snooping bill HR 1981," *The New York Daily News*, http://www.nydailynews.com/news/house-panel-approves-isp-snooping-bill-hr-1981-article-1.155716#ixzz2btWkNZpw The Protecting Children from Internet Pornographers Act of 2011, (H.R. 1981).

274 Charlie Savage, "U.S. Tries to Make It Easier to Wiretap the Internet," *The New York Times*, September 27, 2010, http://newmediaethics.pbworks.com/f/U.S.+Tries+to+Make+It+Easier+to+Wiretap+the+Internet+-+NYTimes.com.pdf (accessed: August 5, 2013).

275 Federal Bureau of Investigation, "Statement Before the House Judiciary Committee: Subcommittee on Crime, Terrorism, and Homeland Security Washington, D.C.," General Counsel Valerie Caproni, February 17, 2011, (accessed: August 10, 2012). http://www.fbi.gov/news/testimony/going-dark-lawful-electronic-surveillance-in-the-face-of-new-technologies

Statement Before the House Judiciary Committee, Jennifer Lynch, "Newly Released Documents Detail FBI's Plan to Expand Federal Surveillance Laws," *Electronic Frontier Foundations*, February 16, 2011, https://www.eff.org/deeplinks/2011/02/newly-released-documents-detail-fbi-s-plan-expand (accessed: August 4, 2013).

[276] David Kravets, "Internet 'Kill Switch' Legislation Back in Play," *Wired*, January 28, 2011, http://www.wired.com/threatlevel/2011/01/kill-switch-legislation/ (accessed: August 4, 2013).

[277] Mark Klein," *C-SPAN Video*, November 8, 2007, http://www.c-spanvideo.org/program/201508-6 (accessed: August 3, 2013).

"Exclusive: National Security Agency Whistleblower William Binney on Growing State Surveillance," *Democracy Now!* April 20, 2012, http://www.democracynow.org/2012/4/20/exclusive_national_security_agency_whistleblower_william

Dan Farber, "U.S. v. Whistleblower Tom Drake," *CBS News*, October 18, 2012, http://www.cbsnews.com/8301-503544_162-20122207-503544/thomas-drake-the-dark-side-of-data-and-the-nsa/

"Exclusive: Did U.S. Spy On Journalists?" *Countdown with Keith Olbermann*, MSNBC, January 21, 2009, http://www.youtube.com/watch?v=vqigfE0nBs0 *(accessed: August 4, 2013).*

[278] Siobhan Gorman, "NSA Killed System That Sifted Phone Data Legally
Sources say project was shelved in part because of bureaucratic infighting," *The Baltimore Sun, May 18, 2006,* http://www.commondreams.org/headlines06/0518-07.htm (accessed: August 13, 2013).
Seymour M. Hersh, "Listening In," *The New Yorker,* May 29, 2006, http://agriculturedefensecoalition.org/sites/default/files/pdfs/1S_2006_Seymour_Hersh_New_Yorker_May_29_2006_Listening_In_National_Security.pdf (accessed: August 13. 2012).
Dana Priest and William Arkin, "Top Secret America," *The Washington Post,* http://projects.washingtonpost.com/top-secret-america/ (accessed: August 13, 2013).
James Risen, *State of War: The Secret History of The CIA and the Bush Administration,* (New York: Free Press, 2006).
Bamford, *The Shadow Factory.*
"Exclusive: National Security Agency Whistleblower William Binney on Growing State Surveillance."

[279] Ted Ullyot, "Facebook Releases Data, Including All National Security Requests", Newsroom, Facebook, June 14, 2013, http://newsroom.fb.com/News/636/Facebook-Releases-Data-Including-All-National-Security-Requests

[280] Hepting v. AT&T No. 09-16676, U.S. District Court for the Northern District of California. June 3, 2009.

[281] Jewel v. National Sec. Agency, 673 F. 3d 902 - Court of Appeals, 9th Circuit 2011.

[282] American Civil Liberties Union et al., v. National Security Agency / Central et al., 493 F.3d 644, 6th Cir. 2007

Clapper v. Amnesty International USA, 132 S. Ct. 2431 - Supreme Court 2012

[283] Russ Buettner, "A Brooklyn Protester Pleads Guilty After His Twitter Posts Sink His Case," *The New York Times*, December 12, 2012, http://www.nytimes.com/2012/12/13/nyregion/malcolm-harris-pleads-guilty-over-2011-march.html?_r=0 (accessed: August 4, 2013).

[284] United States v. Drew, 259 F.R.D. 449 (C.D. Cal. 2009)

"Developing a Policy On the Use of Social Media in Intelligence And Investigative Activities: Guidance and Recommendations," *IACP Center for Social Media*, February 2013, http://www.iacpsocialmedia.org/Portals/1/documents/SMInvestigativeGuidance.pdf

[285] Federal Trade Commission, "Trade Commission: A History," http://www.ftc.gov/opa/history/ (accessed: August 4, 2013).

[286] In Re Facebook Internet Tracking Litigation, 844 F. Supp. 2d 1374 - Judicial Panel on Multidistrict Litigation 2012

[287] [292]Federal Trade Commission, "FTC Approves Final Settlement with Facebook," August 10, 2012, http://ftc.gov/opa/2012/08/facebook.shtm (accessed: August 4, 2013).

Federal Trade Commission. In the Matter of Facebook, Inc. Agreement Contain Consent Order, http://www.ftc.gov/os/caselist/0923184/111129facebookagree.pdf

[288] United States Senate, "Sen. Franken Presses Facebook, Government to Safeguard Privacy as Facial Recognition Technology Quickly Advances," July 18, 2012, http://www.franken.senate.gov/?p=press_release&id=2144 (accessed: August 4, 2013).

[289] United States Senate, "Rockefeller Seeks Information About Data Brokers' Practices," *Democratic Press Office,* October 10, 2012, http://www.commerce.senate.gov/public/index.cfm?p=PressReleases&ContentRecord_id=a42a865a-be30-4171-8278-86ee0a8c76fb&ContentType_id=77eb43da-aa94-497d-a73f-5c951ff72372&Group_id=505cc3fa-a767-40f4-8ac2-4b8326b44e94&YearDisplay=2012r (accessed: August 5, 2013).

[290] Mali Friedman, "Court Won't Undo Dismissal of in re Facebook Privacy Litigation," *Inside Privacy,* Covington & Burlington LLP, February 28, 2012, http://www.insideprivacy.com/united-states/court-wont-undo-dismissal-of-in-re-facebook-privacy-litigation/

In re Facebook Privacy Litigation, 791 F. Supp. 2d 705 - Dist. Court, ND California 2011

[291] "Remembering Lane v. Facebook, Inc.: An Important Online Privacy Lawsuit," Aaron Kelly Law, October 28, 2011, http://www.aaronkellylaw.com/online-privacy-laws/remembering-lane-v-facebook-inc-an-important-online-privacy-lawsuit/ (accessed: August 5, 2013)

[292] Cohen v. Facebook, Inc., 798 F. Supp. 2d 1090 - Dist. Court, ND California 2011

[293] Venkat Balasubramani, "Court Dismisses Misappropriation Claims Against Facebook Over Its Friend Finder Service -- Cohen v. Facebook". *Technology & Marketing Law Blog.* June 29, 2011, http://blog.ericgoldman.org/archives/2011/06/court_dismisses_2.htm (accessed: August 5, 2013).

[294] Cohen v. Facebook, Inc., 798 F. Supp. 2d 1090 - Dist. Court, ND California 2011

[295] Fraley v. Facebook, Inc., 830 F. Supp. 2d 785 - Dist. Court, ND California 2011

[296] Tatro v. University of Minnesota, 816 NW 2d 509 – Minn.: Supreme Court 2012

[297] Sumien v. CareFlite, No. 02-12-00039-CV, Tex. App. Ct., 2nd Dist. 2012

[298] Ibid.

[299] Ibid.

[300] "Defense Electronics," *Open Secrets.org,* http://www.opensecrets.org/pacs/industry.php?txt=D02&cycle=2012 (accessed: August 5, 2013).

[301] Cecilia Kang. "Facebook Forms PAC for Political Donations". *The Washington Post.* September 27, 2011, http://www.washingtonpost.com/blogs/post-tech/post/facebook-forms-pac-for-political-donations/2011/09/26/gIQAHhmW0K_blog.html (accessed: August 5, 2013).

[302] "Facebook Inc. Summary," *Open Secrets.org,* http://www.opensecrets.org/pacs/lookup2.php?strID=C00502906 (accessed: August 5, 2013).

[303] "Facebook Inc., Contributions to Federal Candidates," *Open Secrets.org,* http://www.opensecrets.org/pacs/pacgot.php?cmte=C00502906&cycle=2012 (accessed: August 5, 2013).

[304] Ibid.

[305] Oracle Corp Summary, Open Secrets, http://www.opensecrets.org/pacs/pacgot.php?cmte=C00323048&cycle=2012 (accessed: August 20, 2013).

Microsoft Corp Contributions to Federal Candidates, Open Secrets, http://www.opensecrets.org/pacs/pacgot.php?cmte=C00227546&cycle=2012 (accessed: August 20, 2013).

Google Inc. Contributions to Federal Candidates, Open Secrets, http://www.opensecrets.org/pacs/pacgot.php?cmte=C00428623&cycle=2012 (accessed: August 20, 2013).

[306] Data Use Policy, Facebook, December 11, 2012, http://www.facebook.com/about/privacy (accessed: August 5, 2013).

FTC Policy Statement on Deception, "There Must Be a Representation, Omission, or Practice That is Likely to Mislead the Consumer", Federal Trade Commission, October 14, 1983, http://www.ftc.gov/bcp/policystmt/ad-decept.htm (accessed: August 3, 2013).

[307]Facebook Changes Privacy Policy After Pushback from Users, PBS, May 26, 2010, http://www.pbs.org/newshour/bb/media/jan-june10/facebook_05-26.html

Richard Wray, Facebook forced to tighten up privacy rules, The Guardian, August 27, 2009, http://www.theguardian.com/technology/2009/aug/27/facebook-privacy-canada

A Privacy Policy Re-imagined For Users Like You, Facebook, February 25, 2011 https://www.facebook.com/note.php?note_id=10150434660350301

Heather Kelly, Voting closes on Facebook policy changes, only 299 million votes short, CNN, http://www.cnn.com/2012/12/10/tech/social-media/facebook-policy-vote

[308] Kara Brandeisky, Six Ways Congress May Reform NSA Snooping, *ProPublica,* July 25, 2013, http://www.propublica.org/article/six-ways-congress-may-reform-nsa-snooping

[309] The White House "Remarks by the President in a Press Conference ," *Office of the Press Secretary*, August 09, 2013, http://www.whitehouse.gov/blog/2013/08/09/president-obama-holds-press-conference (accessed: August 13, 2013).

[310] Aubrey Bloomfield, "ACLU NSA Lawsuit: PRISM Violates the First and Fourth Amendments Of the Constitution," *Policy Mic*, http://www.policymic.com/articles/48195/aclu-nsa-lawsuit-prism-violates-the-first-and-fourth-amendments-of-the-constitution

Natalie Huet, "French lawsuit targets NSA, FBI, tech firms over Prism," Reuters, July 11, 2013, http://www.reuters.com/article/2013/07/11/usa-security-france-idUSL6N0FH3N320130711

Joanna Hausemann, "The $20 Billion PRISM Lawsuit: 5 Fast Facts You Need to Know," *The Heavy,* June 12, 2013, http://www.heavy.com/news/2013/06/the-20-billion-prism-lawsuit-5-fast-facts-you-need-to-know/

[311] James Bamford, "The NSA Is Building the Country's Biggest Spy Center (Watch What You Say)," *Wired,* March 15, 2012, http://www.wired.com/threatlevel/2012/03/ff_nsadatacenter/ (accessed: August 5, 2013).

[312] Larry Magid, "What Are SOPA and PIPA and Why All The Fuss?" *Forbes*, January 18, 2012, http://www.forbes.com/sites/larrymagid/2012/01/18/what-are-sopa-and-pipa-and-why-all-the-fuss/

Smith, Lamar. "Stop Online Piracy Act," *US Government,* 2011. Protect Intellectual Property Act 112th Congress (2011-2012) S.968

[313] Christina DesMarais, "SOPA, PIPA Stalled: Meet the OPEN Act," *PCWorld*, Jan 21, 2012 http://www.pcworld.com/article/248525/sopa_pipa_stalled_meet_the_open_act.html (accessed: August 8, 2013).

H.R. 3782 (112th): Online Protection and Enforcement of Digital Trade Act

[314] Hill, Kashmir, "Your Internet Service Provider Is Being Deputized," *Forbes,* July 30, 2012, http://www.forbes.com/sites/kashmirhill/2012/07/30/your-internet-service-provider-is-being-deputized/ (accessed: August 18, 2012).

[315] Community Standards, Facebook, http://www.facebook.com/communitystandards (accessed: August 5, 2012).

316 Sauvik Das and Adam Kramer, "Self-Censorship on Facebook," Computer Human Interaction: Mobile Privacy Security Lab, http://cmuchimps.org/uploads/publication/paper/122/self-censorship_on_facebook.pdf (accessed: August 14, 2013). As cited in Alexis C. Madrigal, "71% of Facebook Users Engage in 'Self-Censorship," *The Atlantic,* April 15, 2013, http://www.theatlantic.com/technology/archive/2013/04/71-of-facebook-users-engage-in-self-censorship/274982/ (accessed: August 5, 2013).

317 Community Standards, Facebook, http://www.facebook.com/communitystandards (accessed: August 5, 2013).

318 Open Graph Overview, Facebook Developers, https://developers.facebook.com/docs/opengraph/overview/ (accessed: August 5, 2013).

319 Nick Fielding and Ian Cobain, "Revealed: US spy operation that manipulates social media Military's 'sock puppet' software creates fake online identities to spread pro-American propaganda," *The Guardian,* March 17, 2011, http://www.guardian.co.uk/technology/2011/mar/17/us-spy-operation-social-networks (accessed: August 5, 2013).

320 Ibid.

321 Matthew Fraser and Soumitra Dutta, "Obama's win means future elections must be fought online," *The Guardian,* November 7, 2008, http://www.theguardian.com/technology/2008/nov/07/barackobama-uselections2008 (accessed: August 5, 2013).

322 "2008 Facebook Statistics on American Politics," *Inside Facebook,* January 2, 2008, http://www.insidefacebook.com/2008/01/02/2008-statistics-on-american-politics-on-facebook/(accessed: August 5, 2013).

323 Aaron Smith and Lee Rainie, "The Internet and the 2008 Election", *Pew Internet Research*, June 15, 2008, http://www.pewinternet.org/Reports/2008/The-Internet-and-the-2008-Election.aspx (accessed: August 5, 2013).

324 Matthew Fraser & Soumitra Dutta, "Obama's win means future elections must be fought online," *The Guardian*, November 7, 2008, http://www.theguardian.com/technology/2008/nov/07/barackobama-uselections2008 (accessed: August 5, 2013).

325 Cassie Whitt, "Facebook posts Year in Review highlighting 2012's top trends," *Alternative Press*, December 12, 2012, http://www.altpress.com/news/entry/facebook_posts_year_in_review_highlighting_2012s_top_trends (accessed: August 5, 2013).

326 "KONY 2012", *Invisible Children*, YouTube, March 5, 2012, http://www.youtube.com/watch?v=Y4MnpzG5Sqc (accessed: August 5, 2013).

327 Cassie Whitt, "Facebook posts Year in Review highlighting 2012's top trends,"

328 Gangnam Style, *officialpsy,* YouTube. July 15, 2012, *www.youtube.com/watch?v=9bZkp7q19f0 (accessed: August 5, 2013).*

329 "Madsen: Social networks are linked to CIA," Russia Today, 2011, http://www.youtube.com/watch?v=oTb3F5H2bdY

330 Oliver Stone and Peter Kuznick, *The Untold History of the United States*, (New York: Gallery Books, 2012), 338.

331 Ward Churchill and Jim Vander Wall, *The COINTELPRO Papers: Documents from the FBI's Secret Wars Against Dissent in the United States* 1st Edition, (South End Press; 1990)

332 "Enemies: A History of the FBI": Tim Weiner Explores a Century of Secrets, Snooping and subterfuge, *Democracy Now!* April 4, 2012, http://www.democracynow.org/2012/4/4/enemies_a_history_of_the_fbi

333 Federal Bureau of Investigation, "History," http://www.fbi.gov/about-us/history/directors (accessed: August 14, 2013).

334 James Bamford. *Body of Secrets: The Anatomy of the Ultra Secret National Security Agency from the Cold War to the dawn of a new century, (New York: Anchor Books, 2001).*

[335] Peter Eisler, "Terrorist watch list hits 1 million," *USA Today*, March 10, 2009. http://usatoday30.usatoday.com/news/washington/2009-03-10-watchlist_N.htm (accessed: August 14, 2013).

[336] Joyce Lee "Mark Ruffalo Reportedly Placed on U.S. Terrorist Watch List," *CBS News*, November 29, 2010,http://www.cbsnews.com/8301-31749_162-20024001-10391698.html (accessed: August 14, 2013).

Formal calls for probe into reporter's name on no-fly list, *CNN*, July 17, 2008, http://www.cnn.com/2008/US/07/17/watchlist.chertoff/ (accessed: August 14, 2013).

Rachel L. Swarns, "Senator? Terrorist? A Watch List Stops Kennedy at Airport." *The New York Times*, August 20, 2004, http://www.nytimes.com/2004/08/20/national/20flight.html

[337] Federal Bureau of Investigation, "Terrorist Screening Center," http://www.fbi.gov/about-us/nsb/tsc/tsc (accessed: August 14, 2013).

[338] Jonathan Weisman. "Scrutiny of Political Nonprofits Sets Off Claim of Harassment", *The New York Times*, March 6, 2012, http://www.nytimes.com/2012/03/07/us/politics/irs-scrutiny-of-political-groups-stirs-harassment-claim.html?_r=0 (accessed: August 14, 2013)

[339] Sean Captain, "Occupy Geeks Are Building a Facebook for the 99%", *Wired*, .December 27, 2011, http://www.wired.com/threatlevel/2011/12/occupy-facebook/2/

Adario Strange, "Occupy Wall Street Protesters Used Alternative Social Networks", *PCMAG*, October 3, 2011, http://www.pcmag.com/article2/0,2817,2394043,00.asp

Charlie Osborne, "Occupy Facebook: A new social network for the 99%", *ZDNet*, December 28, 2011, http://www.zdnet.com/blog/igeneration/occupy-facebook-a-new-social-network-for-the-99/14086

Gloria Goodale, "Social media drive Occupy Wall Street. Do they also divulge its secrets?" October 2, 2011, *Christian Science Monitor*, http://www.csmonitor.com/USA/Politics/2011/1012/Social-media-drive-Occupy-Wall-Street.-Do-they-also-divulge-its-secrets (accessed: August 5, 2013).

[340] Occupy Wall Street, http://occupywallst.org/ (accessed: July 25, 2013).

[341] David Simon, "The Audacity of Despair," YouTube, September 10, 2008, http://www.youtube.com/watch?v=nRt46W3k-qw (accessed: August 5, 2013).

[342] Chris Hogg, "Digital Journal Editorial Guidelines," *Digital Journal*, Aug 23, 2007, http://www.digitaljournal.com/article/220179#ixzz2OxhJlPN5 (accessed: August 5, 2013).
 "Frequently Asked Questions," *Ground Report*, http://www.groundreport.com/info.php?action=faq&questionID=11

[343] Ibid.

[344] Ching-man Au Yeung, Ilaria Liccardi, Kanghao Lu, Oshani Seneviratne, Tim Berners-Lee, "Decentralization: The Future of Online Social Networking," *World Wide Web Consortium*, http://www.w3.org/2008/09/msnws/papers/decentralization.pdf (accessed: August 5, 2013).

[345] Dolf Zantinge and Pieter Adriaans, *Managing Client/Server*, (Harlow, England, Addison-Wesley, 1996), 235

[346] Jacob Appelbaum and Dmitry Kleiner, "Resisting the Surveillance State and Its Network effects," *re:publica*, 2012, http://www.youtube.com/watch?v=Y3h46EbqhPo (accessed: August 5, 2013).

[347] Orin Kerr, "Digital Evidence and the New Criminal Procedure," *Cybercrime: Digital Cops in a Networked Environment*, (New York: University Press. 2007).

[348] Eben Moglen, "Freedom in The Cloud: Software Freedom, Privacy, and Security for Web 2.0 and Cloud Computing," at the Internet Society New York Chapter, February 5, 2010, http://www.youtube.com/watch?v=QOEMv0S8AcA (accessed: August 6, 2013).

[349] "About AOL," AOL, http://corp.aol.com/about-aol/overview (accessed: August 5, 2013).

[350] "Overview," Yahoo, http://pressroom.yahoo.net/pr/ycorp/overview.aspx (accessed: August 5, 2013).

[351] "About Match.com," Match.com, http://www.match.com/help/aboutus.aspx?lid=4 (accessed: August 5, 2013).

[352] "Our Brands", IAC, http://iac.com/ (accessed: August 5, 2013).

[353] "About Match.com," Match.com, http://www.match.com/help/aboutus.aspx?lid=4 (accessed: August 5, 2013).

[354] "The History of Microsoft", Channel 9, MSDN, July 7, 2009, http://channel9.msdn.com/Series/History/The-History-of-Microsoft-1996 (accessed: August 5, 2013).

[355] "MSN, Costco offer low-cost Net access," *CNET*, August 10, 1999, http://news.cnet.com/Microsofts-ISP-strategy/2009-1023_3-229667.html (accessed: August 5, 2013).

[356] "World Internet Usage And Population Statistics," *Internet Usage Statistics*, June 30, 2012, http://www.internetworldstats.com/stats.htm (accessed: August 5, 2013).

[357] About AOL," AOL, http://corp.aol.com/about-aol/overview (accessed: August 5, 2013).

[358] Danah M. Boyd and Nicole B. Ellison, "Social Network Sites: Definition, History, and Scholarship," *Journal of Computer-Mediated Communication,* Volume 13, Issue 1, pages 210–230, December 17, 2007, http://onlinelibrary.wiley.com/doi/10.1111/j.1083-6101.2007.00393.x/full (accessed: August 3, 2013).

[359] "Interview of Andrew Bein with Leslie Walker," .COM – LIVE, The Washington Post, March 25, 1999, http://www.washingtonpost.com/wp-srv/business/talk/transcripts/walker/walker032599.htm (accessed: August 8, 2013).

[360] Ibid.

[361] Danah M. Boyd and Nicole B. Ellison, "Social Network Sites: Definition, History, and Scholarship," *Journal of Computer-Mediated Communication,* Volume 13, Issue 1, pages 210–230, December 17, 2007, http://onlinelibrary.wiley.com/doi/10.1111/j.1083-6101.2007.00393.x/full (accessed: August 3, 2013).

[362] Sarah Lacy, Once Your Lucky Twice Your Good: The Rebirth of Silicon Valley and the Rise of Web 2.0, (New York: Gotham Books, 2008), 56.

[363] Danah M. Boyd and Nicole B. Ellison, "Social Network Sites: Definition, History, and Scholarship."

[364] Max Chafkin, "How to Kill a Great Idea!" *Inc. Magazine*, June.1, 2007, http://www.inc.com/magazine/20070601/features-how-to-kill-a-great-idea_pagen_2.html (accessed: August 2, 2013).

[365] Interview with Jonathan Abrams on ThisWeekInStartUps #303, November 6, 2012, http://www.youtube.com/watch?v=GDs2nJf6lro (accessed: August 3, 2013).

[366] Max Chafkin, "How to Kill a Great Idea!"

[367] Kirkpatrick, 87.

[368] Max Chafkin, "How to Kill a Great Idea!"

[369] Interview with Jonathan Abrams on ThisWeekInStartUps #303, November 6, 2012, http://www.youtube.com/watch?v=GDs2nJf6lro (accessed: August 3, 2013).

[370] Jeff Rothschild, "High Performance At Massive Scaled, Lessons Learned At Facebook," at Calit2 Auditorium, University of California, San Diego, YouTube. January 16, 2013, http://www.youtube.com/watch?v=KIRzk08NMNo (accessed: August 5,

2013).

[371] Ibid.

[372] Kirkpatrick, *The Facebook Effect*, 116.

[373] Interview with Jonathan Abrams on ThisWeekInStartUps #303, November 6, 2012, http://www.youtube.com/watch?v=GDs2nJf6lro (accessed: August 3, 2013).

[374] Robin Wauters, "Social Network Pioneer Friendster To Erase All User Photos, Blogs And More On May 31," *TechCrunch*, March 26, 2011, http://techcrunch.com/2011/04/26/social-network-pioneer-friendster-to-erase-all-user-photos-blogs-and-more-on-may-31/

[375] Liz Gannes, "Facebook Buys Friendster Patents for $40M," Gigaom, Aug. 4, 2010, http://gigaom.com/2010/08/04/facebook-buys-friendster-patents-for-40m/ (accessed: September 1, 2013).

[376] Ibid.

[377] Brian Chatfield, *The MySpace.com Handbook: The Complete Guide for Members and Parents.* (Atlantic Publishing Group, 2008).

Marcia Amidon Lüsted, *Social Networking: MySpace, Facebook, & Twitter,* (Abdo Publishing. 2011), 14.

[378] T. Brian Chatfield, *The MySpace.com Handbook: The Complete Guide for Members and Parent, (*Atlantic Publishing Company. 2008), 220.

[379] Patrick Bromley, "Dane Cook – Biography," *About.com Guide*, http://comedians.about.com/od/currentcomedians/p/danecook.htm

[380] Julia Angwin, *Stealing MySpace: The Battle to Control the Most Popular Website in America,* (New York: Random House, 2009),1,25, 193-194

[381] Ibid, 197.

[382] Christopher Soghoian, DEFCON 18: Your ISP and the Government: Best Friends Forever, YouTube, October 26, 2010, http://www.youtube.com/watch?v=t0aQojDGSD4

[383] "Law Enforcement & The Social Networks", Sunnyvale Department of Public Safety, SMILE, February 6, 2013, http://smileconference.com/live.

[384] Angwin, *Stealing MySpace,* 197.

[385] Ibid. 6-8.

[386] "Mark Zuckerberg On Innovation," *Business Insider*, September 15, 2010, http://www.youtube.com/watch?v=PWXZjFd8STo

[387] "Interview of Andrew Bein with Leslie Walker," .COM – LIVE, The Washington Post, March 25, 1999, http://www.washingtonpost.com/wp-srv/business/talk/transcripts/walker/walker032599.htm (accessed: August 8, 2013).

[388] Jacob Appelbaum and Dmitry Kleiner, "Resisting the Surveillance State and Its Network effects," *re:publica*, 2012, http://www.youtube.com/watch?v=Y3h46EbqhPo (accessed: August 5, 2013).

[389] Ibid.
[390] Ibid.
[391] Interview with Dmitry Kleiner at the conference "Economy of Crisis Capitalism and Ecology of the Commons," November 22.-24, 2012, Zagreb, Goethe Institut (Vukovarska str. 64) http://www.youtube.com/watch?v=CK319sIWwbA

[392] Daniel Alef, *Mark Zuckerberg: The Face Behind Facebook and Social Networking*, (Jersey City, NJ: Titans of Fortune Publishing 2013), 2.

[393] Jose Vargas, "The Face of Facebook,' *The New Yorker*, September 20, 2010, http://www.newyorker.com/reporting/2010/09/20/100920fa_fact_vargas?currentPage=all

[394] Alef, *Mark Zuckerberg,* 3

[395] Vargas, "The Face of Facebook."

[396] Michael M. Grynbaum, "Mark E. Zuckerberg '06: The Whiz Behind thefacebook.com," *Harvard Crimson*, June 10, 2004, http://www.thecrimson.com/article/2004/6/10/mark-e-zuckerberg-06-the-whiz/

[397] *Mark Zuckerberg The Real Face Behind Facebook,* STP Productions, 2012, .http://www.youtube.com/watch?v=U6akOK7Bupg
[398] "Did Mark Zuckerberg's Inspiration for Facebook Come Before Harvard?" *ReadWrite*, May 10, 2009, http://readwrite.com/2009/05/10/mark_zuckerberg_inspiration_for_facebook_before_harvard

[399] Suzanne Reese, "Top Ten College Prep and Boarding Schools in the U.S.," *Yahoo! Voices*, May 13, 2010, http://voices.yahoo.com/top-ten-college-prep-boarding-schools-us-6013386.html

[400] *Mark Zuckerberg The Real Face Behind Facebook*

[401]. Vargas, "The Face of Facebook."

[402] Aaron Greenspan, "Chapter 30: The Other Folder," September 19, 2012, http://www.thinkpress.com/authoritas/housesystem/20040602.zuckerberg.html (accessed: August 18, 2013).

[403] Grynbaum, "Mark E. Zuckerberg '06".

[404] Alexia Tsotsis, "Zuckerberg vs. D'Angelo, 'Before They Were Stars' And 'Where Are They Now'?" *Tech Crunch*, October 31, 2010, http://techcrunch.com/2010/10/31/zuckerberg-d-angelo/ (accessed: August 3, 2013).

[405] Ben Mezrich, *The Accidental Billionaires: The Founding of Facebook, A Tale of Sex, Money, Genius and Betrayal*, (New York: Random House, 2010), 15

[406] Michael M. Grynbaum, "Mark E. Zuckerberg '06

[407] *Mark Zuckerberg The Real Face Behind Facebook.*

[408] Justin C. Worland, "Legacy Admit Rate at 30 Percent," *Harvard Crimson*, May 11, 2011, http://www.thecrimson.com/article/2011/5/11/admissions-fitzsimmons-legacy-legacies/

[409] Rebecca O'Brien, "The Truth Behind 'The Social Network," *The Daily Beast*, September 8, 2010, http://www.thedailybeast.com/articles/2010/09/08/mark-zuckerberg-at-harvard-the-truth-behind-the-social-network.html

[410] *Mark Zuckerberg The Real Face Behind Facebook*, 2012, STP Productions, .http://www.youtube.com/watch?v=U6akOK7Bupg

[411] Mezrich, *The Accidental Billionaires*, 16.

[412] Alan J. Tabak, "Hundreds Register for New Facebook Website Facemash creator seeks new reputation with latest online project," *The Harvard Crimson*, February 9, 2004.

[413] Susan Dobinick, Mark Zuckerberg and Facebook, (New York: Rosen Publishing Group, 2013), http://books.google.com/books?id=fd3-Y7fehZIC&pg=PA24&dq=mark+zuckerberg+course+match&hl=en&sa=X&ei=kmo-UazUGLKJ0QHIhYDACQ&ved=0CDMQ6AEwAA#v=onepage&q=mark%20zuckerberg%20course%20match&f=false (accessed: August 3, 2013), 24.

281

[414] Mezrich, *the Accidental Billionaires*, 44.

[415] Vargas, "The Face of Facebook."

[416] James Breyer/ Mark Zuckerberg Interview, Stanford University, October 26, 2005, http://www.youtube.com/watch?v=WA_ma359Meg (accessed: August 18, 2013).

[417] Ibid.

[418] "Did Mark Zuckerberg's Inspiration for Facebook Come Before Harvard?" *ReadWrite*, May 10, 2009, http://readwrite.com/2009/05/10/mark_zuckerberg_inspiration_for_facebook_before_harvard (accessed: August 18, 2013).

[419] Alan J. Tabak, "Hundreds Register for New Facebook Website: Facemash creator seeks new reputation with latest online project" Crimson Staff Writer, February 9, 2004 http://www.thecrimson.com/article/2004/2/9/hundreds-register-for-new-facebook-website/ (accessed: August 18, 2013).

[420] *Mark Zuckerberg The Real Face Behind Facebook.*

[421] Alyson Shontell, "A Grudge 8 Years in the Making: The Full Story Behind The New, Leaked Zuckerberg IMs," *Business Insider*, September 19, 2012, http://www.businessinsider.com/the-story-behind-aaron-greenspans-alleged-new-zuckerberg-ims-2012-9#ixzz2aGRmXy8N (accessed: August 18, 2013).

[422] "Mark Zuckerberg On Innovation," *Business Insider*, September 15, 2010, http://www.youtube.com/watch?v=PWXZjFd8STo

"Young Mark Zuckerberg Interview: "We Ran the Site Originally for $85 a Month," *Fast Company*. September 1, 2010. http://www.youtube.com/watch?v=dW3CNdsE_k4

[423] Mezrich, 67-68.

[424] Nicholas Carlson, "In 2004, Mark Zuckerberg Broke Into A Facebook User's Private Email Account," Business Insider, March 5, 2010, http://www.businessinsider.com/how-mark-zuckerberg-hacked-into-the-harvard-crimson-2010-3#ixzz2N7kV8LsJ (accessed: August 18, 2013).

[425] Nicholas Carlson, "Exclusive: Mark Zuckerberg's Secret IMs From College", *Business Insider,* May 17, 2012, http://www.businessinsider.com/exclusive-mark-zuckerbergs-secret-ims-from-college-2012-5?op=1 (accessed: August 18, 2013).

[426] Ibid

[427] . Carlson, "In 2004, Mark Zuckerberg Broke Into A Facebook User's Private Email Account."

[428] Ibid

[429] Timothy J. Mcginn, "Online Facebooks Duel Over Tangled Web of Authorship". Harvard Crimson, May 28, 2004, http://www.thecrimson.com/article/2004/5/28/online-facebooks-duel-over-tangled-web/ (accessed: August 18, 2013).

[430] Carlson, "In 2004, Mark Zuckerberg Broke Into A Facebook User's Private Email Account."

[431] Nicholas Carlson, "How Mark Zuckerberg Hacked Into Rival ConnectU In 2004," *Business Insider*, March 5, 2010, http://www.businessinsider.com/how-mark-zuckerberg-hacked-connectu-2010-3#ixzz2QrY8xkQJ (accessed: August 18, 2013).

[432]Ibid.
[433] Adam P. Schneider, "Facebook Expands Beyond Harvard; Stanford, Columbia join network, with Yale next in line," *Harvard Crimson,* March 1, 2004. http://www.thecrimson.com/article/2004/3/1/facebook-expands-beyond-harvard-harvard-students/

(accessed: August 18, 2013).

"Manifest Destiny, Facebook Style Detractors at Columbia cannot succeed in halting the spread of thefacebook.com", *Harvard Crimson*, March 11, 2004, http://www.thecrimson.com/article/2004/3/11/manifest-destiny-facebook-style-now-that/ (accessed: August 18, 2013).

434 Kirkpatrick, *The Facebook Effect*, 101.

435 Ibid, 101

436 Ibid, 47.

437 Sean Parker at "The Allure of the Hive" held at the Philoctetes Center and moderated by David Kirkpatrick, http://www.youtube.com/watch?v=cyEbnekohRc (accessed: July 28, 2013).

438 Steven Dertoni, "Sean Parker: Agent of Disruption," *Forbes*, September 21, 2011, http://www.forbes.com/sites/stevenbertoni/2011/09/21/sean-parker-agent-of-disruption/4/

439 Ibid.

440 Sean Parker at "The Allure of the Hive" held at the Philoctetes Center and moderated by David Kirkpatrick, http://www.youtube.com/watch?v=cyEbnekohRc (accessed: July 28, 2013).

441 Audio Podcast: From Harvard to the Facebook, Stanford.

442 Mezrich, 165-168.

443 David Kirkpatrick, "With a Little Help From His Friends", *Vanity Fair*, October 2010, http://www.vanityfair.com/culture/features/2010/10/sean-parker-201010

444 Kirkpatrick, *The Facebook Effect,* 89.

Kirkpatrick, *The Facebook Effect, 46.*

445 Julianne Pepitone and Stacy Cowley, "Facebook's first big investor, Peter Thiel, cashes out", *CNN*, August 20, 2012, http://money.cnn.com/2012/08/20/technology/facebook-peter-thiel

446 Audio Podcast: From Harvard to the Facebook. Stanford.

447 Sean Parker at "The Allure of the Hive" held at the Philoctetes Center and moderated by David Kirkpatrick, http://www.youtube.com/watch?v=cyEbnekohRc (accessed: July 28, 2013).

448 Book Discussion on The Accidental Billionaires, *C-SPAN Video Library*, November 21, 2010, http://www.c-spanvideo.org/program/296688-3 (accessed: July 31, 2013).

449 Nicholas Carlson, "Exclusive: How Mark Zuckerberg Booted His Co-Founder Out Of The Company", *Business Insider*, May 15, 2012, http://articles.businessinsider.com/2012-05-15/tech/31706573_1_ceo-mark-zuckerberg-billionaire-facebook-eduardo-saverin

450 Ibid.

451. Mezrich, *The Accidental Billionaires*, 16, 170.

452 Ibid, 170

453 Nicholas Carlos, "Exclusive: How Mark Zuckerberg Booted His Co-Founder Out Of The Company."

[454]"Chapter 30: The Other Folder," Aaron Greenspan, September 19, 2012, http://www.thinkpress.com/authoritas/housesystem/20040602.zuckerberg.html

[455] Mezrich, 192

[456] VC Industry Overview, National Venture Capital Association, http://www.nvca.org/index.php?option=com_content&view=article&id=141&Itemid=589 (accessed: August 8, 2013).

[457] "Angel Investors: How the Rich Invest," *Forbes*, March 12, 2013, http://www.forbes.com/sites/tanyaprive/2013/03/12/angels-investors-how-the-rich-invest/ (accessed: August 1, 2013)

[458] Personal Finance and Investing All-in-One For Dummies, UK Edition edited by Faith Glasgow, John Wiley & Stands, 2007.

[459] "Mark Pincus," *Forbes*, http://www.forbes.com/profile/mark-pincus/(accessed: August 1, 2013).

[460] Kirkpatrick, *The Facebook Effect*, 86.

[461] Thomas Hellmann, "Venture Capitalists: The Coaches of Silicon Valley," Sauder School of Business, February 2000, http://strategy.sauder.ubc.ca/hellmann/pdfs/coaches04.pdf (accessed: July 31, 2013).

[462] Vanessa Grigoriadias, "Ol' Mark Pincus Had a Farm…," *Vanity Fair*, June 2011, http://www.vanityfair.com/business/features/2011/06/mark-pincus-farmville-201106 (accessed: July 31, 2013).

[463] Alexia Tsotsis, "Mark Pincus Used to be Sean Parker's Boss," *Tech Crunch*, October 18, 2011, http://techcrunch.com/2011/10/18/mark-pincus-uscd-to-be-sean-parkers-boss/ (Date of Access: July 31, 2013).

[464] Kirkpatrick, *The Facebook Effect, 125.*

[465] "Jim Breyer," Accel Partners. http://www.accel.com/#people/jim-breyer (accessed: August 4, 2013).

[466] Ellen Rosen, "Student's Start-Up Draws Attention and $13 Million", *The New York Times*, May 26, 2005, http://www.nytimes.com/2005/05/26/business/26sbiz.html (accessed: August 1, 2013).

[467] Jim Breyer," Accel Partner, http://www.accel.com/global/people/specialty/all/Jim_Breyer (accessed: August 1, 2013).

[468]Ibid.

Erick Schonfeld, "Jim Breyer's Midas Touch. Two Acquisitions in 24 Hours (Marvel and BNN)," *Tech Crunch*, September 1, 2009, http://techcrunch.com/2009/09/01/jim-breyers-midas-touch-two-acquisitions-in-24-hours-marvel-and-bbn/ (accessed: August 1, 2013).

[469] BBN Web Monitoring System Version 2. BBN Technologies, http://bbn.com/products_and_services/web_monitoring_system/ (accessed: July 31, 2013).

[470] Accel Partners, Crunchbase Profile, http://www.crunchbase.com/financial-organization/accel-partners (accessed: August 15, 2013).

[471] "Facebook Sees $25M from Greylock," WebProNews, April 19, 2006, http://www.webpronews.com/facebook-sees-m-from-greylock-2006-04 (accessed: July 31, 2013).

[472] "Companies," Greylock Partners, http://www.greylock.com/companies (accessed: July 31, 2013).

[473] "Teams," Greylock Partners, http://www.greylock.com/teams (accessed: July 31, 2013)

[474] Founders Fund, http://www.foundersfund.com/ (accessed: July 31, 2013).

[475] Dan Primack. "Exclusive: Facebook investor Meritech raises $425 million," CNN. April 27, 2011, http://finance.fortune.cnn.com/2011/04/27/exclusive-facebook-investor-meritech-raises-425-million (accessed: August 4, 2013).

[476] Meritech Capital, http://www.meritechcapital.com/investments (accessed: July 31, 2013).

[477] Emil Protalinski. "IPG sells half of Facebook stake at $65.50 billion valuation", ZDNet, August 15, 2011, http://www.zdnet.com/blog/facebook/ipg-sells-half-of-facebook-stake-at-65-50-billion-valuation/2664 (accessed: August 18, 2013).

[478] "About", Interpublic Group, http://www.interpublic.com/about/overview (accessed: July 31, 2013).

[479] Microsoft invests $240 million in Facebook," NBC, Oct 24, 2007, http://www.nbcnews.com/id/21458486/ns/business-us_business/t/microsoft-invests-million-facebook/ (accessed: July 31, 2013).

Andrew Gumbel, "Internet: Mark Zuckerberg has one friend- but he's worth 500 Million," Independent, Sept 30, 2007, http://www.independent.co.uk/news/science/internet-mark-zuckerberg-has-one-friend-ndash-but-hes-worth-500m-403935.html (accessed: July 31, 2013).

[480] "Customer Relationship Management," Microsoft Dynamics, http://www.microsoft.com/en-us/dynamics/crm.aspx (accessed: August 1, 2013).

[481] "Windows Embedded," Microsoft, http://www.microsoft.com/windowsembedded/en-us/windows-embedded.aspx (accessed: August 1, 2013).

[482] "New York City Police Department and Microsoft Partner to Bring Real-Time Crime Prevention and Counterterrorism Technology Solution to Global Law Enforcement Agencies," Microsoft, August 8, 2012, http://www.microsoft.com/en-us/news/press/2012/aug12/08-08nypdpr.aspx (accessed August 1, 2013).

Paul Harris, "NYPD And Microsoft Launch Their Very Own 'Minority Report' Crime Fighting Surveillance System," Business Insider, August 8, 2013, http://www.businessinsider.com/nypd-and-microsoft-launch-their-very-own-minority-report-crime-fighting-surveillance-system-2012-8#ixzz23TA07tJQ (accessed: August 8, 2013).

[483] Emil Protalinski, "Facebook taps Microsoft Bing for Page content translation," ZDNet, October 6, 2011. http://www.zdnet.com/blog/facebook/facebook-taps-microsoft-bing-for-page-content-translation/4436 (accessed: August 15, 2013).

[484] Spencer E. Ante, "Facebook: Friends with Money," BusinessWeek, May 9, 2008, http://www.businessweek.com/stories/2008-05-09/facebook-friends-with-moneybusinessweek-business-news-stock-market-and-financial-advice (accessed: August 1, 2013).

[485] "Li Kai Shing," Crunchbase, http://www.crunchbase.com/person/li-ka-shing (accessed: August 1, 2013).

[486] The Li Kai Shing Foundation, "About Us," http://www.lksf.org/en/about/foundation (accessed: August 1, 2013).

[487] Michael Arrington, "Breaking: Samwer Brothers Invest In Facebook," TechCrunch, January 15, 2008, http://techcrunch.com/2008/01/15/breaking-samwer-brothers-invest-in-facebook/ (accessed: August 1, 2013).

[488] "LinkedIn Raises $12.8 Million from Bessemer Venture Partners and European Founders Fund to Accelerate Global Growth Palo Alto, CA," LinkedIn, January 29, 2007, http://press.linkedin.com/79/linkedin-raises-128-million-bessemer-venture-partners-and-european-founders-fund-accelerate (accessed: August 1, 2013).

[489] Matt Cowan, "Inside the clone factory: The story of Germany's Samwer brothers," Wired, March 2, 2012 / http://www.wired.co.uk/magazine/archive/2012/04/features/inside-the-clone-factory?page=all (accessed: August 18, 2013).

[490] "Debt Financing," Investopedia, http://www.investopedia.com/terms/d/debtfinancing.asp (accessed: August 18, 2013).

[491] Rich Miller, "Facebook Borrows $100 Million to Buy Servers", Data Center Knowledge, May 12, 2008, http://www.datacenterknowledge.com/archives/2008/05/12/facebook-borrows-100-million-to-buy-servers/ (accessed: August 1,

2013).

[492] Ibid.

[493] "Representative Customers". Triple Point Capital. http://www.triplepointcapital.com/track-record/representative-customers (accessed: August 1, 2013).

[494] Joseph Galante, "Facebook Receives Investment from Digital Sky Technologies", Bloomberg, May 26, 2009, http://www.bloomberg.com/apps/news?pd5=newarchive&sid+aaVK4mbgY.U8 (accessed: August 1, 2013).

[495] Chris Rovzar, "Yuri Milner: "Google, Wikipedia, and Facebook Will Last 100 Years," Vanity Fair, March 9, 2013, http://www.vanityfair.com/online/daily/2013/03/yuri-milner-google-facebook-100-years

[496] Executive Profile: Yuri Milner, Business Week, http://investing.businessweek.com/research/stocks/private/person.asp?personId=1042788&privcapId=31315493 (accessed: August 18, 2013).

[497] "Interview of Mark Zuckerberg and Yuri Milner by Michael Arrington," TechCrunch, May 26, 2009, http://www.youtube.com/watch?v=ZRMkt8xYQz0 (accessed: August 8, 2013).

[498] "Facebook Raises $1.5 Billion Downloads", Newsroom, Facebook, January 21, 2011, http://newsroom.fb.com/News/131/Facebook-Raises-1-5-Billion (accessed: August 18, 2013).

[499] Clara Shih, The Facebook Era.

[500] "The Stages in Venture Capital Investing," Investopedia, http://www.investopedia.com/exam-guide/cfa-level-1/alternative-investments/venture-capital-investing-stages.asp (accessed: August 15, 2013).

[501] David Faber, "Latest Facebook Investment Values Company at $65 Billion".

[502] "Investment Team", Elevation, http://www.elevation.com/EP_IT_FLASH.asp (accessed: August 15, 2013).

[503] Naomi Klein, The Shock Doctrine: The Rise of Disaster Capitalism, (New York: Picador, 2007), 310.

[504] Brian Womack and Douglas MacMillan, "Goldman Sachs Said to Invest $450 Million in Facebook," Bloomberg, January 3, 2011, http://www.bloomberg.com/news/2011-01-03/facebook-valued-at-50-billion-as-goldman-is-said-to-invest-450-million.html (accessed: August 18, 2013).

[505] Goldman Sachs," Crunchbase, http://www.crunchbase.com/financial-organization/goldman-sachs (accessed: August 18, 2013).

[506] "The Anti-Social Network," The Daily Show with Jon Stewart, Jan 6, 2006

[507] David Faber, "Latest Facebook Investment Values Company at $65 Billion."

[508] Scott Austin, "Kleiner Perkins Invests In Facebook At $52 Billion Valuation," The Wall Street Journal, February 14, 2011, http://blogs.wsj.com/venturecapital/2011/02/14/kleiner-perkins-invests-in-facebook-at-52-billion-valuation/ (accessed: August 18, 2013).

[509] "Companies", Kleiner, Perkins, Caulfield and Byers, http://www.kpcb.com/companies (accessed: August 6, 2013).

[510] Michael Arrington, "The Kleiner Perkins sFund: A $250 Million Bet That Social Is Just Getting Started," October 21, 2010, http://techcrunch.com/2010/10/21/the-kleiner-perkins-sfund-a-250-million-bet-that-social-is-just-getting-started/ (accessed: August 18, 2013).

"$250 Million sFund Initiative Announcement," Kleiner Perkins Caufield &Byers, October 21, 2010, http://www.youtube.com/watch?v=oG-WkZVHL4U (accessed: August 15, 2013).

[511] Portfolio Companies, Andreessen Horowitz, http://a16z.com/portfolio/portfolio-venture-growth/ (accessed: August 18, 2013).

[512] Connie Guglielmo and Tommie Geron, "Andreessen, Horowitz: Capital's New Bad Boys", Forbes, ,May 2, 2012, http://www.forbes.com/forbes/2012/0521/feature-midas-list-ben-horowitz-marc-andreesen-silicon-valley-vc-capital-bad-boys_4.html (accessed: August 15, 2013).

[513] Board of Directors," Investor Relations, Facebook, http://investor.fb.com/directors.cfm   (accessed: July 31, 2013).

[514] Mary Pilon, "T. Rowe Price Invests in Facebook," The Wall Street Journal, April 16, 2011 http://online.wsj.com/article/SB10001424052748704495004576264730149910442.html (accessed: August 15, 2013).

[515] Kyle Alspach, "5 Fidelity funds with $$ in Facebook", Biz Journals, February 2, 2012, http://www.bizjournals.com/boston/blog/startups/2012/02/5-fidelity-funds-with-in-facebook.html (accessed: August 15, 2013).

[516] David Faber, "Latest Facebook Investment Values Company at $65 Billion."

[517] Julianne Pepitone, "Facebook IPO: What the %$#! happened?" CNNMoney, May 23, 2012, http://money.cnn.com/2012/05/23/technology/facebook-ipo-what-went-wrong/ (accessed: August 18, 2013).

[518] Cristina Alesci, "Facebook Underwriters Said to Split About $176 Million in Fees," Bloomberg, May 18, 2012, http://www.bloomberg.com/news/2012-05-18/facebook-underwriters-said-to-split-about-176-million-in-fees.html (accessed: August 18, 2013).

[519] Alistair Barr, "Insight: Morgan Stanley cut Facebook estimates just before IPO," Reuters, May 22, 2012, http://www.reuters.com/article/2012/05/22/us-facebook-forecasts-idUSBRE84L06920120522 (accessed: August 18, 2013).

[520] "Unfriended: The Facebook IPO Debacle," The Wall Street Journal, June 10, 2012,   http://live.wsj.com/video/unfriended-the-facebook-ipo-debacle/557F9142-E127-43CB-BA02-38E29383BAD0.html#!557F9142-E127-43CB-BA02-38E29383BAD0 29383BAD0 (accessed: August 18, 2013).

[521] Ibid.

[522] Facebook Inc. (NASDAQ:FB), http://www.google.com/finance?q=NASDAQ:FB (August 18, 2013).

[523] Brigitte Yuille, "Short Selling: What Is Short Selling?" Investopedia, http://www.investopedia.com/university/shortselling/ (accessed: August 18, 2013).

[524] "Facebook," Crunchbase, http://www.crunchbase.com/company/facebook (accessed: August 1, 2013).

[525] Rich Miller, "Facebook Looks to Sublease Data Center Space in Santa Clara," Data Center Knowledge, June 6, 2013, http://www.datacenterknowledge.com/archives/2013/06/06/facebook-seeking-to-sublease-excess-space-in-santa-clara/ (accessed: August 4, 2013).

[526] "Mark Zuckerberg," Management Team, Investor Relations, Facebook, http://newsroom.fb.com/Management (accessed: August 5, 2013)

[527] "David Ebersman," Management Team, Investor Relations, Facebook, http://newsroom.fb.com/Management (accessed: August 5, 2013).

[528] Sheryl Sandberg," Management Team, Investor Relations, Facebook, http://newsroom.fb.com/Management (accessed: August 5, 2013).

[529] Mike Schroepfer," Management Team. Investor Relations, Facebook, http://newsroom.fb.com/Management (accessed: August 5, 2013).

[530] "Chris Cox," *Fast Company*. http://www.fastcompany.com/most-creative-people/2011/chris-cox-facebook (accessed: August 18, 2013).

[531] "People," Facebook Inc., *Reuters*, http://www.reuters.com/finance/stocks/companyOfficers?symbol=FB.O (accessed: August 18, 2013).

[532] "Lori Goler," *Crunchbase*, http://www.crunchbase.com/person/lori-goler (accessed: August 15, 2013).

[533] "Dan Rose," *Forbes*, http://www.forbes.com/profile/dan-rose/ (accessed: August 4, 2013).

[534] "People," Facebook Inc., *Reuters*, http://www.reuters.com/finance/stocks/companyOfficers?symbol=FB.O (accessed: August 18, 2013).

[535] 2013 Proxy Statement, Investor Relations, Facebook, 2013, https://materials.proxyvote.com/Approved/30303M/20130409/NPS_166824/ (accessed: August 18, 2013).

[536] Ibid.

[537] "Board of Directors," Investor Relations, Facebook, http://investor.fb.com/directors.cfm   (accessed: July 31, 2013).

[538] Ibid.
[539] Ibid.
[540] Ibid.

[541] Ibid.

[542] Ibid.

[543] 2013 Proxy Statement, Investor Relations, Facebook 2013, https://materials.proxyvote.com/Approved/30303M/20130409/NPS_166824/ (accessed: August 5, 2013).

[544] "Careers at Facebook," Facebook, https://www.facebook.com/careers/ (June 25, 2013).

[545] "Careers at Facebook," Facebook, https://www.facebook.com/careers/university (June 25, 2013).

[546] Ibid.

[547] "Facebook", *Glassdoor*, http://www.glassdoor.com/facebook (accessed: August 18, 2013).

[548] Emily Shur, "Inside Facebook Headquarters," *Time*, http://www.time.com/time/photogallery/0,29307,1990443_2140543,00.html (accessed: August 18, 2013).

[549] Scott Martin, "Perk wars: Facebook, Zynga, Google jockey for top talent," *USA TODAY*, July 4, 2012, http://www.usatoday.com/tech/news/story/2012-07-04/silicon-valley-perks/56021130/1 (accessed: August 18, 2013).

[550] "Secret Facebook Millionaire Video ," ABC News, February 11, 2012, http://www.youtube.com/watch?v=MtazR6Iu2yE (accessed: August 16, 2013).

[551] Julia Boorstin and Paul Toscano, "Inside Facebook Headquarters," *CNBC*, May 18, 2012, http://www.cnbc.com/id/46236670/page/2 (accessed: August 16, 2013).

[552] "Culture", Newsroom, Facebook, http://newsroom.fb.com/Culture (accessed: July 31, 2012).

[553] Emily Shur, "Inside Facebook Headquarters."

[554] "Facebook Reviews," *Glassdoor*, http://www.glassdoor.com/Reviews/Facebook-Reviews-E40772.htm (accessed: August 16, 2013).

[555] Quentin Hardy, "Technology Workers Are Young (Really Young)," *The New York Times*, July 5, 2013, http://bits.blogs.nytimes.com/2013/07/05/technology-workers-are-young-really-young/?_r=0

[556] "Culture," Newsroom, Facebook, http://newsroom.fb.com/Culture (accessed: July 31, 2013).

[557] "Facebook Reviews," *Glassdoor*, http://www.glassdoor.com/Reviews/Facebook-Reviews-E40772.htm (accessed: 16, 2013).

[558] Will Oremus, "Do Facebook Interns Make more Money Than You?" *Slate*, December 13, 2012, http://www.slate.com/blogs/future_tense/2012/12/13/facebook_interns_make_5_600_a_month_glassdoor_report_says.html (accessed: June 20, 2013).

[559] Facebook Software Engineer Entry, *Glassdoor*, http://www.glassdoor.com/Salary/Facebook-Software-Engineer-Palo-Alto-Salaries-EJI_IE40772.0,8_KO9,26_IL.27,36_IC1147434.htm (accessed: 16, 2013).

[560] Will Oremus, "Do Facebook Interns Make more Money Than You?"

[561] Ten Things To Know Before Interviewing at Facebook," *Forbes*, http://www.forbes.com/pictures/fddh45ekff/be-prepared-to-sign-a-non-disclosure-agreement (accessed: August 18, 2013).
[562] "Infrastructure," Facebook, http://newsroom.fb.com/Infrastructure (accessed: August 18, 2013).

[563] Sharing Our Footprint, Newsroom, Facebook, August 1, 2012, https://newsroom.fb.com/News/412/Sharing-Our-Footprint (accessed: August 16, 2013).

[564] James Glanz, "The Cloud Factories Power, Pollution and the Internet", *The New York Times*, September 22, 2012, http://www.nytimes.com/2012/09/23/technology/data-centers-waste-vast-amounts-of-energy-belying-industry-image.html?pagewanted=2&ref=us (accessed: August 18, 2013).

[565] Ibid.
[566] "Sharing Our Footprint, Newsroom," Facebook, August 1, 2012, https://newsroom.fb.com/News/412/Sharing-Our-Footprint (accessed: July 31, 2013).

[567] James Glanz, "The Cloud Factories Power, Pollution and the Internet."

[568] Angwin, *Stealing MySpace, 227*

[569] Data Centers, Google, http://www.google.com/about/datacenters/inside/locations/index.html (accessed: July 31, 2013).

[570] "About Us," LinkedIn, http://www.linkedin.com/about-us (accessed: August 8, 2013).

[571] Twitter Statistics, Statistics Brain, May 7, 2013. http://www.statisticbrain.com/twitter-statistics/ (accessed: August 16, 2013).

[572] Matt Clark, "Report: Google+ Bigger than Twitter with 359 Million Active Users," *IGN*, May 2, 2013, http://www.ign.com/articles/2013/05/02/report-google-bigger-than-twitter-with-359-million-active-users (accessed: July 31, 2013).

[573] "Pinterest Is Worth $2 Billion Because Its 25 Million Users Are Rich, Female, And Like To Spend,". *Business Insider*, February 28, 2013, http://www.businessinsider.com/pinterest-is-worth-2-billion-because-its-25-million-users-are-rich-female-and-like-to-spend-2013-2

[574] Facebook, *Crunchbase*, http://www.crunchbase.com/company/Facebook (accessed: August 16, 2013).

[575] Kirkpatrick, *The Facebook Effect. 87.*

[576] Microsoft, *Crunchbase*, http://www.crunchbase.com/company/microsoft (accessed: August 16, 2013).

Google, *Crunchbase*, http://www.crunchbase.com/company/microsoft (accessed: August 16, 2013).

577 Form 10-K Annual Report. FACEBOOK, INC. February 1, 2013, http://investor.fb.com/secfiling.cfm?filingID=1326801-13-3&CIK=1326801 (accessed: August 4, 2013).

578 Bobbie Johnson and Robert Andrews, "Facebook doesn't just want world domination: it needs it," *Gigom*, May 19, 2012, http://gigaom.com/2012/05/19/facebook-international-growth/ (accessed: August 4, 2013).

579 Form 10-K Annual Report, Facebook, Inc., Feb 1, 2013, http://investor.fb.com/secfiling.cfm?filingID=1326801-13-3&CIK=1326801

580 "World Internet Usage and Population Statistics," *Internet Usage Statistics*, June 30, 2012, http://www.internetworldstats.com/stats.htm (accessed: August 5, 2013).

581 Matt Cowan, "Inside the clone factory, The Story of Germany's Samwer Brothers."

Eric Eldon, "Attack of the Facebook clones: Russia's VKontakte," *VentureBeat*, September 5, 2007, http://venturebeat.com/2007/09/05/attack-of-the-facebook-clones-russias-vkontakte/ (accessed: August 6, 2013).

582 "Facebook Localization Tools," Facebook Developers, https://developers.facebook.com/docs/internationalization/ (accessed: August 7, 2013).

583 "Facebook's Foreign Clones. Competitors poke at the social networking site's lead," Jun 24, 2008, www.thedailybeast.com/newsweek/ 2008/ 06/ 24/ facebook-s-foreign-clones.html (accessed: August 15, 2013

584 Eldon, "Attack of the Facebook clones: Russia's VKontakte

585 World Internet Usage and Population Statistics," *Internet Usage Statistics*, June 30, 2012, http://www.internetworldstats.com/stats.htm (accessed: August 5, 2013).

586 Michael Parenti, *Against Empire,* (San Francisco: City Light Books, 1995), 11.

587 Gary Blight, Sheila Pulham, and Paul Torpey, "Arab Spring: An Interactive Timeline of Middle East Protests," *The Guardian*, January 5, 2012. http://www.guardian.co.uk/world/interactive/2011/mar/22/middle-east-protest-interactive-timeline (accessed: July 25, 2013).

588 Wael Ghomin, *Revolution 2.0: A Memoir and a Call to Action,* (Boston, New York: Houghton Mifflin. 2012).

589 Ibid.

590 Ibid.

591 Dhiraj Murthy, *Twitter: Social Communication in the Digital Age,* (Cambridge: Polity, 2013), 68

Wael Ghomin, *Revolution 2.0: A Memoir and a Call to Action,* (Boston: Houghton Mifflin, 2012), 143.

592 Ibid.

593 Ibid.

594 Kenneth Griffiths, "Chinese Censors Report Facebook Blocked in North Korea, Iran, Cuba and 'Another Country'," *Shanghai List*, March 28, 2013, http://shanghaiist.com/2013/03/28/cowardly_chinese_censors_wont_admit_that_they_block_facebook.php (accessed: July 20, 2013).

595 Paul Sawers, "Access denied: Facebook is banned...where, exactly?" *The Next Web,* Nov 25, 2010, http://thenextweb.com/socialmedia/2010/11/25/access-denied-facebook-is-banned-where-exactly/ (accessed: August 18, 2013).

[596] Asia Internet Use, Population Data and Facebook Statistics, *Internet World Stats*, June 30, 2012, http://www.internetworldstats.com/stats3.htm (accessed: August 18, 2013).

[597] Oliver August, "The Great Firewall: China's Misguided-- and Futile — Attempt to Control What Happens Online," *Wired*, October 23, 2007. http://www.wired.com/politics/security/magazine/15-11/ff_chinafirewall?currentPage=all (accessed: August 18, 2013).

[598] Noah Shachtman, "U.S. Spies Buy Stake in Firm That Monitors Blogs, Tweets," *Wired*, October 19, 2009, http://www.wired.com/dangerroom/2009/10/exclusive-us-spies-buy-stake-in-twitter-blog-monitoring-firm/ (accessed: July 5, 2012).

[599] Rosa Golijan, "Google Refuses to Continue Censoring Results in China," *Gizmodo*, January 12, 2010, http://gizmodo.com/5446712/google-refuses-to-continue-censoring-results-in-china (accessed: August 8, 2013).

[600] Tencent Announces 2013 First Quarter Results", Tencent, March 31, 2013, http://www.tencent.com/en-us/content/at/2013/attachments/20130515.pdf

[601] RenRen and Viki Bring Subtitled Global TV to Renren's 160 Million Users on 56.com," RenRen, July 13, 2012, http://www.renren-inc.com/en/news/89.html

Renren.com, *Alexa*, http://www.alexa.com/siteinfo/renren.com

[602] Sarah Lai Stirland, "Cisco Leak: 'Great Firewall' of China Was a Chance to Sell More Routers," *Wired*, May 20, 2008, http://www.wired.com/threatlevel/2008/05/leaked-cisco-do/ (accessed: August 18, 2013).

[603] International Center for Social Media, "Building Your Presence with Facebook Pages, a Guide for Police Departments." http://www.iacpsocialmedia.org/Portals/1/documents/FacebookPagesGuide.pdf (accessed: August 18, 2013).

[604] Olga Khaza, "In The entire world is increasingly using Facebook", *The Washington Post*, January 4, 2013, http://www.washingtonpost.com/blogs/worldviews/wp/2013/01/04/the-entire-world-is-increasingly-using-facebook/ (accessed: July 25, 2013).

[605] Kirkpatrick, *The Facebook Effect*, 101.

[606] Ibid.

[607] Freedombox, http://freedomboxfoundation.org/learn/ (accessed: July 25, 2013).

[608] Rob Van Kranenburg and Sean Dodson, "The Internet of Things: A critique of ambient technology and the network of all seeing RFIDs," *Institute of Network Cultures* Sept. (2008), 29.

[609] "Active vs. Passive," Atlas RFID solutions, http://www.atlasrfid.com/Technology/ActivevsPassive.aspx (accessed: August 19, 2013).

[610] Kevin Mahaffey, "Passive RFID Security," *Blackhat*, July 2005, http://www.blackhat.com/presentations/bh-usa-05/bh-us-05-mahaffey.pdf (accessed: August 19, 2013).

[611] RFID Glossary, AIM Global, http://www.aimglobal.org/?rf_glossary#NO (accessed: August 15, 2013).

[612] RFID Tags & Readers, Texas Instruments, http://www.ti.com/rfid/faqs.shtml

[613] Matrix QR codes make link between real, virtual worlds", *CBC News*, November 5, 2010, http://www.cbc.ca/news/technology/story/2010/11/03/f-qr-code-2d-barcode-matrix.html (accessed: August 19, 2013).

[614] Dodson, Sean. "The Internet of Things: A tiny microchip is set to replace the barcode on all retail items but opposition is growing to its use." The Guardian, October 8, 2003. .http://www.guardian.co.uk/technology/2003/oct/09/shopping.newmedia (accessed: June 7, 2012).

[615] Chana R Schoenberger, "The Internet of Things", *Forbes,* March 18. 2012, http://www.forbes.com/forbes/2002/0318/155.html (Date of Access: July 20, 2012)

[616] Katherine Albrecht and Liz McIntyre, *SpyChips: How Major Corporations and Government Plan to Track Your Every Purchase and Watch Your Every Move, (*Nashville, Tennessee, Plume. 2006), xii, 43.

[617] U.S. Passport Card, U.S. State Department, http://travel.state.gov/passport/ppt_card/ppt_card_3926.html

[618] Radiation Emitting Products, FDA, http://www.fda.gov/Radiation-EmittingProducts/RadiationSafety/ElectromagneticCompatibilityEMC/ucm116647.htm

[619] Bob Violino, "RFID in the Global Cattle Industry RFID in the Global Cattle Industry," *RFID Journal,* July 18, 2004, http://www.rfidjournal.com/articles/view?1034

[620] Todd Lewan, "Chip Implants Linked to Animal Tumors," *The Associated Press,* September 8, 2007, as reported in the *Washington Post,* http://www.washingtonpost.com/wp-dyn/content/article/2007/09/08/AR2007090800997_pf.html (accessed: August 19, 2013).

[621] Katherine Albrecht and Liz McIntyre, *The SpyChips Threat: Why Christians Should Resist RFID and Electronic Surveillanc*e, (Nashville: Nelson Current, 2006).

[622] Matthew Malone, "Did Wal-Mart love RFID to death?" *Smartplanet,* February 14, 2012, http://www.smartplanet.com/blog/pure-genius/did-wal-mart-love-rfid-to-death/7459 (July 25, 2013).

U.S. State Department, "U.S. Passport Card," http://travel.state.gov/passport/ppt_card/ppt_card_3926.html (accessed: August 19, 2013).

[623] Malone, "Did Wal-Mart Love RFID to Death?"

[624] Active RFID Tags, http://www.sagedata.com/learning_centre/active-rfid-tags.html (accessed: August 19, 2013).

C H A P T E R 6: RFID Tag Considerations, in *RFID Tag Technology*, CISCO, http://www.cisco.com/en/US/docs/solutions/Enterprise/Mobility/wifich6.pdf (accessed: August 19, 2013).

[625] Albrecht and McIntyre, *SpyChip*s, 26.

[626] "Virtualize Your IT Infrastructure," VMware, http://www.vmware.com/virtualization/ (accessed: August 19, 2013).

[627] "Steve Jobs Introducing The iPhone At MacWorld 2007," January 9, 2007, .http://www.youtube.com/watch?v=x7qPAY9JqE4, (accessed: August 19, 2013).

[628] "Key Global Telecom Indicators for the World Telecommunication Service Sector in 2012," MobiThinking, http://mobithinking.com/mobile-marketing-tools/latest-mobile-stats/a#subscribers (accessed: August 19, 2013).

[629] Chris Velazco, "Carrier IQ: How To Find It, And How To Deal With It," *TechCrunch,* December 1, 2011, http://techcrunch.com/2011/12/01/carrier-iq-how-to-find-it-and-how-to-deal-with-it/ (accessed: August 19, 2013).

[630] Carrier IQ Part #2, YouTube, November 28, 2011, https://www.youtube.com/watch?v=T17XQI_AYNo (August 3, 2013).

[631] "Key Global Telecom Indicators for the World Telecommunication Service Sector in 2012," *MobiThinking*, http://mobithinking.com/mobile-marketing-tools/latest-mobile-stats/a#subscribers (accessed: August 19, 2013).

[632] Smart Meter, General Electric, http://www.gedigitalenergy.com/Meters.htm (accessed: August 19, 2013).

Smart Grid, Texas Instruments, http://www.ti.com/lsds/ti/apps/smartgrid/end_equipment.page (accessed: August 19, 2013).

Utilities/Smart Grid, Cisco, http://www.cisco.com/web/strategy/energy/external_utilities.html (accessed: August 19, 2013).

[633] Jonathan Collins, "Self-Checkout Gets RFID Upgrade," *RFID Journal*, Aug 13, 2004, http://www.rfidjournal.com/articles/view?1082 (accessed: August 19, 2013).

[634] "Bill Buxton at TechFest 2013: Designing for Ubiquitous Computing," Microsoft, March 18, 2013, http://www.youtube.com/watch?v=ZQJIwjlaPCQ (accessed: August 19, 2013).

[635] Foursquare, https://foursquare.com/ (accessed: July 31, 2013).

[636] Yelp, http://www.yelp.com/ (accessed: July 31, 2013).

[637] Swipely, https://www.swipely.com/; Square, https://squareup.com/; Google Wallet, http://www.google.com/wallet/index.html (accessed: August 19, 2013).

[638] Richard Gray, "Minority Report-style advertising billboards to target consumers," *The Telegraph,* August 1, 2010, http://www.telegraph.co.uk/technology/news/7920057/Minority-Report-style-advertising-billboards-to-target-consumers.html (accessed: August 15, 2013).

[639] Fourth Quarter 2012 Earnings Call Facebook, Inc. Investor Relations, Facebook, January 30, 2013, http://files.shareholder.com/downloads/AMDA-NJ5DZ/2449166033x0x631892/cc895d21-303f-4afe-a564-dd2641a04ab9/Facebook_Q412EarningsTranscript.pdf (accessed: July 31, 2013

[640] "Board of Directors," Investor Relations, Facebook, http://investor.fb.com/directors.cfm

[641] Press Center, PayPal, https://www.paypal-media.com/about (accessed: August 15, 2013).

[642] "Seed," Andreessen Horowitz, http://a16z.com/portfolio/a16z-seed/ (accessed: July 25, 2013).

[643] "Board of Directors," Investor Relations, Facebook, http://investor.fb.com/directors.cfm

[644] Albrecht and McIntyre, *Spy Chips*, 60.

[645] Ben Popper, "Why Google Keeps Losing Employees to Facebook," *CBS,* November 2, 2010, http://www.cbsnews.com/8301-505124_162-43341335/why-google-keeps-losing-employees-to-facebook/

[646] David Ebersman," Management Team, Investor Relations, http://newsroom.fb.com/Management

[647] Kieron O'Hara and Nigel Shadbolt, *The Spy in the Coffee Machine: The End of Privacy As We Know It*, Oneworld, Oxford, 2008

[648] The Internet of Things 2012 New Horizons Ian G Smith Technical Editors: Ovidiu Vermesan Peter Friess Anthony Furness, IERC, - Internet of Things European Research Cluster 3rd edition of the Cluster Book. http://www.internet-of-things-research.eu/pdf/IERC_Cluster_Book_2012_WEB.pdf (accessed: August 19, 2013).

[649] Annalee Newitz, "The RFID Hacking Underground," *Wired*. May 5, 2006 http://www.wired.com/wired/archive/14.05/rfid.html (accessed: August 19, 2013).

[650] Matthew Malone, "Did Wal-Mart love RFID to death?

[651] Annalee Newitz, "The RFID Hacking Underground."

[652] Ibid.

[653] Ibid.

[654] Campbell, Das, Kleinschmidt, and Thornton, *RFID Security, 84-85.*

[655] Annalee Newitz, "The RFID Hacking Underground."

[656] The RFID Question," Adam Savage at the Hotel Pennsylvania in New York City, July, 18-20 2008, YouTube,

http://www.youtube.com/watch?v=-St_ltH90Oc (accessed: August 4, 2013).

657 2012 Norton Cybercrime Report, Symantec.

658 Albrecht and McIntyre, *SpyChips,* 164.

659 James Bamford, *The Shadow Factory: The NSA from 9/11 to the Eavesdropping on America,* (New York: Anchor Books. Random House, 2008), 166-168.

660 Ward Churchill and Jim Vander Wall, *The COINTELPRO Papers,* (Cambridge, MA: South End Press Classics, 2002), xlviii.

661 Bamford, *The Shadow Factory, 161-163.*

662 E. Judson Jennings, "Carnivore: US Government Surveillance of Internet Transmissions," *Virginia Journal of Law and Technology,* Summer 2001, http://www.vjolt.net/vol6/issue2/v6i2-a10-Jennings.html

663 "FBI Ditches Carnivore Surveillance System," *Associated Press*, January 18, 2005, http://www.foxnews.com/story/2005/01/18/fbi-ditches-carnivore-surveillance-system/#ixzz2c5QcHTeW

664 Shane Harris, *The Watchers: The Rise of America's Surveillance State,* (New York: The Penguin Press, 2011), 115-128.

665 Dan Farber. "U.S. v. Whistleblower Tom Drake," *CBS News,* October 18, 2012, http://www.cbsnews.com/8301-503544_162-20122207-503544/thomas-drake-the-dark-side-of-data-and-the-nsa/ (accessed: July 25, 2013).

666 Ibid.

667 Ibid.

668 William J. Krouse, "The Multi-State Anti-Terrorism Information Exchange (MATRIX) Pilot Project," Congressional Research Service, August 18, 2004 , included on Federation of American Scientists http://www.fas.org/irp/crs/RL32536.pdf (accessed: August 4, 2013).

669 U.S. Department of Homeland Security, "Report to the Public Concerning the Multistate Anti-Terrorism Information Exchange (MATRIX) Pilot Project," *Privacy Office*, December 2006, http://www.dhs.gov/xlibrary/assets/privacy/privacy-matrix-122006.pdf (accessed: August 4, 2013).

670 Harris, *The Watchers.*

Jeffrey Rosen, "Total Information Awareness", *The New York Times,* December 15, 2002, https://www.nytimes.com/2002/12/15/magazine/15TOTA.html (accessed: May 15, 2013)..

671 Bamford, *The Shadow Factory, 279.*

672, Jessica Yellin, "President Obama defends NSA surveillance", *CNN*, June 7, 2013, http://politicalticker.blogs.cnn.com/2013/06/07/president-obama-defends-nsa-surveillance/ (July 25, 2013.

673 Defense Advanced Projects Research Agency, "Our Work," http://www.darpa.mil/our_work/ (accessed: August 4, 2013).

674 National Science Foundation, (accessed: August 15, 2013).

675 Ibid.

676 Stanford University, "The Original GOOGLE Computer Storage [Page and Brin] (1996)," *Stanford Historical Exhibit*, http://infolab.stanford.edu/pub/voy/museum/pictures/display/0-4-Google.htm (accessed: August 19, 2013).

677 Google, *Crunchbase*, http://crunchbase.com/company/google (accessed: August 19, 2013).

678 Ellen Nakashima, "Google to enlist NSA to help it ward off cyber-attacks," *The Washington Post*, February 4, 2010, http://www.washingtonpost.com/wp-dyn/content/article/2010/02/03/AR2010020304057.html?nav=emailpage (accessed: August 6, 2013).

James Ball, "NSA's Prism surveillance program: how it works and what it can do," *The Guardian*, June 8, 2013. http://www.theguardian.com/world/2013/jun/08/nsa-prism-server-collection-facebook-google (accessed: August 6, 2013).

679 Ben Popper, "Why Google Keeps Losing Employees to Facebook", *CBS*, November 2, 2010, http://www.cbsnews.com/8301-505124_162-43341335/why-google-keeps-losing-employees-to-facebook/ (accessed: August 19, 2013).

680 "The IQT Mission," In-Q-Tel, http://www.iqt.org/about/mission.html (accessed: August 4, 2013)

681 Recorded Future, In-Q-Tel, http://www.iqt.org/portfolio/recorded_future.html (accessed: August 15, 2013)

682 Siobhan Gorman, "How Team of Geeks Cracked Spy Trade," *The Wall Street Journal*, September 4, 2009, http://online.wsj.com/article/SB125200842406984303.html (accessed: August 10, 2013).
.

683 The CIA's In-Q-Tel venture arm invests in Visible Technologies, BizJournals, Oct 19, 2009, http://www.bizjournals.com/seattle/blog/techflash/2009/10/the_cias_in-q-tel_venture_arm_invests_in_visible_technologies.html?page=all

684 Kambiz Foroohar, CIA Venture Fund Focuses on Spy Gadgets Q Adores (Correct)," Bloomberg, October 25, 2007, http://www.bloomberg.com/apps/news?pid=newsarchive&sid=arSqdOLQVK9g

[685] Cecilia Kang, "Silicon Valley's data gurus lure Defense customers," *The Washington Post,* May 24, 2012, http://www.washingtonpost.com/blogs/post-tech/post/silicon-valleys-data-gurus-lure-defense-customers/2012/05/24/gJQAJeF6mU_blog.html (accessed: August 6, 2013).

[686] Alexander Karp, Interview by Charlie Rose, The Charlie Rose Show, PBS, August 11, 2009.

[687] Kevin Freedman, LinkedIn, http://www.linkedin.com/in/kfreedman

[688] Joe Lonsdale, Crunchbase, http://www.crunchbase.com/person/joe-lonsdale
[689] Stephen Cohen, Palantir, http://www.palantir.com/stephen

[690] Nicholas Carlson, "Secretive Startup Palantir Is Now Worth ~$8 Billion, According To Cofounder," January 15, 2013, http://www.businessinsider.com/secretive-startup-palantir-is-now-worth-8-billion-according-to-cofounder-2013-1#ixzz2MafxDVym (accessed: August 19, 2013).

[691] Ken/Howery, Founder Fund, http://www.foundersfund.com/#/team/ken-howery (accessed: August 6, 2013).

Luke Nosek, Founders Fund, http://www.foundersfund.com/#/team/luke-nosek (accessed: August 6, 2013).

Brian Singerman, Founders Fund, http://www.foundersfund.com/#/team/brian-singerman (accessed: August 6, 2013).

Sean Parker, Founders Fund, http://www.foundersfund.com/#/team/sean-parker (accessed: August 6, 2013).

[692] RoboteX, Founders Fund, http://www.foundersfund.com/#/company/robotex (accessed: August 23, 2013)

[693] About RoboteX, http://robotex.com/about-robotex/ (accessed: August 23, 2013).

[694] "Jim Breyer," Accel Partners, http://www.accel.com/global/people/specialty/all/Jim_Breyer

[695] Erick Schonfeld, "Jim Breyer's Midas Touch. Two Acquisitions in 24 Hours (Marvel and BBN)," *Tech Crunch*, September 1, 2009, http://techcrunch.com/2009/09/01/jim-breyers-midas-touch-two-acquisitions-in-24-hours-marvel-and-bbn/ (accessed: August 19, 2013).

[696] "Jim Breyer," Accel Partners, http://www.accel.com/global/people/specialty/all/Jim_Breyer (accessed: August 19, 2013).

[697] Tim Shorrock, *Spies for Hire: The Secret World of Intelligence Outsourcing 1st Edition* (New York: Simon & Schuster; 2008), 147.

[698] "Howard Cox," Harvard Business School Entrepreneurs, http://www.hbs.edu/entrepreneurs/pdf/howardcox.pdf (accessed: August 6, 2013).

[699] "Reid Hoffman, Partner," Team, Greylock Partners, http://www.greylock.com/teams/11-reid-hoffman (accessed: August 19, 2013).

[700] "Facebook Names Sheryl Sandberg Chief Operating Officer Downloads," Newsroom, Facebook, March 4, 2008, http://newsroom.fb.com/News/240/Facebook-Names-Sheryl-Sandberg-Chief-Operating-Officer (accessed: August 1, 2013).

[701] "Erskine Bowles –Bio Fall 2009," Gateway University Research Park. http://www.gatewayurp.com/documents/SpeakerBiographies.pdf (accessed: August 1, 2013).

[702] Nicholas Carlson, "Secretive Startup Palantir is now worth ~$8 Billion, According To Cofounder," *Business Insider*, Jan 15, 2013, http://www.businessinsider.com/secretive-startup-palantir-is-now-worth-8-billion-according-to-cofounder-2013-1#ixzz2MafxDVym (accessed: August 6, 2013).

[703] Kirkpatrick, *The Facebook Effect*, 327.

[704] "People", Facebook Inc., *Reuters,* http://www.reuters.com/finance/stocks/companyOfficers?symbol=FB.O (accessed: August 6, 2013).

[705] Kashmir Hill, "Facebook's Top Cop: Joe Sullivan."

[706] Stephen Levi. *In the Plex: Inside Google.*1st Edition. (New York: Simon & Schuster, 2011), 267-314.

Josh Rogin, "Inside the State Department Arab Twitter Policy, *The Cable,* January 28, 2011, http://thecable.foreignpolicy.com/posts/2011/01/28/inside_the_state_department_s_arab_twitter_diplomacy (accessed: August 6, 2013).

[707] About Bilderberg, Bilderberg Meetings, http://www.bilderbergmeetings.org/index.html (accessed: August 16, 2013).

[708] Ibid.

[709]

[710] Daniel Estulin, *The True Story of the Bilderberg Group*, (New York: Trine Day, 2009).

[711] Bilderberg Meetings, Sitges, Spain 3-6 June 2010, http://www.bilderbergmeetings.org/participants_2010.html

Bilderberg Meetings, St. Moritz, Switzerland, 9-12 June 2011, http://www.bilderbergmeetings.org/participants_2011.html (accessed: July26, 2013).

"Bilderberg 2012: The Official List of Participants," *Infowars.com,* May 31, 2012, http://www.infowars.com/bilderberg-2012-the-official-list-of-participants/

[712] Byers, "The Bilderberg Group's media men," *Politico,* May 21, 2012, http://www.politico.com/blogs Dylan /media/2012/05/the-bilderberg-groups-washington-media-men-124074.html (accessed: August 17, 2013).

 Ellen McGirt, "How Chris Hughes Helped Launch Facebook and the Barack Obama Campaign," *Fast Company,* http://www.fastcompany.com/1207594/how-chris-hughes-helped-launch-facebook-and-barack-obama-campaign (accessed: August 17, 2013).

[713] "Donald E. Graham," Investor Relations, Facebook, http://investor.fb.com/directors.cfm (accessed: August 16, 2013).

[714] Kirkpatrick, *the Facebook Effect, 123-124, 136.*

[715] Mezrich, *The Accidental Billionaires, 108*

[716] Ibid., 125-131

[717] Sheryl Sandberg, *Lean In: Women, Work, and the Will to Lean.* 1st Edition, (New York: Knopf, March 11, 2013), 18, 36-37, 67

[718] Reid Hoffman, LinkedIn, http://www.linkedin.com/in/reidhoffman

[719] Alexander Karp, Interview by Charlie Rose, The Charlie Rose Show, *PBS,* August 11, 2009.

[720] "Sean Parker," Founders Fund, http://www.foundersfund.com/#/team/sean-parker

[721] Portraits of Bilderberg Participants, Daniel Estulin, http://www.danielestulin.com/wp-content/uploads/portraits_bilderberg.pdf

[722] 2012 Bilderberg Meeting Participant List, *Public Intelligence,* May 31, 2012, .http://publicintelligence.net/2012-bilderberg-meeting-participant-list/ (July 31, 2013)

[723] About CFR," *Council on Foreign Relations,* http://www.cfr.org/about/

[724] Jim Marrs. *Rule by Secrecy: The Hidden History That Connects the Trilateral Commission, the Freemasons, and the Great Pyramids.* (William Morrow Paperbacks, 2001), 31-39.

[725] "Membership Roster," Council on Foreign Relations, http://i.cfr.org/content/about/annual_report/ar_2012/Membership_Roster2012.pdf (accessed: December 10, 2012).

[726] Ibid.

[727] David Kirkpatrick. "With a Little Help From His Friends," *Vanity Fair,* October 2010, http://www.vanityfair.com/culture/features/2010/10/sean-parker-201010 (accessed: August 19, 2013).

[728]

[729] "Corporate Members," Council on Foreign Relations, July 29, 2013, http://www.cfr.org/about/corporate/roster.html (accessed: August 19, 2013).

[730] Mary Pilon, "T. Rowe Price Invests in Facebook," *The Wall Street Journal,* April 16, 2011, http://online.wsj.com/article/SB10001424052748704495004576264730149910442.html (accessed: August 19, 2013).

[731] "People," Facebook Inc., *Reuters,* http://www.reuters.com/finance/stocks/companyOfficers?symbol=FB.O

[732] Cassandra Anderson, "Council on Foreign Relations Propaganda," *Infowars.com,* May 12, 2010, http://www.infowars.com/council-on-foreign-relations-propaganda/

[733] Trilateral Commission, http://www.trilateral.org/ (accessed: August 20, 2013).

[734] Marrs, *Rule by Secrecy,* .22-30

[735] Membership, The Trilateral Commission,   http://www.trilateral.org/go.cfm?do=Page.View&pid=6 (accessed: August 20, 2013).

[736] The Trilateral Commission, http://www.trilateral.org/download/file/TC_list_4-13.pdf (accessed: August 20, 2013).

[737] Ibid.

[738] The Trilateral Commission, http://www.trilateral.org/go.cfm?do=Page.View&pid=5 (accessed: August 20, 2013

[739] "History," World Economic Forum, http://www.weforum.org/history (accessed: August 20, 2013).

[740] "Members," World Economic Forum, http://www.weforum.org/members (accessed: August 20, 2013).

[741] "History," World Economic Forum, http://www.weforum.org/history (accessed: August 20, 2013).

[742] "Sheryl Sandberg," World Economic Forum, http://www.weforum.org/young-global-leaders/sheryl-sandberg (accessed: August 20, 2013).

"Peter A. Thiel," World Economic Forum, http://www.weforum.org/contributors/peter-thiel (accessed: August 20, 2013).

"Sean Parker," World Economic Forum, http://www.weforum.org/contributors/sean-parker (accessed: August 20, 2013).

"Mark Zuckerberg," World Economic Forum, http://www.weforum.org/contributors/mark-zuckerberg/ (accessed: August 20, 2013).

"Jim Breyer," World Economic Forum, http://www.weforum.org/contributors/jim-breyer (accessed: August 20, 2013).

"David Kirkpatrick," World Economic Forum. http://www.weforum.org/contributors/david-kirkpatrick (accessed: August 20, 2013).

[743]Barry Neil, "Davos: Part of the problem, or solution?" *CNN,* January 25, 2012, http://edition.cnn.com/2012/01/17/business/davos-relevance (accessed: August 20, 2013).

[744] Key Global Telecom Indicators for the World Telecommunication Service Sector in 2012," MobiThinking, http://mobithinking.com/mobile-marketing-tools/latest-mobile-stats/a#subscribers (accessed: August 4, 2013).

[745] "Who can translate my Facebook Page's posts?" Help Center, Facebook, https://www.facebook.com/help/212642972129076 (accessed: August 4, 2013).

Josh Constine, "Bing Powers New Facebook Page Post Translation Tool," *Inside Facebook,* Oct 5, 2011, http://www.insidefacebook.com/2011/10/05/bing-translate-pages/(accessed: August 16, 2013).

[746] "Gift Basics," Help Center, Facebook, https://www.facebook.com/help/212642972129076#!/help/510469902314404/ (accessed: August 16, 2013).

[747] Naomi Klein, *The Shock Doctrine: The Rise of Disaster Capitalism,* (New York: Picador, 2007), 353.

[748] Kirkpatrick, *The Facebook Effect*, 87.

[749]. Ibid., 95

[750] "A Conversation with Jimmy Fallon and Sean Parker," *Fora TV,* YouTube, June 24, 2011, http://www.youtube.com/watch?v=yCyMz-u-HcQ (accessed: August 6, 2013).

[751] Kirkpatrick, *The Facebook Effect*, 146-147

[752] Official List of Participants for the 2007 Bilderberg Meeting, Public Intelligence, June 12, 2007, http://publicintelligence.net/official-list-of-participants-for-the-2007-bilderberg-meeting/

[753] Ibid.

[754] "Facebook Names Sheryl Sandberg Chief Operating Officer," Newsroom, Facebook, March 4, 2008, http://newsroom.fb.com/News/240/Facebook-Names-Sheryl-Sandberg-Chief-Operating-Officer

[755] "Management Team," Google, http://www.google.com/about/company/facts/management/.(accessed: July 31, 2013).

"Membership Roster," Council on Foreign Relations, http://i.cfr.org/content/about/annual_report/ar_2012/Membership_Roster2012.pdf (December 10, 2012)

2012 Bilderberg Meeting Participant List, *Public Intelligence*, May 31, 2012, .http://publicintelligence.net/2012-bilderberg-meeting-participant-list/

"Eric Schmidt," World Economic Forum, http://www.weforum.org/contributors/eric-schmidt (accessed: July 31, 2013).

[756] *The Google Story: Behind the Hottest Business, Media and Technology Successes of Our Time*, (New York: Bantam-Dell, 2005), 103-111.

[757] Ibid., 175,178, 383.

[758] Dir. Daniel Geller and Dayna Goldfine, *Something Ventured,* Zeitgeist Films, 2011.

[759] Ibid.

[760] "Sheryl Sandberg," Management Team, Investor Relations, http://newsroom.fb.com/Management

Membership Roster, Council on Foreign Relations,

http://i.cfr.org/content/about/annual_report/ar_2012/Membership_Roster2012.pdf

"Sheryl Sandberg," World Economic Forum, http://www.weforum.org/young-global-leaders/sheryl-sandberg

[761] "Sheryl Sandberg Joins Facebook Board," *The Wall Street Journal,* June 25, 2012, http://online.wsj.com/article/SB10001424052702304782404577489003831226744.html, (accessed: July 31, 2013).

[762] "Board of Directors," Investor Relations, Facebook, http://investor.fb.com/directors.cfm (accessed: August 16, 2013).

[763] National Science Foundation, "Cyber Infrastructure: A Brief History of the NSF and the Internet," http://www.nsf.gov/news/special_reports/cyber/internet.jsp (accessed: August 15, 2013).

[764] Donald E. Graham," Investor Relations, Facebook, http://investor.fb.com/directors.cfm (accessed: August 16, 2013

[765] The Kojo Nnamdi Show: Donald Graham on Mark Zuckerberg, May 22, 2012, http://www.youtube.com/watch?v=Zhk0KD0meGI (August 3, 2013

[766] Ibid.

[767] "Board of Directors," Investor Relations, Facebook, http://investor.fb.com/directors.cfm (August 3, 2013).

[768] "Facebook and Microsoft Expand Strategic Alliance," Newsroom, Facebook, Oct 24, 2007, http://newsroom.fb.com/News/232/Facebook-and-Microsoft-Expand-Strategic-Alliance (August 3, 2013).

[769] Katie Rogers, "Netflix goes social with Facebook sharing," *The Guardian,* March 13, 2013, http://www.guardian.co.uk/media/us-news-blog/2012/dec/27/netflix-social-sharing-features-gacebook (August 3, 2013).

[770] "Erskine Bowels," Board of Directors, Facebook, http://investor.fb.com/directors.cfm (August 3, 2013).

[771] "Key Facts," Facebook, http://newsroom.fb.com/Key-Facts (August 3, 2013).

[772] "Products," Facebook, http://newsroom.fb.com/Products (August 3, 2013).

[773] Griswold v. Connecticut 381 U.S. 479 (1965)

[774] Ibid.
[775] Ibid

[776] Bobbie Johnson, "Privacy no longer a social norm, says Facebook founder," *The Guardian,* January 10, 2010, http://www.theguardian.com/technology/2010/jan/11/facebook-privacy (accessed: August 20, 2013).

Eliot Van Buskirk, "Report: Facebook CEO Mark Zuckerberg Doesn't Believe In Privacy," *Wired,* April 28, 2010, http://www.wired.com/business/2010/04/report-facebook-ceo-mark-zuckerberg-doesnt-believe-in-privacy/ (accessed: August 20, 2013).

[777] "Facebook Inc. Summary," *Open Secret.org*, http://www.opensecrets.org/pacs/lookup2.php?strID=C00502906 (accessed: August 20, 2013).

[778] Michael Foucault. *Discipline and Punish: Birth of the Prison* 1st Edition, (Gallimard, 1975), 204.

[779] Cantwell v. Connecticut, 310 U.S.296 (1940)

[780] Media Benjamin, *Drone Warfare: Killing by Remote Control*, (New York; London: Verso, 2012).

Rob Van Kranenburg and Sean Dodson, "The Internet of Things: A critique of ambient technology and the network of all seeing RFIDs," *Institute of Network Cultures,* 2008.

[781] Wills Kerry, Robert Gearty, and Stephen Rex Brown, "NYPD's controversial 'Stop and Frisk' policy ruled unconstitutional," *New York Daily News*, January 8, 2013, http://www.nydailynews.com/new-york/nypd-controversial-stop-frisk-policy-ruled-unconstitutional-article-1.1235578#ixzz2aOLTZcRl

[782] James Risen, *State of War*

[783] Big chill: Obama's Justice Department targets the press," *Pittsburg Post-Gazette*, July 26, 2013, http://www.post-gazette.com/stories/opinion/editorials/big-chill-obamas-justice-department-targets-the-press-696977/#ixzz2aOJYpOIM (August 20, 2013).

[784] Exclusive: National Security Agency Whistleblower William Binney on Growing State Surveillance," *Democracy Now!,* April 20, 2012, http://www.democracynow.org/2012/4/20/exclusive_national_security_agency_whistleblower_william (accessed: August 19, 2013).

[785] "Ex-CIA Agent, Whistleblower John Kiriakou Sentenced to Prison While Torturers He Exposed Walk Free," *Democracy Now!* Jan 30, 2013, http://www.democracynow.org/2013/1/30/ex_cia_agent_whistleblower_john_kiriakou (accessed: August 19, 2013).

[786] John Hudson, "Obama's War on Whistle-Blower's," *The Atlantic Wire*, July 24, 2011, http://www.theatlanticwire.com/politics/2011/05/obamas-war-whistle-blowers/38106/ (accessed: August 20, 2013).

[787] Jeremy Scahill, *BlackWater: The Rise of America's Mercenary,* (New York: Nation Books, 2007).

[788] Tim Shorrock, *Spies for Hire: The Secret World of Intelligence Outsourcing 1st Edition, (*Simon & Schuster; 2008), 12.

[789] Radley Balco, *Rise of the Warrior Cop: The Militarization of America's Police Forces,* (New York: Public Affairs, 2013) , 24, 25.

[790] Naomi Wolf, *The End of America: Letters to a Young Patriot,* (White River Junction, VT: Chelsea Green Publishing, 2007).

[791] William Shirer, *The Rise and Fall of the Third Reich, (New York:* Simon & Schuster, 1960), 144.

[792] John Hudson, "Obama's War on Whistle-Blowers," *The Atlantic Wire*, May 24, 2011, http://www.theatlanticwire.com/politics/2011/05/obamas-war-whistle-blowers/38106/ (accessed: August 20, 2013).

[793] Michael Parenti. *Blackshirts & Reds: Rational Fascism and the Overthrow of Communism*, (San Francisco: City Lights Books, 1997), 2-4, 10-12.

[794] Naomi Klein, *The Shock Doctrine: The Rise of Disaster Capitalism,* (New York: Picador, 2007), 79.

[795] John Perkins, *Diary of An Economic Hitman,* (San Francisco: Plume. 2007), 29, 84-85.

[796] Edwin Black*, IBM and the Holocaust, (*Dialog Press, 2001).

[797] Edwin Black Discusses *IBM and the Holocaust* at Yeshiva University, Feb 26, 2012, http://www.youtube.com/watch?v=kQPiub5Qyqw (July, 25, 2013).

[798] Ibid.

[799] Walter Issacson, *Steve Jobs*, (New York: Simon & Schuster, 2011

[800] 2004 Bilderberg Meeting Participant List, Public Intelligence, http://publicintelligence.net/2004-bilderberg-meeting-

participant-list/ (accessed: August 17, 2013).

801 "Jim Breyer," Accel Partners. http://www.accel.com/#people/jim-breyer (accessed: August 4, 2013).

802 Platform, Newsroom, Facebook, http://newsroom.fb.com/Platform (accessed: August 4, 2013).

803 World Internet Usage and Population Statistics," *Internet Usage Statistics*, June 30, 2012, http://www.internetworldstats.com/stats.htm (accessed: August 5, 2013).

804 Earnings Release FY13 Q4, Investor Relations, Microsoft, (accessed: August 5, 2013).

Apple Reports Third Quarter Results, Press Info, Apple, http://www.apple.com/pr/library/2013/07/23Apple-Reports-Third-Quarter-Results.html (accessed: August 5, 2013).

"Google Inc., Announces Second Quarter 2013 Results," Google, July 18, 2013, http://investor.google.com/earnings/2013/Q2_google_earnings.html (accessed: August 5, 2013).

805 The Internet of Things How the Next Evolution of the Internet Is Changing Everything," CISCO, http://www.cisco.com/web/about/ac79/docs/innov/IoT_IBSG_0411FINAL.pdf (accessed: August 5, 2013).

Albrecht and McIntyre, *SpyChips*

806 Sharon Gaudin, "Study: Facebook use cuts productivity at work Survey finds 77% of Facebookers use the social networking site while on the job," *ComputerWorld,* July 22, 2009, http://www.computerworld.com/s/article/9135795/Study_Facebook_use_cuts_productivity_at_work (accessed: August 4, 2012).

807 Sharing Our Footprint," August 1, 2012, https://newsroom.fb.com/News/412/Sharing-Our-Footprint. (accessed: August 5, 2013).